Cherokee Myths and Legends

T0040355

Cherokee Myths and Legends

Thirty Tales Retold

TERRY L. NORTON

McFarland & Company, Inc., Publishers
Jefferson, North Carolina

LIBRARY OF CONGRESS CATALOGUING-IN-PUBLICATION DATA

Norton, Terry L., 1952–
    Cherokee myths and legends : thirty tales retold / Terry L. Norton.
      p.   cm.
    Includes bibliographical references and index.

    ISBN 978-0-7864-9460-6 (softcover : acid free paper) ∞
    ISBN 978-1-4766-1811-1 (ebook)

    1. Cherokee Indians—Folklore.   2. Tales—North Carolina.   I. Title.
E99.C5N675 2014
398.2089'97557—dc23   2014037060

BRITISH LIBRARY CATALOGUING DATA ARE AVAILABLE

On the cover: *The Historian*, Eanger Irving Couse, 1902 (© 2014 PicturesNow)

Printed in the United States of America

McFarland & Company, Inc., Publishers
   Box 611, Jefferson, North Carolina 28640
   www.mcfarlandpub.com

Contents

Preface   1

*Introduction: Considerations in Adapting Native American
    Traditional Literature*   9

Guide to the Pronunciation of Cherokee Words   55

ORIGINS

The Three Worlds   57

Fire   60

Corn and Game   62

Disease and Medicine   70

The Bear and the Bear Songs   74

Tobacco   76

The Pleiades and the Pine Cone   78

KILLING THE GREAT MONSTERS

The Great Yellow Jacket Ulagu   81

The Leech Place   82

The Uktena and the Shawano Conjuror   84

The Red Man and the Uktena   88

Ustu-tli, the Great Snake of the Cohutta Mountains   90

The Great Hawks   92

The Hunter in the Dakwa   95

SUPERNATURAL AND ANIMAL ADVERSARIES AND HELPERS

Spear-Finger, the Nantahala Ogress	97
The Stone Man of the Mountains	100
The Raven Mockers	102
The Immortals and the Water Cannibals	105
The Man Who Traveled to the World Below	108
Judaculla, the Slant-Eyed Giant of Tanasee Bald	112
Legends of Pilot Knob	117
Yahula	121
The Unseen Helpers	123

LEGENDS FROM HISTORY BY OR ABOUT THE CHEROKEE

The Lost Cherokee	130
Ga'na and the Cherokee	133
The Mohawk Warriors	147
The False Warriors	152
Jocassee	156
Some Heroic Acts in Wars with Whites	165
Cateechee of Keowee: A Ballad of the Carolina Backcountry	169

Sources Used in the Retellings	189
Notes	205
Bibliography	211
Index	217

Invitation

Ye who love the haunts of nature,
Love the sunshine in the meadow,
Love the shadow of the forest,
Love the wind among the branches,
Love the rain-shower and the snow-storm,
And the rushing of the rivers
Through their palisades of pine-trees,
And the thunder in the mountains,
Whose innumerable echoes
Flap like eagles in their aeries; —
Listen to these wild traditions.

—From Introduction, *Song of
Hiawatha*, by Henry Wadsworth
Longfellow, 1855

Preface

Retelling Native American Folklore

An examination of sections on folklore in bookstores and libraries reveals that collections identified with Native Americans readily abound. This circumstance requires anyone offering a new collection to explain what differentiates it from others. The chief distinction between this book and others lies in the approach to authenticity and accuracy when original, print sources related to an indigenous group like the Cherokee are adapted or retold. Although the two terms are not mutually exclusive, authenticity concerns the faithful preservation of the cultural context in which the stories are set, whereas accuracy refers to the maintenance of historical veracity in details of time and place. Authenticity is usually more important in rendering stories of origins, magical transformations, talking animals, supernatural beings, and similar features found in folktales around the world. It must be preserved in adaptations of traditional literature when a work's stated or implicit values do not reflect attitudes of the current dominant culture. Accuracy is more important when a traditional story purports to be a legend or a fictional tale set in a remote but historically identifiable context usually lacking magic and supernatural elements. An adaptation of legendary material should not cavalierly disregard the essential facts of history, insofar as these can be ascertained, even though many legends transposed into literary retellings by identifiable authors do ignore them. Accuracy is vitally important, especially when the writer asserts that the redaction is factually based.

Sources for the Adaptations

As for this book, it contains retellings not only of stories recounted *by* the Cherokee themselves to James Mooney in the 1890s but also of stories told *about* the Cherokee. Two adaptations from Mooney are significantly integrated with accounts from earlier nineteenth century writers, John Haywood and Charles

1

Lanman, both of whom are discussed later in more detail. The stories *about* the Cherokee comprise an anecdote conveyed by an Indian trader to colonial historian James Adair, a tale of the Seneca collected in 1883 by folklorist Jeremiah Curtin, and two upstate South Carolina legends highly reshaped by nineteenth century writers William Gilmore Simms and James Daniel. The adaptation of Daniel's story is supplemented a great deal from research published in 1981 by historian E. Don Herd, Jr.

My method in retelling the material has been to tamper, sometimes heavily, with the original sources in order to render the stories derived chiefly from Mooney, Curtin, and Adair more authentic and those based primarily on Simms and Daniel not only more authentic but also more accurate for current readers. At first blush, such an approach to sources related to an indigenous group like the Cherokee would seem to violate the generally accepted dimensions of authenticity and accuracy, particularly in regard to an ethnographer like Mooney. However, this seeming paradox should resolve itself after a brief discussion of the core sources and aims of their authors.

The great majority of the stories here are adapted from efforts by James Mooney to preserve the folklore and traditions of the Cherokee. In the late 1890s, he arrived at the Qualla Boundary in western North Carolina where the Eastern Band of Cherokee lived, having evaded the requirement of the 1836 Treaty of New Echota that the Old Cherokee Nation be removed to territories west of the Mississippi by May 23, 1838. Mooney lived and worked among the Eastern Cherokee and developed enough trust with them so that he was able to record their myths, folktales, legends, and sacred rituals. Most of the lore was related to him by the few remaining "adepts" and traditionalists living at the time. As an ethnographer from the Bureau of American Ethnography, Mooney tasked himself with recording this material in as nearly an exact a manner as possible based on what native storytellers told him, sometimes through an interpreter. In his quest for accuracy, he had studied the Cherokee language and wrote what is still a valuable early account of the nation—*Historical Sketch of the Cherokee*, often published as a separate book. This body of work he set as a prelude within his longer *Myths of the Cherokee* (1900).

Along with the narratives that he gathered from the Cherokee, Mooney included and acknowledged other written accounts for additional stories in his *Myths*. Among these sources was the work of Henry Schoolcraft—nineteenth century explorer, geologist, early anthropologist, and Indian agent for the Ojibwa. With the help of his wife, Jane, who was part Ojibwa, Schoolcraft had recorded a voluminous amount on the lore of Native Americans. One legend in his *Algic Researches* (1839) inspired Henry Wadsworth Longfellow's popular 1855 epic poem *The Song of Hiawatha*. Sometimes incorporating Schoolcraft's work verbatim and sometimes rearranging it, Mooney often relied on School-craft's 1847 *Notes on the Iroquois* if the material contained legends about conflicts with other tribes and if these related to the Cherokee. Mooney also used verbatim anecdotes from Adair's 1775 *The History of the American Indians* and rearranged stories from the then unpublished manuscript of 1883 by Curtin on tales of the Seneca which the latter had collected for the Bureau of American Ethnology. Again, if the work of these two authors pertained to the Cherokee, Mooney included it in his *Myths*. He relied on other writers as well but usually for additional commentary or alternative versions of stories, material which he injected into his accompanying Notes and Parallels at the end of *Myths*. As previously noted, two of these authors, who are used in the present collection and whose anecdotes are fused with two of Mooney's stories, are the jurist and historian John Haywood, considered the father of Tennessee history, and the painter and travel writer Charles Lanman. Both produced works in the first half of the nineteenth century.

In contrast to the selections taken from Mooney, Curtin, Adair, Haywood, and Lanman, two of the stories retold here are, in their original versions, much more fictionalized and elaborately developed and derive from the work of white authors from South Carolina: antebellum literary giant William Gilmore Simms and the Reverend James Walter Daniel, who served as a Methodist minister in Abbeville toward the end of the nineteenth century. Their purposes were very different from those of Mooney, Curtin, and Adair, who aimed for accuracy and authenticity inasmuch as possible. Having literary aspirations, Simms and Daniel took local legends by white settlers that had slight historical references to the Cherokee of the eighteenth century. These writers then turned this material into highly remolded, romanticized adaptations in which the Cherokee are filtered through the lens of the Euro-American culture of the time. In his research, Mooney himself refers briefly to these pre–Revolutionary War legends from South Carolina as being connected with "local names upon which the whites who succeeded to the [Cherokee] inheritance have built traditions of more or less doubtful authenticity."[1]

From material associated with Toxaway Creek in the western corner of South Carolina, Simms fabricated his literary retelling "Jocassee, a Cherokee Legend." He included it in *The Wigwam and the Cabin*, his 1856 collection of stories about the state's colonial frontier, African American slaves, other Native American groups like the Choctaw and the Catawba, and Spanish slave catchers and fortune seekers like Lucas de Ayllon, who in the early sixteenth century preyed upon Native Americans along the Florida coast and the Gulf of Mexico. Set during the time when Moytoy of Great Tellico was acknowledged by the British as "emperor" of the Cherokee between 1730 and 1741, Simms' "Jocassee" is not unduly burdened with inaccuracies. Indeed, there are few factual details except as related to the geography of the area and a smattering of Cherokee names like Emperor Moitoy [Moytoy] and the famous diplomat, peace chief, and later emperor Attakulla [Attakullakulla], neither of whom have any documented connection with the events Simms recounts. Instead, more severe issues concern some incredulous cultural details and Simms' florid style, frequently escalating into purple patches, and his sometimes bemused attitude of condescension toward his indigenous subject matter. The Introduction to the present collection gives more information about the both the problems and provenance of this literary legend adapted from Simms as well as the story retold from Daniel.

Much more egregious in regard to accuracy than Simms' tale is Daniel's 1898 publication, *Cateechee of Keeowee: A Descriptive Poem*. The work takes place primarily during the Anglo-Cherokee War of 1759 to 1761 in upstate South Carolina in the areas around the colonial stockade and trading post at Ninety Six and the Lower Cherokee town of Keowee located near present-day Clemson University but now submerged beneath Lake Hartwell. The poem is full of fanciful embellishments on people and places, slipshod recounting of historical events, blatantly incorrect explanations of the names of upstate South Carolina creeks and streams, misinterpretations of Cherokee life, stereotypical Indian characters like King Kuruga of Keowee, and absurd instances of the pathetic fallacy in which "Dame Nature"[2] possesses a surfeit of human emotions. This long narrative of doggerel versifying purports, as Daniel avers in his opening Inscription to the poem, to be "a historical fact" recounted "in a style similar to Longfellow's *Hiawatha*."[3]

Like Simms' "Jocassee," Daniel's *Cateechee*, despite its numerous flaws, has taken hold in the popular imagination of local residents down to today, whether they are familiar with all of the particular details in the legends shaped by these two authors. Some Web sites related to recreational opportunities on the Duke Energy impoundment of Lake Jocassee provide brief versions of the tragic legend of Jocassee, in all likelihood as part of advertising to make their offerings seem all-the-more special, but never mention Simms. (See www.customboattours.com and www.jocasseelaketours.com.) The Web site for the National Society for the Daughters of the American Revolution, Cateechee Chapter, Anderson, South Carolina, states that the local organization's name "is in commemoration of the noble Choctaw maiden, one of the spoils of war and a slave of the old Cherokee Chief Kuruga, around whom tradition has woven this story of love and courage." (See http://scdar.org/CateecheeDAR.) This statement might be interpreted to suggest that these were two individuals from history, and yet unlike the aforementioned Moytoy and Attakullakulla in Simms, names which derive from real personages of the past, neither Cateechee nor Kuruga are to be found in colonial accounts of the two Cherokee attacks at Ninety Six. Neither is Cateechee's love interest, Allan Francis, who probably never existed. Daniel's poem and other narratives of the day seem to be the source of the characters' existence. The Introduction that follows explores in further detail the provenance the Cateechee legend.

Purpose of the Adaptations in This Collection

As listeners are learners, so readers are learners also. Learners bring different backgrounds of experience that determine how well they will construct meaning when they hear a story or read it in a book. Once the stories of the Cherokee passed from the spoken into the printed word, they became removed in varying degrees from the cultural context of their indigenous audiences who more than likely would have understood passing references to the specific mountains, rivers, valleys, and settlements of their land. Such listeners would also have been likely to catch a storyteller's allusions to characters and plot details based on other tales from their traditional canon heard on various occasions. Contemporary readers do not have these advantages of background to aid their comprehension of passing geographical, historical, and cultural references contained in the stories of ethnographers like Mooney, folklorists like Curtin, and historians like Adair. Neither will readers today likely possess the background necessary to have a more in-depth understanding of the intrinsically interesting and action-packed local legends transposed by Simms and Daniel. Such knowledge is especially needed as a counterweight to the excessive amount of misinformation contained in the last author's work.

The purpose of this book, therefore, is to render the stories taken from Mooney, Curtin, and Adair—and to a lesser degree from Haywood and Lanman—more understandable through adding or expanding authentic and accurate background details. For the stories derived from Simms and Daniel, the goal has been to make them more historically and geographically accurate, stylistically accessible, and less stereotypical and condescending in regard to Native Americans. As opposed to the usual method of having exterior explanatory headnotes or notes and glossaries at the end of the book or footnotes at the bottom of each page, the background knowledge for each selection is provided within the text itself, thus preempting the need to interrupt the reading and fracture the full impact of the stories. Readers curious about supplemental information integrated into the folktales and legends adapted here should consult Sources Used in the Retellings that follows the adaptations.

In regard to the aim of this book, suffice it to say in a preface that the ideas of literary critic Louise Rosenblatt, cognitive psychologist Jean Piaget, sociolinguist Lev Vygotsky, and various writers on translation theory have provided the theoretical framework and scholarly discipline for the approach used in the retellings. Rosenblatt, Piaget, and Vygotsky hold that learning is a process in which humans seek to create meaning. The implication for readers is that meaning occurs through their interaction with text in an effort to comprehend. The more background readers bring from their life experiences, including education and language ability, the more they are able to construct meaning. This meaning derives as much from the learner as it does from the text itself and comes about through a transaction between the reader and the printed page. Therefore, the more background readers have, the more they comprehend what they read because they have the cognitive wherewithal to "make connections beyond what a text states or implies."[4] Especially for the selections adapted from Mooney, Haywood, Lanman, Curtin, and Adair, the inclusion of elaborated background information within the text allows readers to experience the stories in a manner more akin to the context of their original audiences and deepens understanding. Likewise, adapting the narratives from Simms and Daniel by embedding cultural, historical, and geographical background details or correcting falsehoods enhances comprehension of this material.

Ideas in rhetoric and translation theory have further informed the method for adapting the core stories that make up this collection. One concern has been how to create stylistic approximations in English for the ritual language used by Native Americans in conveying stories, particularly those of a sacred nature. Insightful suggestions for creating such a style come from Virginia Tufte's study in rhetoric, *Artful Sentences: Syntax as Style*. Her discussion of creating "ritualistic prose"[5] has been extremely valuable. Also helpful have been ideas concerning translation as delineated by Denis Diderot and Jean-Baptiste le Rond d'Alembert of France and by Friedrich Schleiermacher and Wilhelm von Humboldt of Germany. According to Hugo Friedrich, these thinkers, who spanned the eighteenth and nineteenth centuries, enjoined the translator (here the adaptor) to avoid everyday language just as the original literature avoided it.[6] Failure to follow this advice is often a pitfall for those who retell Native American stories and who mistakenly believe that they are adhering to authenticity by narrowly following renditions by ethnographers and folklorists. As Dennis Tedlock mused in his essay "On the Translation of Style in Oral Narrative," those who read Native American stories produced by the disciples of anthropologist Franz Boas may "wonder whether the original style of these narratives was as choppy and clumsy as that of most English translations."[7] Although he preceded Boas, these kinds of problems plague Curtin's work. Anyone who reads *Myths of the Seneca* immediately realizes that he cared not in the least for stylistic considerations in his barebones redactions and understands why Mooney, who was a much better prose stylist, rearranged every legend that he borrowed from Curtin's manuscript.

Additional Issues Presented

Further analysis of authenticity, accuracy, and appropriate style as well as methods to accomplish these ends is provided in the Introduction. It also describes the variety among Native American cultures, the difficulty of defining and categorizing traditional indigenous literature, and the sometimes seeming strangeness of this literature to modern audiences because of the common underlying *mythopoeic* worldview that it shares with pre-scientific societies.

In addition, the Introduction explores concerns related to adapting traditional multicultural literature of Native Americans in general and the Cherokee in particular. Among these is the issue of ownership or sovereignty regarding this material, especially as found in simplistic debates about preserving the purity of a particular indigenous group's stories. Such discussions assume that the various native cultures of the new world existed in isolation both *before* and *after* contact with whites, as though there were no developments within particular cultures, modifications brought about through interchanges among them, and later radical upheavals caused by contacts with European invaders during several centuries of travel, trade, intermarriage, warfare, continued outbreaks of virulent diseases introduced by whites, captivity, enslavement, divided intertribal loyalties, and treaty negotiations. Still another issue examined as part of the debate about authenticity, accuracy, style, sovereignty, and cultural integrity is the way storytelling normally works among oral cultures and how source transcriptions by anthropologists, ethnographers, and folklorists often decontextualize or remove traditional literature from its original settings, whether American Indian or otherwise.

Commonalities Among Selections

One common denominator among the selections is that all have more intricate plots than many traditional stories connected with the Cherokee and other American Indian groups. The original core narratives, on which the retellings are based, are comparatively well-developed tales of creation and origins, animal monsters, supernatural and animal adversaries and helpers, and legends more or less based on history. Not included are the seemingly truncated, although frequently, anthologized Native American narratives of one or two paragraphs about talking animals or of abbreviated *pourquoi* stories that explain how something came to be or why something is the way it is in the natural world. Although not a commonality among all of the stories selected, a large number have specific local settings. Except for "The Three Worlds," "Fire," "The Pleiades and the Pine Cone," "The Red Man and the Uktena," "The Stone Man of the

Mountains," and "The Raven Mockers," the remainder of the thirty selections, as adapted here, contain identifiable places in the traditional lands of the Cherokee in Georgia, the Carolinas, and Tennessee. Another predominant feature is that the legends based on history, as with other frontier narratives, often have a raw violence about them, perhaps making them more suitable for mature readers, if such categories based on age and worldliness have much meaning for today's audiences. And finally, many of the stories reveal Native Americans as not always at home in the world of nature but frequently afraid of its dark and unpredictable forces that could disrupt settled life.

In completing this book, I am indebted to Professor Louise Pettus (retired) from the Department of History at Winthrop University for guiding me toward the research of Charles Hudson on Indians of the southeastern United States; to Professor Jane White (retired) who lent her expertise in anthropology as she read and offered suggestions on substantial portions of the manuscript; to Robert Gorman, Susan Silverman, Michaela Volkmar, Nancy White, and Trey Woodring of the Ida Jane Dacus Library at Winthrop University; and to Gina Price White of the library's Louise Pettus Archives and Special Collections, all of whom were helpful in securing some of the more obscure documentary sources on the Cherokee and other southeastern Native Americans. I am also grateful to Courtney Niskala for designing the two maps for the book. Any flaws contained within the book are mine alone.

Introduction

Considerations in Adapting Native American Traditional Literature

Beyond the Myths: Native American Diversity

In a 1956 essay titled "Myths That Hide the American Indian," anthropologist and the author of the Pulitzer Prize winning novel *Laughing Boy,* Oliver La Farge wrote "Part of the myth about the first Americans is that all of them, or most of them, had one culture and were at the same stage of development."[8] However, the most cursory examination of their traditional stories should be enough to explode this popular preconception, for anyone who delves into the folklore of North American Indians has to be astonished at the sheer variety of the material. Such was my case several decades ago when I began teaching university courses in children's and adolescent literature at the graduate and undergraduate levels to teachers and librarians. The traditional literature of Native Americans, as adapted for younger readers, was a part of those courses in the examination not only of myths, legends, and folktales but also of multicultural literature from around the globe.

I was aware from past reading and study that Native American stories often concerned animals, contained themes of respect for and living in harmony with nature, and explained how the world came into being and why things are as they are. Yet, until I began to encounter more and more of the adaptations of these tales, I had little idea of their immense diversity in form, subject matter, and themes. Among influences contributing to this variety are the longevity of storytelling traditions among the indigenous, numerous patterns of socio-political organization and culture, wide differences in geographic areas, and diverse expression in artistic form and style—with all of these mutually affecting one another. In the words of Kenneth L. Donelson and Alleen Pace Nilson, it is "a gross simplification" to talk about Native Americans "as if they were one people holding the same religious and cultural views."[9]

9

**CHEROKEE & NEIGHBORING
NATIVE AMERICANS OF THE COLONIAL ERA**

Going back many millennia, Native American literature has at least a 28,000-year-old tradition of storytelling. Unfortunately, several decades ago, those who have known little of Native American literature and the oral tradition have said, "The Indians lacked a stable and literate tradition which could easily be absorbed" into the dominant English culture of the colonial era.[10] Such now outdated views upheld the notion that American literature in what is now the United States began in the 1600s with John Smith and the Jamestown colonists

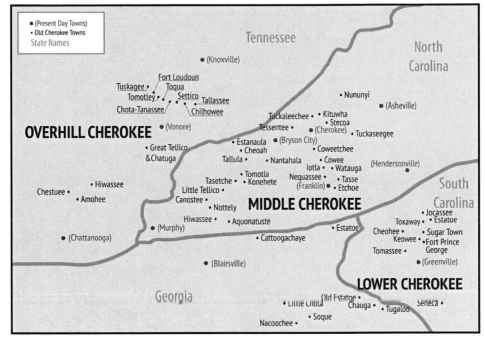

MAJOR CHEROKEE REGIONS

of Virginia (1607) and with the Pilgrims of Plymouth (1620) and Puritans of the Massachusetts Bay Colony (1630–1643). Ron Querry, however, has argued more recently that American literature really started in the rich oral and communal literature of Indian peoples.[11] Thousands of years before Europeans arrived on the North American continent, their storytellers were the historians of each tribe, and from their early days, they absorbed the tales told by the elders and imparted the fundamental beliefs shared by their communities.[12]

Although similar story patterns of plot, character, and motif may be found across cultures around the world, the hundreds of different indigenous polities in North America both before and after contact with Europeans, along with their sharing of tales through proximity to one another or through distant travel and trade, gave enormous variety to the stories told. In *From Abenaki to Zuni: A Dictionary of Native American Tribes*, Native American writer Evelyn Wolfson notes that, of the sixty-eight groups discussed in her book, she has presented "only a fraction" living in North America when Europeans first arrived.[13] Historian Alvin M. Josephy, Jr., states that before the coming of Columbus, the continent may have had an Indian population of as many as forty million and that their customs, environment, and forms of political and social organization "played a role in giving each nation an individual identity and directing it along an individual path."[14] In Charles F. Kovacik and John J. Winberry's *South Carolina: A Geography*, a map showing the location of Indians at the founding of the English colony of South Carolina in 1670 names twenty-six separate groups within the borders of the present state.[15] Among them are two surviving tribes today, the Catawba and the Cherokee.

Of course, an accurate numbering of Native American nations is difficult to achieve. According to Walter Edgar's *South Carolina: A History*, older accounts indicate that, before contact with Europeans, more than forty separate nations were in South Carolina. Yet problems with such counts abound. Over time, some could have been combined and duplicated in later reports. Some nations on the coast may have moved inland and have been called by new names.[16] Furthermore, European names were not always what Indian groups called themselves, nor were the names consistently used by the colonists and, of course, the newcomers' conception of a nation was not necessarily the same as that of aboriginal peoples. Decades ago, anthropologists such as John R. Swanton were aware of the problems in identifying indigenous ethnic and linguistic groups.[17]

One example of the difficulty of determining an exact count of so-called native nations occurs with the Catawba. In her history of the tribe, Douglas Summers Brown counts forty-seven separate names used for this group.[18] Edgar says that the current name did not appear among whites until around 1715. About thirty years later, the Indians themselves had adopted the appellation, and it generally referred to a loose collection of towns in the upper Piedmont of North and South Carolina composed of the Esau, Sugaree, Nassaw, and Cheraw.[19] Historian Lawrence Lee observes that, following unrest and bloodshed with North and South Carolina, the Cheraw left their settlements on the upper Neuse River in North Carolina and moved toward the west into South Carolina near the Catawba.[20] Like many other instances from history, this blending of tribes demonstrates the complicated, manifold, and continuously evolving nature of native cultures as some dissipated and later coalesced with other groups.

Separate Cultures, Divided Aims

Interestingly enough, the conflict between the Cheraw and the Carolinas demonstrates that, based on colonial records, the first Americans often did not share the same political, economic, and military aims. In fighting the Cheraw, the province of North Carolina in 1718 organized four military companies, each composed of ten whites and ten Indians.[21] Indeed, Indian allies of Europeans sometimes outnumbered the white militias and colonial troops whom they accompanied in campaigns against other tribes as in the second war (1712–1715) between forces from South Carolina sent against the Tuscarora who resided along the lower Neuse River and Contentea Creek in the inner coastal plain of North Carolina. Laurence Lee numbers the troops from South Carolina as consisting of only thirty-three whites but around eight hundred and fifty assorted Indian auxillaries.[22] Promises of trade, scalps, and slaves were the usual enticements for the colonists' native allies as Lee makes clear in describing the 1711–1712 first war with the Tuscarora[23] and the later Cheraw conflict of 1718 already mentioned. According to Alan Gallay's *The Indian Slave Trade*, winner of the Bancroft Prize in American History, South Carolina forces of one thousand and five hundred men, primarily composed of Chickasaw, Creek, and Yamasee warriors, also launched an invasion in 1711 to the distant west of the province to destroy and enslave the Choctaw, who were aligned with the French whose goal was imperial domination of Native American trade along the Mississippi River. The expedition proved to be successful because of the close cooperation between the Indians and Carolina's English traders, with each group expecting to profit from it.[24]

The reader who knows the history of the Spanish conquests of the Aztecs by Cortes in Mexico and of the Incas by Pizarro in Peru will not be surprised at European and Indian alliances against other Indians in North America. The Indian domains to the south had already experienced such events on a grander scale in the sixteenth century. Once the Tlaxcalans, a tributary people to the Aztecs, made peace with Cortes, his tiny army of a few hundred grew by many thousands so that he could more readily defeat the Aztecs, who were the hated enemies of his allies. In the words of historian and documentary filmmaker Michael Wood, "More even than the superiority of European technology, it would be the support given by Native American peoples which would eventually lead to Cortes' victory."[25] In their history and art, the modern citizens of the city of Tlaxcala today still defend their choice to help overthrow their detested Aztec overlords.[26] Further south in the Inca Empire of Tawantinsuyu, the sons of Emperor Wayna Capac—Atahuallpa and Huascar, both dual claimants to their father's throne—were fighting a brutal civil war. According to Charles C. Mann's *1491: New Revelations of the Americas Before Columbus*, this conflict allowed Pizarro to exploit the divided Inca society, already weakened by a virulent smallpox epidemic that had prepared the way for victory by the conquistador's tiny force of 168 men.[27]

At any rate, bands both large and small that lived or ranged throughout the Carolinas and other parts of North America also had their dissensions with one another. These emerged frequently not just between separate tribes but within the same tribe. The two wars with the Tuscarora of North Carolina illustrate this point. Led by Chief Tom Blount, one branch of the Tuscarora, who lived along the upper Neuse, Tar, and Roanoke Rivers, opposed fighting the English. During the Second Tuscarora War, this group aided colonial invaders and turned over Chief Hancock of the lower settlements to his white enemies and their native allies. As a reward for cooperation, the colony of North Carolina provided the Upper Tuscarora with a reservation. The defeated segment of the tribe left the colony, moved to New York, and joined their Iroquoian relatives of the Five Nations to form the Six Nations.[28]

One among many instances of an on-going record of divided aims within the Cherokee of the eighteenth century occurred in July of 1777 with the Treaty of Long Island. Historian Stanley Hoig recounts that at Fort Patrick Henry on the Holston River in Virginia, the peace party of Corn Tassel, Raven, Oconostota, Attakullakulla, and almost twenty other headmen signed away all of their land in upper east Tennessee and western North Carolina. Opposing the terms of the treaty and not one of its signatories, the war chief Dragging Canoe persuaded dissident Overhill headmen to abandon their settlements on the Little Tennessee and to establish new ones farther south on the Tennessee River.[29] With almost a thousand warriors, what historian John P. Brown calls "practically the entire fighting strength" of the Cherokee nation, Dragging Canoe established himself and his followers in eleven settlements along Chickamauga Creek near the present location of Chattanooga. This pro-war faction became the much-feared Chickamaugans. From their remote location, Dragging Canoe and other prominent leaders like Bloody Fellow, Glass, Hanging Maw, Little Owl, Kitegista, Little Turkey, Lying Fish, Man Killer, Middlestriker, Richard Justice, Young Tassel, and other less well-known headmen conducted raids along the frontiers of Georgia, North and South Carolina, and Virginia. These nativitists referred to their nation's accommodators and treaty signers as "Virginians and rogues" and looked upon themselves as the true Cherokee people.[30] Indeed, throughout most of the 1700s, Cherokee leaders "remained dichotomized into peace and war factions."[31]

Lest anyone think that Native Americans were always manipulated by unscrupulous whites, evidence suggests the contrary. Noted social anthropologist and expert on Native American cultures of the Southeast, Charles Hudson has called the eighteenth century Indian trader and historian James Adair "a well-educated man who had perhaps the best understanding of the southeastern Indians of any man of his time."[32] Having lived and traded for thirty-three years among the Indians of the colonial Southeast, Adair provides a strong antidote to the fallacy that indigenous people were the puppets of Europeans. In his 1775 *History of the American Indians*, he observed that "they are very deliberate in their councils, and never give an immediate answer to any message sent by strangers, but suffer some nights first to elapse. They reason in a very orderly manner, with much coolness and good-natured language, though they may differ widely in their opinions."[33] He described how all their national affairs were debated by "every father of a family speaking in his house on the subject, with rapid, bold language, and the utmost freedom that a people can use. Their voices, to a man, have due weight in every public affair, as it concerns their welfare alike."[34] In his 1775 "Narrative of an Adventure in Kentucky," Felix Walker gave an account of meeting the distinguished Cherokee chief Attakullakulla, at that time approximately ninety years of age. Walker described him as "the Solon of his day" who was "the most celebrated and influential Indian among all the tribes then known."[35] Called by whites the Little Carpenter, Attakullakulla derived this name from his skill in negotiating treaties. According to Walker, the chief's diplomatic abilities were like an artful joiner who could make "every notch and joint" of wood fit seamlessly together.[36] Attakullakulla was certainly adroit in manipulating Virginia and South Carolina, one against the other, to advance Cherokee economic interests.[37] In writing not only of Attakullakulla but of other Cherokee leaders as well, Hoig avers that they were rarely "defeated in their contests with the government on the merits of their case but usually by the unwillingness of government officials to adhere to their own ethics and written laws."[38] Yet Cherokee leaders often colluded with whites in dispossessing their communities of commonly held lands. Boundaries settled by treaty mattered little when headmen like Oconostota, Saluy, and others worked to give the half–Indian sons of white traders huge slices of territory. One attempted land grant in the upper Saluda valley of South Carolina in the late 1760s encompassed 144 square miles. Another at this time was a twelve square-mile tract. Officials of the crown overturned both grants, but the larger one was later approved in the same provincial court at Ninety Six that had originally denied title to it.[39]

As with the Cherokee, numerous divisions occurred within other Native American groups, a salient example being one among the nineteenth century Lakota, or Sioux, of the northern Great Plains. In *Bury My Heart at Wounded Knee*, historian Dee Brown describes their lack of cohesion during the second half of the nineteenth century. At the beginning of the Civil War, the leader of the Oglala Sioux was Red Cloud, an outstanding and shrewd war chief whose military prowess in the late 1860s drove white intruders and the United States Army from the Powder River country. However, Spotted Tail of the Brule, although not always pleased with incursions by outsiders into traditional Sioux territory, opposed warfare and counseled peace at this time.[40] And yet by 1876, after the defeat of Custer, both men and their followers signed an agreement, although under duress, ceding the Black Hills and the Powder River lands to the United States, while Sitting Bull and his Hunkpapa band rejected the treaty and decided to remain free of reservations and live a traditional life of hunting by going to Canada.[41]

Variances in Language and Literature: Problems in Defining and Classifying

Along with differing geo-political interests, the great variances in languages and the arts further affected the diversity of the indigenous literature just as the literature influenced these cultural components. Even as late as 1887, three distinct dialects of the Cherokee language could still be found among the Eastern Band in western North Carolina.[42] Citing Charles Hudson's work, Edgar indicates that four hundred years ago, near the time of the founding of South Carolina, the colony had four Native American linguistic groups and that these bore as much resemblance to one another as Chinese would to English today.[43] An anecdote from early eighteenth century explorer John Lawson corroborates this linguistic diversity. In his 1709 journal, a major source for early documentary evidence on southeastern Indians, Lawson describes traveling to visit the Congarees of South Carolina. Lawson notes how they spoke a language which was "quite different" from neighboring tribes that lived no more than ten or twenty miles away.[44] In discussing the variety of ceramics among the indigenous of the Carolinas, Edgar points out that the largest group of Indians living there, the Cherokee, geographically dispersed as they were into their towns of the Lower, Middle, Valley, and Overhill regions, produced different styles of pottery. That of the Overhill towns along the Tennessee River possessed a shiny glaze, whereas that of the Lower towns along the Keowee and its tributaries had stamped designs.[45]

Despite the variety within and between groups, even in relatively small places like South Carolina, commonalties do emerge in the literature surviving today in written form. Both Mooney with Cherokee narratives and later Swanton with tales from other southeastern Indians like the Creek, Hitchiti, Alabama, Koasati, and Natchez commented on variants of the same storyline found among these different groups.[46] Native American stories also partake of common motifs across wider cultural areas. In analyzing adaptations for younger readers, Zena Sutherland classifies the stories into five types, although all may have overlapping characteristics causing them not to fit tidily into one category.[47] These include creation myths, or stories of how the world came into being and who or what made it; trickster stories, sometimes humorous, with a human or animal protagonist; journeys to other worlds, often a type of threshold tale or one as Donna E. Norton says that allows a character to move between the worlds of human and animal, child and adult, or the everyday and spiritual[48]; hero stories, in which an individual must overcome great obstacles as tests of courage; and tales in which a human unites in marriage to an animal or spirit.

Other writers use similar groupings but sometimes give additional categories. For instance, anthropologist Alfonso Ortiz and storyteller Richard

Erdoes in their anthology, *American Indian Myths and Legends*, subdivide creation stories into those pertaining to humans and those relating to the world. Besides trickster and hero tales, they also have those of war, of the Great Spirit as expressed in nature, of love and lust, of the supernatural realm of ghosts and spirits, and of individual deaths and apocalyptic endings.[49]

Because Native American stories have such variety, anyone expecting a logically consistent basis of classification will be disappointed. When the Bureau of American Ethnology issued *Myths of the Cherokee* in 1900, the collection made by Mooney, he divided the stories into cosmogonic myths; quadruped, bird, snake, fish, and insect myths; wonder stories; historical traditions; and miscellaneous myths and legends.[50] Today, Mooney's scheme does not appear systematic when compared to the more comprehensive and internationally accepted cataloging devised in 1910 by Finnish scholar Antii Aarne and enlarged and translated by Stith Thompson of Indiana University in 1928. Revised in 1961, *The Types of Folktales: A Classification and Bibliography* is now a standard research tool that contains five basic categories of tales with some 2,499 tale types.

A Common Mythopoeic Worldview

Whatever might be the content or the various classification schemes used, however, authorities are in agreement about one thing: the world of nature in its manifold forms permeates a significant number of the tales of native peoples.[51] In describing the overarching theme of their collection of Native American legends, Edmunds and Clark speak of the way that different tribes believed that all of nature possessed an in-dwelling spirit. Not only man but the heavens above and the earth below—its lakes and streams, mountains and hills, plants and animals—all were visible manifestations of spirit within.[52] According to this pantheistic religion, humans should live in harmony with nature, and communication with its objects and forces was nothing out of the ordinary. Summarizing research on the Cherokee and other Indians of the southeastern United States, Edgar says,

> When a young man killed his first animal and caught his first fish, he did not eat them. This was so as not to offend their spirits into denying him good hunting or fishing in the future. Even in the gathering of herbs, such as ginseng, there was a ritual and a prayer. Every living thing and every force in nature had a spirit. Each needed to be mollified in order to maintain the balance and harmony of the natural world.[53]

This worldview of the indigenous is similar to the mythopoeic conceptions found in the cradle of western civilization in Egypt and the Fertile Crescent. As

Henri and H. A. Groenwegen Frankfort have explained, humanity and nature for the ancients could not be compartmentalized. Every event that they encountered in nature was rife with cosmic meaning, not to be logically analyzed through impersonal, scientific causes detached from events but to be explained through personal causes and related as story.[54] Nothing was ever as it appeared to the limitations of human senses.

The same holds true in Greco-Roman mythology and Cherokee lore. The rendition of classical myths recounted in *Metamorphoses,* by the first century Roman poet Ovid, relates how the young hunter Actaeon accidentally comes upon what seems to be a woman and her attendants bathing in a pool in the valley of Gargaphie, "all dark and shaded with pine and cypress."[55] Yet these are no mortals but the goddess Diana and her nymphs. As punishment for his accidentally seeing her nakedness, the goddess turns Actaeon into a stag, and his own hounds attack and kill him. In *The Golden Fleece,* an adaptation from Greek mythology of Jason and the Argonauts for juvenile readers by Irish storyteller Padraic Colum, the young hero leaves his mentor, the centaur Chiron, and travels down Mount Pelion, where he comes to the flooded and swift-flowing Anaurus River. Unable to cross the swollen stream, he meets an old woman who offers to carry him over it on her back. She does, and, lo, and behold, on the opposite bank she suddenly becomes the great goddess Hera who stands before him in a "wondrous light." No longer an old crone, she wears "a golden robe and a shining crown."[56]

In Mooney's recording of the Cherokee story "The Man Who Married the Thunder's Sister,"[57] retold here as "The Man Who Traveled to the World Below," a young warrior follows two women to their home. They enter a river, which turns out to be a grassy path leading to the cave of their brother who personifies the Thunder Spirit of Tallulah Gorge.

In all of these mythopoeic experiences, anything can and does happen without the necessity of seeking logical explanation. Perhaps for this reason, traditional Native American literature sounds strange to contemporary ears. Yet there are additional reasons for this otherness besides similarity to an ancient worldview that is different from a modern, scientific one. When compared to well-known, time-honored European folktales like Charles Perrault's "The Sleeping Beauty" of 1697 or Jacob and Wilhelm Grimm's "The Elves and the Shoemaker" of 1812, Native American stories do not usually have the same highly structured plots.

In *The World of Manabozho: Tales of the Chippewa Indians*, adapter Thomas B. Leekley calls Amerindian folklore "a great collection of anecdotes, jokes, and fables" with plots generally composed of one episode perhaps connected to another in a relationship like that of "two beads on one string, seldom that of two bricks in one building."[58] Erdoes and Ortiz echo this description and add that at times the tales start and end abruptly, "spinning out a single image or episode" with the stories "often told in chains, one word, character, or idea bringing to mind a related one."[59]

Simple and Complex Story Structure

These characterizations, however, do not seem entirely accurate of all the Cherokee folktales found in Mooney's seminal collection. Yes, some of the stories have sudden beginnings and endings, and some are loosely plotted with only one or two episodes. These features seem to predominate among such talking animal and trickster fables as "The Rabbit Dines the Bear"[60] or the very brief *pourquoi* stories that offer explanations like "Why the Mink Smells."[61]

Yet many of the stories have more fully developed plot lines. Mooney's rendition of the Cherokee legend of "The Bear Man" does indeed abruptly begin with "A man went hunting in the mountains and came across a black bear, which he wounded with an arrow."[62] The tale also concludes just as quickly with "If they [the people in the village] had kept him [the hunter who had turned into a bear] shut up and fasting until the end of the seven days he would have become a man again and would have lived."[63]

This particular story, though, does have several highly interconnected episodes, seven to be precise, matching the number seven that figures prominently at the end of the tale. Along with four, this number was sacred to the Cherokee.[64] The seven episodes are as follows:

1. A hunter in the mountains meets a friendly "medicine bear" that possesses great powers.
2. The hunter follows the bear to huge cave that is like a council house full of all kinds of other bears who discover that, because of their claws, they are unable to use bows and arrows to hunt.
3. The hunter and the bear then travel to another cave where the bear lives and where he feeds the hungry man chestnuts and berries.
4. The bear and man stay together during the winter as the man slowly transforms into a bear, during which time the bear predicts that hunters will kill and skin him but that they will take the man back with them.
5. The hunters come and do as the bear predicted, and as they depart, the man gathers leaves and covers the bloody spot where they had killed the bear so that he can be reborn as another bear.
6. Back in the village, the man tells what had happened, and the people lock him up for seven days and nights so that he will lose his bear nature and become a man again.

7. Unfortunately, the hunter's wife releases him before the seven days are over, and he dies because he had not fully completed his transformation back into a man.[65]

Other stories in Mooney have even more complicated plots and also use conventional beginnings like the "once upon a time" openings of European folktales. The tale of Spear-Finger, the terrible female monster who lurked along the gorge of the Nantahala River, starts "Long, long ago,"[66] while "The Hunter in the Dakwa," a Jonah story about a fish large enough to swallow human beings, begins "In the old days there was a great fish...."[67]

Conventional endings with formulaic stylistic devices of the "happily ever after" type rarely appear, and the stories where humans have crossed thresholds into animal or spiritual realms generally close abruptly and sadly as in the death of the main character in "The Bear Man" previously discussed. In "The Underground Panthers," a hunter meets a mountain lion in the woods and learns the human and animal worlds are not dissimilar. Both hunt deer, both celebrate the green corn dance, both live in towns with their own kind, and both have a physical ceremonial space in their respective communities for sacred festivals. After staying for a part of the night in the underground village of the panthers, dancing with them in the green corn celebration, the hunter leaves their mountain cave and discovers that he has been away for several days in another place where time is not the same as it is among people. He returns to his settlement and unfortunately dies within seven days, as does the hunter in "The Bear Man," because he had begun to assume the nature of a panther and can no longer live in the human world.[68] This type of ending is common in Cherokee stories in which individuals cross thresholds between animal and human or human and spirit realms and in which they do not undergo ritual cleansing by such means as fasting, usually for seven days, though sometimes for four. A good example of this kind of story contained within the present collection is "The Man Who Traveled to the World Below."

However, tales in which a hero or group attempts to set the world in order by killing a monster that threatens human life usually do end happily even if they do not have a stylistic tag underscoring the point that all is now safe as a result of the monster's destruction. These stories are also comparable to myths in other cultures. In his *Age of Fable or Beauties of Mythology*, Thomas Bulfinch describes Heracles' ridding the ravaged countryside of Argos of the nine-headed Lernaean hydra; Theseus' destroying the savage Periphetes, armed with his iron club, or the conquering the evil marauder Procrustes, who stretched his captives or chopped them up to fit his iron bed; and Apollo's slaying the gigantic serpent Python that lurked in the rocky recesses of Mount Parnassus.[69] Many of the retellings of Cherokee stories in the present book, classified under the headings of Killing the Great Monsters and Supernatural Adversaries and Helpers also have similarly safe conclusions.

Decontextualized Tales

Besides the mythopoeic assumptions about reality and the often terse plots with sudden beginnings and endings, another reason that much of Native American folklore seems unusual to readers today is that the written transcriptions lack the authentic context that would have rendered the original oral versions meaningful to their indigenous listeners. Kiefer, Hepler, and Hickman point out that this body of literature "would have been heard by insiders who understood these tales within the context of a large interlocking set of stories."[70] For example, in Mooney's "The Water Cannibals," the first sentence of the story refers to the "friendly" Nunnehi and then immediately turns to "the race of cannibal spirits, who stay at the bottoms of the deep rivers and live upon human flesh, especially that of little children."[71] The story next proceeds to tell of a dying man who is helped by an old woman. A stranger, she comes to visit the man and then takes him to an underwater village of the cannibals. He is unaware of who they are. She offers him a slice of human flesh, but he refuses to eat it. This offering serves as a test which he passes so that she then offers regular human food—cornbread and beans. Over time, he revives, and the old woman points the way for him to return home. Until this man's experience, no one knew about the vicious water cannibals. Although the story does not say so directly, the mysterious old woman was a Nunnehi or one of the Immortals, beings who are spirits, who live everywhere, and who often serve as protectors to the Cherokee. Through her help and the man's later recounting his experience to his fellow villagers, after he has waited for the appropriate seven days, the Cherokee were able to learn of the Water Cannibals and warn (or frighten) their children against the predations of these hunters of humans.

In *The Scribal Society,* Alan C. Purves comments on formulating the meaning of a text, whether oral or print. In one passage, he notes that texts from past worldviews took their meaning from communities that shared a common set of reference points in relation to their tales and common "ways of talking about them and interpreting them."[72] Hearing "The Water Cannibals" within the context of Cherokee society, native listeners would have recognized, based on their shared knowledge of other tales, that the old woman was one of the their spiritual protectors. However, to those outside this context—that is, today's readers of the story's written version—it appears disjointed, truncated, incomplete, or decontextualized, thereby lacking the fuller meaning it once had for those from another time and place. If contemporary readers have experienced other stories in Mooney's collection that more fully convey information concerning the Immortals—stories such as "The Nunnehi and Other Spirit Folk"[73]—or have looked in his Glossary of Cherokee Words[74] or have studied relevant sections of his Notes and Parallels to Other Myths,[75] they would likely be able to infer the meaningful connections between the old woman and the spirit helpers of the nation. Today's readers might also make such connections if they had studied authorities on southeastern Indians like anthropologist Charles Hudson. In any event, such knowledge would have been assumed by tribal storytellers. However, it is missing from the printed page isolated from a past Cherokee context in which the stories arose, an important consideration for anyone adapting this material for modern audiences, whether children, adults, or crossover readers. A fuller discussion of the ramifications of an audience's prior knowledge follows in the section Beyond Transcription: Recreating Authenticity.

Recreating Authentic Storytelling in Print

Another significant contextual aspect for an adapter to consider is the physical setting in which native peoples heard their stories and the accoutrements of voice, gesture, and objects accompanying them. Some adapters of Native American folklore forget this point and have suggested that the style for retelling these stories should be, as Ella Clark has said, one of "simplicity, sincerity, a conversational tone or one of oral quality, and the variety of rhythms in everyday speech."[76] According to Anne Pellowski, one of the foremost authorities on the history of storytelling and the variety of forms it has taken from around the world, Clark's suggestion is in line with the observations of ethnologists, folklorists, and anthropologists who transcribed many of the tales and who noted their often brief plots and thin descriptions.[77]

Yet does this suggested manner of retelling necessarily match actual storytelling events? Pellowski argues that this characterization of the style of Native American literature is incorrect. In *The World of Storytelling*, she offers a cogent summary of research on some indigenous styles of oral presentation from the past to support her contention. Among the Clackamas Chinook tribes of the Pacific Northwest, one of their storytellers did not convey a character's emotions with words but acted them out with tone of voice and movement. During another observed rendition, a raconteur of the Coeur d'Alene, whose lands originally spanned parts of Washington, Idaho, and Montana, arose from his chair, went outside, got on his stomach on the porch, and crawled back inside, pantomiming the effect of sneaking up on a tent at night. A Navajo man told his tales in an older, more formal, less conversational style than he would have used in everyday speech. He also indicated that, if an audience were not present, the stories tended to be less interesting.[78]

This sampling from Pellowski's findings obviously undermines notions that oral presentations of Indian storytelling were necessarily the conversational, simple, and unemotional affairs that they appear to be from some of the transcriptions and modern adaptations. Such a perception may inadvertently lend support to an aspect of what La Farge calls the "oldest myth" about Indians, that of "the Noble Red Man or the Child of Nature."[79] In this fantasy, they are endowed with the tendency to speak in "flowery oratory of implacable dullness or else with an imbecilic inability to converse in anything more than grunts and monosyllables."[80] It is this later component of the laconic Indian that strippeddown retellings seem to reinforce, and even though they may be word-for-word recordings by transcribers, they are devoid of a living context that captures the spirit in which the stories were told in times past.

This discussion of print versions of indigenous stories, removed from their traditional oral context, relates to important concerns in selecting and adapting stories originating in various cultures. These considerations began to receive growing attention during the Civil Rights movement in the 1960s. Since then, there has been an ever-increasing awareness of the need for diversity education. Its ideas embrace the treatment of all ethnicities and nations, once on the periphery, as equals within the human family.[81] In *Multicultural Children's Literature*, Donna Norton provides an account of further issues in diversity, particularly with respect to both contemporary and traditional Native American literature. Among these are authenticity, sovereignty, and literal versus metaphorical meanings.[82] Knowledge of such issues, their implications, and certain flaws in assumptions of what is deemed acceptable retellings of Native American literature are important for understanding how an adapter might render a treatment of selected material.

The Myth of the Frozen Traditional Culture

Authenticity concerns whether the text, along with illustrations, if these are included, is an accurate depiction of the particular culture. Yet this idea is not as straightforward as it sounds. No culture is fixed but is constantly changing, sometimes at rates faster than others, and, unless completely isolated, is constantly interacting with others. It influences it neighbors, and it borrows from its neighbors. They assimilate one another's ideas and artifacts, and they accommodate themselves to outside influences by forming new ideas and artifacts. The process might be compared with the Hegelian dialectic of thesis encountering antithesis to form a new synthesis.

Even before the arrival of Europeans, the aboriginal populations did not remain isolated from one another and were connected through travel, trade, hunting, and war. According to Charles Hudson's authoritative study, *The Southeastern Indians*, a web of trails linked tribes like the Cherokee to St. Augustine in the south, to the lower Mississippi in the southwest, and to Ohio and the Great Lakes in the north. The indigenous also made extensive use of waterways, and some had large vessels. Spanish chronicles of the sixteenth century report the de Soto expedition being attacked by Indians in huge canoes that could hold 75 to 80 paddlers and warriors.[83] One of the earliest English sources on Indians east of the Appalachians is Robert Beverley's *The History of Virginia in Four Parts*. Originally published in 1705, this work includes valuable ethnographic information, according to historian Alan Gallay.[84] Beverley's revised 1722 edition mentions the great distances that local native populations traveled on foot, making "no provision for their journey but their gun or bow, to supply them with food for many hundreds of miles together."[85] Adair's 1775 *The History of the Native Americans* makes the same point in regard to travel related to warfare.[86]

As with other societies around the world, such extensive travel in the pursuit of trade, hunting, and war would have allowed different tribes to share stories about creation, heroic feats, and nature. In his discussion of Cherokee stories, Mooney asserts that Indians are "great wanderers, and a myth can travel as far as a redstone pipe or a string of wampum."[87] He adds that sometimes among eastern tribes an entire band or village would visit another one for weeks or months in order to dance, feast, trade, and swap stories. He further adds that the tribes had a "trade jargon or sign language," thus indicating extensive commerce between them.[88] Moreover, Mooney's research indicates an admixture among the Cherokee of eastern tribes such as the Creek, Catawba, Natchez, Iroquois, and others.[89] This intermingling of native strains tends to render dubious oversimplified assertions about story authenticity, if the term is understood to mean an accurate and true narrative depiction originating from a single ethnic group.

Changes to southeastern indigenous cultures came much faster once they encountered alien European societies from Spain, France, and England. Before European contact, the native culture from roughly 800 C.E. to 1600 C.E. was what archaeologists have termed "Mississippian," a period during which a greater reliance on the cultivation of corn brought about highly organized societies where power became centered in rulers whose status was higher than that of their people. Populations grew. Military rivalries expanded. People lived in towns surrounded by castellated wooden palisades, sometimes complete with towers and moats. Chiefs justified their positions by building great burial mounds and claiming descent from such deities as the Sun. These leaders often had so much authority that, when de Soto and his army invaded their domains, his strategy was sometimes to make the ruler a prisoner. To control the body, he controlled the head. If this maneuver failed, his superior arms and the natives' fear of his cavalry did not, for the Indians did not have horses at the time and possessed stone-age weapons such as bows and flint- or horn-tipped arrows, and occasional shields and body armor of woven cane and wooden slats.[90]

Once European contact occurred, the Mississippian world began to collapse in what anthropologist Robbie Ethridge calls "a shatter zone" at points of entry along the Atlantic coast.[91] As a result, "shock waves" began "emanating out of the east and reverberating throughout the lower South to the Mississippi River valley and beyond."[92] Changes to indigenous societies did not occur at once. Sometimes disruptions were concentrated, and sometimes they were gradual. Intense disruptors were primarily caused by European diseases like smallpox that broke out from time to time. Slower disruptors stemmed from commercial traffic based on exchanges for indigenous commodities such as hides and Indian slaves in return for European firearms, gunpowder, and other trade goods. Competition for trade, especially to capture slaves to sell to English colonists in Jamestown and Charleston, led to increased violence and warfare among Indians beyond white settlements and the formation of reorganized native societies that often coalesced with one another into new groups for self-protection, self-preservation, or greater aggression.[93]

The Cherokee provide a case in point. In his *Historical Sketch of the Cherokee*, Mooney dates their first contact with Europeans a year after de Soto's 1539 landing at Tampa Bay. In May 1540, his expedition reached what in the eighteenth century were traditional Cherokee settlements in the Blue Ridge Mountains.[94] After Juan Pardo's later exploration of the interior in two expeditions between 1566 and 1568 of western South and North Carolina, the Spanish appear to have established mining operations for gold and other ores in Cherokee territory. Mooney reports the remains of European style shafts and fortifications, indicating a Spanish presence following the expeditions of de Soto and Pardo.[95]

Ninety years after Mooney's work, Hudson's analysis of Juan Pardo's explorations through *La Florida*, a vast area claimed by Spain, extending up and down the Atlantic coast from Newfoundland to the Florida peninsula and stretching all the way to Mexico, strongly suggests from linguistic evidence that the Spanish made contact with Indians who were more than likely Cherokee speakers.[96] Pardo's first foray went as far west as the eastern Blue Ridge Mountains where he then headed north and northeast before returning to his base at Santa Elena on the South Carolina coast near present-day Beaufort. Near the Indian town of Joara, Pardo built a tiny fort in 1567 and garrisoned it with a small company under Sergeant Moyano.[97] Hudson thought the construction to be near Marion in McDowell County, North Carolina, but recent archaeological evidence now places the site, known as Fort San Juan, near Morganton in Burke County.[98] On his second trip, Pardo crossed the Blue Ridge and in 1568 built four additional small forts. By May of that year, about two months after Pardo had left the interior, word arrived on the coast that the forts had collapsed, overrun by the natives. Only one Spaniard is known to have survived and returned to Santa Elena.[99]

Mooney indicates that the impression on the Cherokee from this early contact with the Spanish must have been "considerable," though difficult to estimate.[100] Hudson's later research, however, provides more concrete information about the effects of the de Soto and Pardo expeditions on indigenous peoples of the interior of the Southeast. Earlier Spanish explorers like Ponce de Leon, Ayllon, and Narvaez gave no indication of populations devastated by disease. Citing archaeological evidence from Mississippian paramount chiefdoms like Coosa, Hudson notes in the latter part of the 1500s that people there and elsewhere perished in large numbers as evidenced by fewer settlements and the fact that the ones remaining became smaller as refugee populations coalesced.[101] Before de Soto, the polity of Coosa, whose descendants later became the Upper Creek who lived south of the Cherokee and with whom they had contact, was among the most powerful chiefdoms of the Southeast and was heavily populated.[102] Thus, the European "stewpots of disease" in these tiny forts, missions, and other settlements that the Spanish established in their vast claim of *La Florida* brought unknown maladies to the indigenous societies that one writer of the time described as *una como pestilential*, meaning "like a plague."[103] Indian traders from these places went into the interior and returned, perhaps with slaves. Native fugitives, fleeing to the hinterlands from the rigorous work requirements and stultifying life imposed by the Spanish mission system, were also likely carriers of pestilences that caused Southeast Indian societies to collapse. Hudson says that the native polities that emerged over the next hundred years were nothing like what Pardo had experienced among these cultures on his forays into the interior.[104]

By the time of English contact in the 1670s, two of the principal activities of the Cherokee—what Grace Steele Woodward has called their "beloved" occupations[105] of hunting and war—were undergoing transformation. According to accounts from a 1673 trade embassy made by James Needham and Gabriel Arthur from Virginia, the Upper Cherokee at their remote mountain capital of Chota, an Overhill settlement on the Little Tennessee River, were in possession of guns. In writing about the expedition, Arthur mentions that the Cherokee had been raiding Spanish settlements in Florida. They had likely obtained the weapons there.[106]

The procurement of gunpowder and firearms over the next sixty years of contact with the English brought even more profound alterations to the traditional culture and enabled the Cherokee to follow war and hunting with a vengeance unknown in earlier times, for the manner and style of both changed. As Duane King, Ken Blankenship, and Barbara Duncan have noted, "The Cherokee economy was dependent on a steady supply of European manufactured goods and the security of the British colonies in the Southeast was dependent on a strong Indian ally in the interior to serve as a bulwark and buffer against French incursions from the Ohio and Mississippi valleys."[107] In *The Cherokee Nation*, Robert J. Conley describes how the Cherokee abandoned the making and use of traditional weapons and turned from hunting in order live to living in order to hunt. Their trade with the whites, especially in South Carolina, became a grand commercial enterprise, with the native and colonial economies becoming interdependent in the first half of the eighteenth century. As a result of the proliferation of commerce, the old skills of the tribe languished. The Cherokee became more and more dependent on European cooking utensils, cloth, and other trade goods, and the makers of bows and arrows, pottery, baskets, and other items found themselves more and more superfluous.[108]

Documentary evidence from the first quarter of the eighteenth century indicates that the Cherokee and their indigenous neighbors appeared satisfied with the changes that had occurred and were occurring. In 1715 and again in 1725, the provincial government of South Carolina sent Colonel George Chicken on embassies to the Cherokee. These missions were to strengthen military alliances and trade. In attempting to broker a peace between the Cherokee and their traditional enemies the Creek, Chicken recorded in his 1715 journal that he counseled the Cherokee against fighting the Creek because the latter had had time to prepare for war and had secured their goods, wives, and children so that there was no advantage to the Cherokee for the "taking of slaves or any plunder."[109] An Indian spokesman replied that these were not important considerations. In regard to their Creek enemies, he told Chicken that the chief reason for war with the Creek was "to cut them off."[110] Chicken's advice nonetheless implied that slaves and booty were common reasons for engaging in warfare. Another parley occurred the next day at the Overhill town of Chota. In reference to the Creek, the Cherokee unequivocally declared to Chicken that, if they made peace, they then "should have no way in getting of slaves to buy ammunition and clothing and that they were resolved to get ready for war."[111]

During his second mission, Chicken recounted in his 1725 journal a speech made by King Crow at the Lower settlement of Tomassee. In the council house, King Crow reminded those assembled "what a good thing it was to be friends with the English ... and bid them [the Cherokee] to remember what good times it was now to what it had been before the English came among them."[112] Ten days later a meeting took place with the Head Warrior of the principal Overhill town of "Tunissee," sometimes spelled as Tanassee, from which Tennessee derives. In addressing the assembly of the town, the Head Warrior commented on the changes among the Cherokee that he had witnessed over the years. He asked that the people "consider that all their old men were gone" and that the current generation had "been brought up after another manner than their forefathers and that they must consider that they could not live without the English."[113]

These kinds of parleys about war, slaves, plunder, firearms, ammunition, other trade goods, and concomitant changes echoed throughout other negotiations during the eighteenth century. In addition to Chicken's 1725 mission, South Carolina also sent Captain Tobias Fitch in the same year on an embassy to the Creek. This journey overlapped with Chicken's trip into the interior. The purpose of Fitch's expedition was to have the Creek make restitution to a white trader named John Sharp. They had attacked and robbed him while he had been with the Cherokee. The marauders had seriously injured Sharp and stolen his property—a slave woman and her children, "his best case of pistols," and other trade items. Scolding the Creek for their actions, Fitch reminded them of how they had benefited from commerce with Charleston. Before, they had nothing with which to war and hunt except bows and arrows, but now they had firearms to kill deer and fight enemies. Before, they had only stone tools, but now they had metal hoes and axes. Before, they wore only skins, but now they dressed in cloth garments.[114] About three weeks after this episode, while Fitch was among the Lower Creek, there arrived in the town of Kawita (Coweta) three Seneca warriors of the Iroquois League, a polity noted for its expansionism and slaving activities.[115] Interfering with Fitch's efforts at peace between the Creek and Cherokee, the Seneca embassy made clear to the people of Kawita that, if they concluded a treaty with the Cherokee, the Seneca nation would regard the Creek as enemies as great as the Cherokee. The Seneca warriors added that the current state of hostilities was best, for at present their people had no one "to war against nor yet no meal to eat but the Cherokee."[116] This instance and others are indicative of how war furnished native peoples the means of trade and livelihood.

Between 1715 and 1717, South Carolina was embroiled in a desperate war for survival with the Yamassee and their confederates. Thereafter, Indian slaves became less important for the province as it began importing greater numbers of Africans for its growing agricultural economy.[117] Trade in hides, however, continued to increase. According to Edgar, commerce became such a preoccupation among Cherokee men that some trade goods like iron kettles conferred great status in much the same manner as war had in the past. The metal could be used for agricultural tools like hoes. Because of the huge demand in England for deer leather procured though the Indian trade, South Carolina went from exporting sixty-four thousand hides at the end of the seventeenth century to shipping from Charleston 150,000 skins in 1750. This figure comprised twenty percent of the exports leaving the port.[118] Hudson compares the slaughter of deer in the Carolinas to that of the buffalo on the Great Plains during the nineteenth century[119] and has declared that the tremendous commerce in whitetail deer hides throughout the colonial era eventually brought about the demise of indigenous nations like the Cherokee. This trade allowed the colonists to "increase their power rapidly over the Indians, eventually dispossessing them of all their land."[120]

Correspondence from the frontier to James Glen during his 1738–1756 tenure as royal governor of South Carolina often contains references to reliance by the Cherokee and other Indians on English provinces. One report of 1754 from George Johnson to Glen relates an address by a Cherokee headman to Creek ambassadors. The headman praises the "Governor of Carolina" for his presents of "axes, hoes, knives, guns, or ammunition" and Glen's encouragement of the Cherokee "to hunt briskly to kill plenty of deer, that with the skins they might buy clothes for their wives, and with the flesh that they might feed their children, that they might grow up stout men and good hunters and that they might become a numerous and powerful people."[121] In the same year, another frontier report from trader Ludovic Grant to Glen summarizes comments from Old Hop, the Cherokee emperor. According to Grant, Old Hop had lamented that the governor of Virginia had not shipped "ammunition and war utensils." This failure by the governor to fulfill his promises had caused the emperor and his people to be unable to make "powder and bullets and other things they very much wanted, and paper alone, meaning the [governor's] letters, would not defend them from their enemies."[122]

Commerce with the Cherokee, of course, brought white traders who lived among them during the colonial period. These men took Cherokee wives. In addition, both male and female white captives were incorporated into the tribe and intermarried with the native population as did escaped African slaves and slaves held by the Cherokee themselves. They also adopted other Native Americans into the tribe such as the Delaware, Natchez, Creek, and Chickasaw.[123]

These incorporations replenished the Cherokee population as it constantly dwindled because of wars and continued outbreaks of devastating epidemics like smallpox. The integration of other groups also may have caused changes in segments of religious observance and mythology. As a result of war with the French, Choctaw, and Chickasaw, the Natchez of Louisiana ceased to exist by 1736 as an independent people, and their remnants coalesced with the Creek and Cherokee. Worship of the Sun was fundamental in the religious belief of the Natchez, and the Sun as a deity may have received greater emphasis among the Cherokee as part of their veneration of Divine Fire because of Natchez influences.[124]

The influence of traders living among the Cherokee further changed the nature of their warfare throughout the eighteenth century. Before extensive contact with whites, warfare was primarily conducted by small parties in retaliatory raids of one tribe against another. Theda Perdue's research indicates that the increased desire for manufactured trade goods led large and powerful groups like the Cherokee to wage incessant war against smaller, weaker tribes. Encouraged by traders and colonial governments, the Cherokee could conduct raids against other Indians for barter or bounties, thus fattening the coffers of Charleston slave merchants. The decimation of tribes supposedly hostile to colonial interests allowed further white encroachment and imperial expansion onto traditional Indian territories.[125] Perdue notes that the trade in both humans and European manufactured goods increased the status of warriors in Cherokee society and brought about disparities in wealth as they accumulated more and more individual possesions and became more like Europeans in their views on individual as opposed to communal ownership of property.[126] As with other Indians of eastern North America, the culture of the Cherokee and the colonists had become intertwined and complicated as a result of capitalist networks connecting the southern frontier and the provinces to the eighteenth century Atlantic world of England and to a lesser degree of France and Spain

The American Revolution resulted in additional transformations to southeastern indigenous people. The vast majority of Creek and Cherokee headmen supported the imperial cause against the colonies because of Britain's desire to regulate the frontier and protect native lands from advancing white settlements. Another reason for native leaders to ally themselves with Britain was that commerce had slowed because of differences between the colonies and the mother country. A British triumph would reopen the needed flow of trade goods. And besides, the Indians had come to trust crown officials like John Stuart, superintendent of Indian affairs for the southern provinces of North America. In contrast to private individuals like the colonial traders, Native Americans believed that Stuart did not have ulterior motives in regard to their interests, with some Creek leaders requesting that one of Stuart's deputies regulate the rum trade because of its detrimental effects on tribal life.[127]

One consequence of the alliance between Britain, the Cherokee, and other southern tribes was that the frontier swarmed with Tories. In his study of black slavery among the Cherokee, Halliburton reports that, with the outbreak of the American Revolution, the Loyalists were often slaveholders and brought their chattel with them. As allies to the crown, they and the Cherokee joined forces to raid white border settlements. Virginians, Georgians, and Carolinians retaliated, destroying numerous Middle, Valley, and Overhill towns. The result was a further diluting of the traditional hunting and warrior culture and the establishment of farming on an individual instead of communal basis.[128] The war and additional contact with whites thus brought about a more settled existence in the nineteenth century and increased the use of black slaves. Even the great Sequoyah, inventor of the Cherokee syllabary and "a stout traditionalist," was of mixed blood, tended dairy cows in his youth, and became a silversmith in later years.[129]

Along with material changes, an evolution in religious beliefs seems to have occurred among southeast indigenous peoples. The fusion of Natchez remnants with the Cherokee has already been mentioned as perhaps influencing increased veneration of the Sun. Yet a more profound evolution in religious emphasis began in the seventeenth century and continued throughout the eighteenth and nineteenth. Ethridge summarizes archaeological evidence suggesting that, throughout the historic period of European contact, the former Mississippian mythology for understanding the cosmos underwent a shift. Religious focus appears to have turned gradually to a preoccupation with human existence in This World and away from supernatural elements found to a greater degree in the Mississippian Above and Below Worlds. At least architecture and pottery suggest such a reorientation. Mounds, once burial places of the elite, lost significance and ceased to be built, replaced by the more egalitarian public square, and such pottery motifs as the sacred looped square, once used exclusively on vessels of chiefs and ruling families, now appeared as iconography on ceramics used by common people.[130]

As with other Indians of the Southeast, changes among the Cherokee until the nineteenth century were not necessarily voluntary. They simply happened, with the leaders and the people adapting to the pressures of new circumstances. Between 1819 and 1827, however, Cherokee leaders undertook a united and determined effort to transform the culture. They constructed public schools, hired teachers, and brought in missionaries. They established a national newspaper, written in both Cherokee and English, and they formed a national government modeled after that of the United States. The more well-to-do emulated white southern planters by living in fine homes and using black slaves to work the land.[131] Conducted by the War Department of the United States, the Cherokee census of 1835 showed that out of a total population of 16,542, the Eastern Cherokee had a slave population of 1,592. These were owned by 7.4 percent of the tribe's membership.[132] Such developments ushered in a new perception of the natural world. By this time, many Cherokee regarded the forest as "necessary to the functioning of a homestead," a place for hogs and cattle to forage, small game to be hunted or trapped, fuel to be gathered, and timber to be harvested for buildings and fences.[133]

Unfortunately, many whites of considerable power were not convinced by the concerted efforts of the Cherokee to prove they were civilized. Popular politicians such as congressman Andrew Jackson and governor John Sevier, who were both from Tennessee, had fought against the tribe. The more they boasted of their battles and professed their continued hatred of the Cherokee, the more their fame and fortunes rose. Other states like North and South Carolina and Georgia had their share of haters as well. Once President Jefferson signed the Compact in 1802, agreeing to purchase all Indian land within Georgia's boundaries, all of these states clamored to be rid of the tribe.[134] Outcries for removal were particularly vociferous in Georgia. Woodward has phrased the ensuing turn of events well:

> Denouncing the Cherokees as savages, Georgia abandoned both dignity and ethics, and through her government, press, and courts began, in 1820, a vicious attack upon the Cherokees that was to continue for eighteen years, or until the Cherokees' final removal west of the Mississippi in 1838–39.[135]

The aforementioned events of history should instill great skepticism concerning assertions about authentic American Indian literature. Querry defines it as "literature *by* as opposed to that *about*" Native Americans and classifies it into "traditional, transitional, and modern."[136] According to Querry's description, modern Native American literature includes "works of fiction (both long and short), nonfiction, drama, and poetry, written in English by Indian Americans, most of whom speak no other language."[137] Although modern literature is not within the purview of the present discussion, traditional and transitional are. Querry's delineates these as follows:

> Traditional literature is defined as that which was composed in an Indian language for an Indian audience at a time when tribal cultures were intact and contact with whites was minimal. It was a literature made up of sacred stories, myths, legends and songs. Transitional literature is generally represented by translations of the great Indian orators of the nineteenth century and by memoirs of the Indian experience as it related to white dominance.[138]

At this point, the intellectual laziness and inadequacy of such oversimplified definitions should be clear as should pious attempts to conceptualize what is meant by an *intact culture*. As already demonstrated, once contact with Europeans transpired, Mississippian chiefdoms collapsed, and native peoples of the Southeast thereafter coalesced into more rapidly evolving new societies.

An examination of the history of when Indian literature began to be collected in written form raises further definitional difficulties, for not until the nineteenth century did Euro-American scholars begin to record it. Although the United States government instituted a Bureau of Indian Affairs supposedly to protect Indians, its efforts encouraged them to cast aside their traditions and become white. As Alice Marriott and Carol K. Rachlin have described the situation in *American Indian Mythology*, the dominant American culture derived from Europe believed itself superior not only materially but non-materially as well. The general expectation was that just as travois or pole-and-lever mode of transportation of Native Americans must yield to the wheel, so must their religions and arts give way to the creative genius of western culture.[139] Not until the 1830s was any serious effort made to gather Indian stories, as white Americans began to emulate what the Brothers Grimm and other European collectors had done for the tales of the common folk of their lands.[140] Relying on "informants" or Native American storytellers and interpreters who had knowledge of both the storyteller's language and English, collectors began to transcribe in decontextualized settings what was left of the Indians' original oral literature. What remains today are "reconstructed fragments of auditory archaeology."[141] When reduced to the printed page and divorced from the oral storytelling context, even though various degrees of content may survive, the best result is "a satisfactory translation."[142] Describing the translations by anthropologists influenced by the German born and educated Frank Boas (1858–1942), fellow anthropologist Dennis Tedlock says that readers seeking authenticity will not find it in the scholarly collections of native folklore and will be left to wonder whether the originals had styles as awkward as the versions rendered into English.[143] Tedlock's statement is, of course, hyperbolic but does contain some truth.

By the time Mooney collected Cherokee stories of the Eastern Band in the late 1890s, the numerous influences of more than four hundred years of history, from the time of the early Spanish explorers and contact with the French of Louisiana and particularly the English after the settlement of Jamestown and Charleston, had rendered the older ways of life nearly defunct. Many tribal stories from the past had been lost or were fragmentary recollections by the few remaining storytellers. In discussing his collection and the informants on whom he relied, Mooney admits to these kinds of problems. He says that the national genesis myth of the Cherokee had been nearly forgotten, although it may have still been intact as late as the middle of the 1700s.[144] Of the few reliable storytellers available to him, "chief in the list" was Ayunini, known as "Swimmer," who was born in 1835, a few years before the Cherokee removal to Oklahoma.[145] Descendants of Swimmer still live in western North Carolina today.

Swimmer had been trained by the holy men of the tribe. He possessed a wealth of information and as an informant provided about three-fourths of the tales, yet he died in 1899 before Mooney could complete his work.[146] Mooney's other major informant was Itagunahi, or John Ax, who was nearly one hundred. He, too, did not speak English, and, in Mooney's words, "age had dulled his faculties" so that his memory was failing.[147] Ax was the source for the wonder stories of giants, monsters, and spirit beings,[148] many of which have been adapted for the present anthology. Mooney did use other informants, but these individuals seemed to have functioned primarily as interpreters or for the purpose of confirming or supplementing what he was told by Swimmer and Ax.[149]

The Teller and the Tale: The Myth of Sovereignty

In addition to debates about authenticity in regard to indigenous literature, conflicts have developed about sovereignty. This issue revolves around who should retell the literature of Native Americans. Donna Norton indicates that questions raised in journals and other scholarly publications are frequently about such concerns as to whether only the members of a particular indigenous group may tell the stories of that group, who is the targeted audience for the literature, and whether Indian writers should be the voices for their group alone or should they feel free to write about other topics.[150] In certain literary genres like contemporary realism, autobiography, and poetry, the right to sovereignty from an Indian viewpoint seems more easily defensible on the basis of accurately depicting the reality of lives lived as verified from an author's cultural or personal experiences. Yet in genres like historical realism, biography, other informational accounts, or mythology and legends from an era long ago, the confines of one's own experience, whether derived from an identity group or from limited personal knowledge as an individual, hardly endow an author to possess sufficient background to create verisimilitude, to flesh out obscure and often fragmented details referred to in stories from a remote and misty mythological past, or to reconstruct circumstances that provide a broader and deeper understanding of events and other people embedded in a more immediate though complex time of a bygone legendary day. In short, neither ethnicity nor personal experience guarantees accuracy, depth of analysis, or objectivity. Such endowments may even be an impediment to the last consideration of lack of bias.

Sovereignty also has little meaning if the term suggests that only members of a particular group possess exclusive purview over traditional stories attributed to that group. The previous discussion of willing and unwilling cultural comingling by Native American populations through travel for hunting, for war to obtain slaves or to get captives for possible adoption into a tribe's dwindling members, for trade with one another or with Europeans, or for finding new homelands demonstrates the fallacy of that idea. So does the fact that Indian societies like the Cherokee, before their stories were written, were influenced for hundreds of years by growing contact with whites. Sovereignty, moreover, lacks meaning when considered from the perspective of how storytellers across cultures have worked as they heard stories, adapted them, made them their own, and passed them on to others.

In her classic work, *The Way of the Storyteller,* Ruth Sawyer talks about how, once a story leaves a storyteller and "becomes impaled for all time on clay tablets or the written and printed page," it suffers "a kind of death," no longer breathed from the mouth of one storyteller "to be drawn in on the breath of another."[151] In oral societies, each person who heard and then told stories must have infused them with individual traits—whether of voice inflection, gesture, pantomime, pause, and pace—and not engaged in slavish imitation, even if the words were rendered exactly as those from the original source. For those who retell Native American stories today through print or oral expression, the challenge, is to "create it again into living substance," as it is with all stories, according to Sawyer.[152] Surely, the task is not to consider the field anthropologists' collections, divorced from the societies in which the stories were told, as dry, dead flowers, pressed forever between the covers of a book.

Indeed, authorities on storytelling emphasize making a story one's own.[153] When told aloud, an exact rendition of the printed word is unnecessary except perhaps for literary fairy tales or stories purposefully created by a master of style who is a renowned author like Hans Christian Andersen. But folktales, as handed down from one person to another, are always adapted or retold. Folklorist, storyteller, and librarian Margaret Read MacDonald states, "there is *no correct* version of a folktale." The printed version itself "represents only one telling of one teller at one moment in time."[154] Averring that "memorizing is wrong," authorities like Sawyer recommend that the method for learning a story is "incident by incident, or picture by picture."[155] This method is the same that Baker and Greene term "the visual approach."[156] In this way, the storyteller preserves the incidents of the plot and, at the same time, brings a new spontaneity to the recreation of the traditional work.[157] When print adapters follow this advice from the folkcraft of storytelling, they cease to be what Jamake Highwater (a.k.a. Jay Marks) calls a "stenographer or enthnologist who tends to value verbatim transcriptions."[158] To borrow Highwater's metaphor, the adapter thus becomes a weaver who still weaves traditional designs but does so with new hands or words.[159]

Beyond Transcriptions: Recreating Authenticity

How then should the new hands weave in adapting stories from the Cherokee? One way focuses on the ongoing oral tradition among living storytellers and attempts to convey their renditions onto the printed page. Two collections come to mind: Jack and Anna Kilpatrick's 1964 *Friends of Thunder: Folktales of the Oklahoma Cherokees* and Barbara Duncan's 1998 *Living Stories of the Cherokee.*

The Kilpatricks' work contains stories transcribed and translated from Cherokee speakers' exact words, including nonstandard English and omitting "irrelevant" information or anything that "might jeopardize the anonymity of the speaker."[160] Words added to clarify meaning for the reader are included in brackets within the narratives. Although not explicitly stated by the Kilpatricks, the storytellers in their collection appear to be bilingual. Therefore, any code switching from Cherokee to English during the taping and before translating the original language is indicated in italics.[161] This kind of presentation thus uses print cues in an effort to capture the flavor of the storytelling moment. Brief explanatory notes, exterior to the narratives themselves, introduce not only categories of selections such as stories about birds but also individual tales like "Why the Rabbit Steals."[162] More scholarly notes and citations follow at the end of the anthology. Emphasis, though, is on the exact preservation of the words of various speakers.

Duncan's more recent book also tries to preserve the words of stories "being told today by living storytellers" who have continued the oral tradition since Mooney's publication in 1900.[163] Duncan states in her Introduction that her book presents the stories "on the page word for word exactly as they were spoken" to convey the tellers' verbal cadences and pauses.[164] Typographical cues attempt to capture these and have their theoretical base in tenets of ethnopoetics, as advocated by Dennis Tedlock, and concepts from sociolinguistics, as espoused by Dell Himes, both writers developing their ideas in the 1970s.[165] Duncan relies on length of line throughout each story to give a sense of her speakers' breaths and pauses. She also uses degree of indentation toward the right side of the page supposedly to impart the level of emphasis and inflection that happens during a live storytelling presentation. Duncan further says that such oral poetics enable the listener "to enter the world of the story" and that they mirror the "culture's aesthetics" and thus reflect "its worldview."[166] These are indeed powerful claims for length of line and indentation.

Duncan's Introduction provides additional information about the different Cherokee storytellers whose renditions she has transcribed. The Introduction also gives a brief history of the Eastern Cherokee Band of North Carolina; discusses the stories as part of Cherokee cultural identity, other arts, and education; describes where and how Duncan collected the selections; contrasts how story meanings change when rendered from Cherokee into English; presents a few similarities and differences between tales from the Eastern and Western Bands; defines some of the more universally accepted folktale genres as well as those particular to Cherokee storytellers; describes unique qualities found in the stories such as patterning related to four and seven, numbers which are sacred and ceremonial to the culture; and ends by briefly summarizing the ancient and still present religious concept of balance.

When considered from the perspective of expression, both of the storyteller's style and culture, the aforementioned efforts by the Kilpatricks and Duncan to render spoken language into print, are legitimate. Yet the art of communication encompasses two broad facets: expression and reception. It is the latter aspect that these collectors neglect—namely, the role of the listener, if the message is oral, and that of the reader, if it is written. For any communication to take place, there must be a meeting of two consciousnesses—that of the speaker or writer and that of the listener or reader—and the last two must negotiate a text, whether oral or written, to derive meaning. Indeed, one of the consciousnesses—that of the writer—need not be alive for the transaction to occur, for once a spoken version is printed, the written text takes on a life of its own, separate and apart from the mind and voice from which it originated.

Based on printed texts of Mooney and earlier writers, the folktales and legends adapted for this book give more consideration to the reader's role than do those found in other anthologies of Native American lore. As mentioned in the Preface, the underpinnings for adapting the material from this perspective derive from translation theory, reader-response theory, and supportive ideas in cognitive psychology and sociolinguistics.

In their overview of how ideas about the nature of translation have developed, Rainer Schulte and John Biguenet point out that "all acts of human communication and that indeed all acts of communication are acts of translation."[167] That is, we receive messages and attempt to make sense of them. Octavio Paz further refines this point by making an analogy between the processes of learning one's mother tongue and learning a second language When children in their own language encounter more difficult concepts, they approximate meanings of harder ideas by translating them into words with which they are already familiar. This process, Paz says, is not essentially different than translating from one language into another.[168] He adds, however, that when translation is literal—namely, a transcription, careful though it may be—then it is not a translation but what he terms "a mechanism, a string of words." Even though it "helps us read the text in its original language," it is little more than "a glossary rather than a translation, which is always a literary activity."[169] Thus there are translations, and then there are translations.

Paz's ideas on translation are applicable to adaptations of folktales in the following way. If a retelling is merely a paraphrase, then the reader gains nothing new from it if it supposedly makes the text more accessible by substituting easier words for more difficult ones and breaking up longer sentences into shorter ones. In fact, shortening more lengthy sentences may increase the inferential burden on the reader. For example, if connectives that show relationships between ideas are omitted, the reader must fill in the gaps. The sentence "I was fired from my job yesterday because I took too many breaks" explicitly states a cause and effect relationship through the subordinating conjunction "because." If recast as two sentences, the statement requires the reader to infer the essential causal relationship that taking too many breaks led to the speaker's being sacked. "I took too many breaks. I was fired from my job yesterday." Here causation is implied. The reader must also decide which sentence is the cause and which one is the effect. Since cause precedes effect in the world of linear time, the reversal of this order in the new version further complicates matters. Furthermore, if the person reading the adaptation is someone without any experience assumed by the world of work in which the two short sentences operate, then there is even less understanding. As with translations, there are adaptations, and then there are adaptations.

The reader's experiential world in considerations of translating or adapting a work has important linkages to reception aesthetics or reception theory. This view of a literary work does not preoccupy itself with the creator (here the storyteller or writer) nor with the independent existence of the work in isolation but looks at what happens when it takes on life in the reader's mind.[170] Once a text is encountered on the printed page, the reader draws conclusions, fills in pieces where the text assumes background knowledge exists, sheds or revises preconceptions, anticipates actions, and makes predictions as "each sentence opens up a horizon which is confirmed, challenged, or undermined by the next."[171] In the specific instance of Native American folklore, once the material takes on the greater permanence of written form, its readers engage in these same activities based on their general knowledge of the world outside the text, their level of education, and the world within the text, the latter of which becomes a series of cues on which the reader's background interacts to create meaning.

Although described in the 1990s as a "fairly novel development,"[172] the importance of the reader in relation to literature is not new. Beginning in 1938 and in the several editions that followed, Louise Rosenblatt in *Literature as Exploration* described the processes of what happens when readers become involved in constructing a text. Known as reader-response or transactional theory, its key tenet is that readers bring to the words and images of a text their personal associations and meanings that will largely govern its interpretation. In her 1978 book, *The Reader, the Text, and the Poem,* she says that, when individuals engage with a text, its written symbols activate "sensations, images, objects, ideas, relationships," all peculiar to the individual reader's cumulative background of experience and current personality, formed by both life and books.[173] The momentary act of reading, however, does not make the reader more important than the work being read. Both are "aspects of the same transaction—the reader looks to the text, and the text is activated by the reader." Both are necessary "in any reading event" which becomes a nonlinear give and take between the two in a transaction that belies the sequential left-to-right and top-to-bottom physical arrangement of words on the page.[174] An inescapable conclusion from transactional theory is that the quality of the meaning that readers construct from a text depends a great deal on the relevance of their background of experience. Otherwise, they can evoke very little from page.[175]

Ideas from Swiss cognitive psychologist Jean Piaget underscore the claims of reader-response theory concerning construction of meaning. Piaget's writings fall within the framework of schema theory which attempts to account for how the mind organizes knowledge in order to make sense of experience and to learn.[176] Although not the first to discuss schema theory, Piaget is perhaps its most-well known exponent through his research on how young children learn and organize their experiences. More than a definition, a schema is a category or concept along with its related attributes and properties. A schema, in turn, is connected to hierarchical networks of information or other schemata. With the acquisition of new knowledge, these undergo revision as the mind develops.[177] According to Piaget, the ability to learn anything new depends on prior learning. For learning to occur, the new information must be integrated into what the learner already knows.[178] One form of integration is assimilation or fitting new information into existing thought. Another is accommodation or revising and reorganizing old patterns of thinking in light of new experiences. These learning processes of assimilation and accommodation are cumulative and ongoing throughout life.[179] Besides being available, previous knowledge must be activated before learning and maintained during learning. Yet the richer one's background of experience, the greater the likelihood that an individual will understand new information.[180]

Research findings corroborate the importance of background knowledge in facilitating comprehension. In his book *Cultural Literacy*, literary critic E. D. Hirsh, Jr., underscores this contention and cites several studies indicating that, without sufficient background information, individuals had difficulty making sense of material they were given to read. Although they were able to decode the words, comprehend separate sentences, and understand vocabulary, they could not interpret contextual references scattered throughout the assigned passages. In other words, they could comprehend bits and pieces but not the meaning of the selection as a whole.[181] Additional evidence consistently supports how accurate and extensive background information gives readers the capacity for better comprehension and that restricted information and mistaken preconceptions impede understanding.[182]

Ideas in the work of Russian sociolinguist Lev Vygotsky also support aspects of Rosenblatt's transactional theory. In analyzing how an individual acquires knowledge, Vygotsky emphasizes the social context of learning and uses the term *zone of proximal development*. He defines this as the difference between the knowledge the learner already has and new knowledge the learner may attain. This attainment is best facilitated through social interaction between a learner and more knowledgeable others who offer guidance and support.[183] According to Vygotsky, these more experienced individuals do not have to be physically present in the situation where the learning takes place.[184] In other words, they may be like the disembodied consciousness of the writer.

Implications for Retellings

Based on the previous discussion of reader-response theory, cognitive psychology, and the social context of learning, there are several implications for an adaptor of folktales to consider. These revolve around the problem for general readers who enter a text derived from another time and place and who lack a sufficient sensibility of its milieu. One way to overcome this difficulty is to create text that aids in the reader's construction of meaning. Good writing obviously should consider its audience, but such audience analysis is likely thin or absent in works conceived in a past far removed from today's circumstances, particularly when these works are presented as autonomous artifacts from another culture to be met on its own terms. To make an adaptation more accessible to its audience, the writer should engage to a greater degree in "intentional acts" to guide the transaction between readers and the printed page and thereby channel their responses in a more informed direction.[185] Such attempts on the part of the writer create a higher "level of congruence" between the work and its readers and significantly affect whether the material is understandable.[186] In other words, has the adaptor presented enough information from the unfamiliar world of which the story is a part to promote a better understanding by a contemporary audience? If so, then the text is what authorities in literacy call "considerate."[187]

One crucial aspect of considerate text is whether it provides topical knowledge or contextual schemata that aid in the recall of specific details and foster the ability to infer ideas not directly supplied. As opposed to knowledge of the conventions of written language and organizational components inherent in narrative, descriptive, expository, or argumentative discourse, contextual schemata concern an individual's knowledge of real or imagined worlds. To create considerate text, the writer must frequently elaborate or amplify ideas to make them more explicit and to show the relationships among them.[188] In striving toward this aim, the writer becomes like Vygotsky's more informed adult or more capable peer who interacts with learners in the social context of reading by guiding and prompting them so that they bring a higher level of knowledge to the page and thus achieve a greater proficiency of understanding. Incorporating topical knowledge into written adaptations in an organized and systematic fashion creates "contextual richness," a quality that Vygotsky considers important in effective learning environments.[189]

Theory and Research Applied to Adaptations

The usual techniques for providing background information for works outside a contemporary context are through exterior explanations and definitions. These are set apart from the narratives in introductions, headnotes, footnotes, endnotes, glossaries, or appendices. These didactic techniques are analogous to direct instruction in learning and are more divorced from the content than information embedded within the world of the narrative itself. My method, however, as an adaptor has been to fuse the underlying topical background within the narratives and render them more immediately meaningful to contemporary readers. I have tried to make such incorporations as seamless and non-intrusive as possible. The goal has been to place the myths and legends in an authentic context, thereby giving readers a similar accessibility to background information that Native American listeners would have brought to a tale before they heard it. Readers themselves will have to judge whether I have accomplished this aim successfully. Below are several examples that illustrate how I have developed interior story context.

One area for the enhancement of topical knowledge concerns geographical settings. Cherokee stories often have specific locales: a mountain range in Georgia, a valley in North Carolina, a river or creek in Tennessee, an indigenous settlement in South Carolina. Yet the original print versions of the stories generally mention these only in passing and as with most folktales continue with their plots unimpeded. The indigenous audience, of course, would have known these locations and not needed a description to have a sense of where they were and what they were like. So, too, would a white audience who had traveled, traded, or settled in the region and who heard a legend about the Cherokee. Mooney gives some information on settings in his Notes and Parallels to Myths. This section follows his collection of stories. Where necessary, I have woven into the structure of the stories geographic details to help the reader understand places named and have used Mooney's Notes and Parallels as well as more updated sources.

Other individuals from whom I have adapted stories—writers like James Daniels, Charles Lanman, and William Gilmore Simms—have embedded in varying degrees details of place within the context of their work. Simms and Daniels provide the least background in their semi-historical recreations of the eighteenth century Carolina backcountry. Because both wrote from a white perspective about the Cherokee, they are discussed later in a separate section. However, the piece titled "Tobacco" about the plant's origin was borrowed from Lanman and fused with a variant from Mooney. Lanman says that the folktale came from a Cherokee informant having the two names of All Bones and Flying Squirrel. Lanman had worked as a newspaperman and librarian. He was also an artist associated with the Hudson River School and did much traveling in order to make sketches for his paintings. Lanman's story about the Cherokee Little People of Hickory Nut Gorge is part of Letter XV from his larger 1849 travelogue, *Letters from the Allegheny Mountains*. Several paragraphs antecedent to the story proper contain vivid depictions the gorge's river and other topography. Nonetheless, I have supplemented his details with more updated information for today's reader. For example, Lanman describes through his painterly eye one sublime feature of the rugged landscape as "an isolated rock, looming against the sky, which is of a circular form" and which "resembles the principal turret of a stupendous castle."[190] This great outcropping of granite is obviously today's tourist attraction of Chimney Rock below Asheville, North Carolina, although in Lanman's day it apparently had not received that name. In the opening paragraph as well as other places in the retelling, I have provided additional details to further clarify Lanman's description.

I have also amplified the text in regard to characters. Unlike most modern readers, a Cherokee audience would have possessed the contextual schemata needed to recognize attributes of characters whether they are monsters, animals, humans, or spiritual beings. Mooney often gives details about such figures in other stories, in his supplementary Notes and Parallels, and sometimes in his glossary, but if readers do not know the other stories or do not refer to the explanatory material, they leave with an inadequate comprehension of a selection. This kind of problem was noted earlier in discussing "The Water Cannibals" with its passing references to the Nunnehi.

A similar instance occurs in "The Red Man and the Uktena,"[191] retold here under the same title. In this story, a hunter helps the Red Man of the Lightning kill a great Uktena, a snakelike monster with whom he is wrestling. In recognition of the hunter's aid, the Red Man rewards him with plentiful game whenever he looks for it. Almost no other details of the Red Man are given in the story. However, in an earlier story, "The Moon and the Thunders,"[192] the Red Man is associated not only with the lightning but also with the rainbow. He is the same as the Great Thunder who lives in the west in the Upper World above the sky vault. In addition, Mooney explains in Notes and Parallels for "The Moon and the Thunders" that the Great Thunder is the mythical hunter Kanati.[193] This character is also the lord of the game and husband of Selu, the corn goddess, both of whom are the focus of yet another story, "Kanati and Selu,"[194] here adapted as "Corn and Game." Unless readers are acquainted with such topical knowledge from these additional sources, they will understand little of the nature of the Red Man as revealed in "The Red Man and the Uktena." As with geographic locales, my goal has been to infuse an organic understanding of such characters into the retellings without the need for consulting other tales or cumbersome cross references and explanatory notes that dilute a single story's impact when these are consulted. My approach has been much like what Betty Rose Nagle describes as the inclusion of "internal glosses" in her translation of Ovid's *Fasti,* thereby making an "allusive text modern and immediately accessible."[195]

Along with elaborated background for places and characters, I have embedded into the narratives information on historical and cultural references. Mooney's version of the legend about the encounter of the Seneca war chief Ga'na with the Cherokee refers to the game of ball play among Native Americans of the Southeast.[196] I have adapted the story as "Ga'na and the Cherokee" and have incorporated not only ancillary information provided by Mooney but also relied heavily on the intricate sacred ceremonies and other activities involved with preparing for and playing the sport as described by anthropologist Charles Hudson in his book *The Southeastern Indians*.[197]

Sometimes two stories are highly connected by a common subject. Such is the case with Mooney's "The Nest of the Tlanuwa" and "The Hunter and the Tlanuwa."[198] Weaving the two together seemed appropriate. The second story tells of a warrior's kidnapping by and his later escape from two great hawks, while the first relates how a shaman ended their predations on a Cherokee settlement. Combining the two gives the myths a kind of finish that each separately does not have. Indeed, tales like these may have been combined at one time or have been part of a story cycle, something not unknown in the folktales of a people. The same could be said for Cherokee tales of lost villages like "The Removed Townhouses," "Kanasta, the Lost Settlement," and "The Legend of Pilot Knob."[199] All seem to be variations of a common plot so that only the last one is retold here as "Legends of Pilot Knob." However, "The Removed Townhouses" contains allusions to war and the impending evil of the 1838 Indian removal. Adding these details to Mooney's "The Legend of Pilot Knob" creates a further dimension because the elaboration offers a powerful explanation telling why some of the people of the Kanuga settlement in this latter story left their homes to live deep inside a mountain with their spiritual protectors, the Nunnehi.

Another aspect to consider in creating an authentic context is to find a language that captures the original ceremonial settings in which stories of a more sacred nature would likely have been performed. As opposed to the historically grounded and more secular legends, all the myths included here are adapted from Mooney. Even though he is not precise as to how the Cherokee would have told these, he does offer suggestions. In discussing sacred myths of creation and national origin, he mentions that only a select few were allowed to hear these and only then if they "observed the proper form and ceremony."[200] And yet in regard to the rituals accompanying the sacred myths, Mooney appears ambiguous in extending their ceremonial settings to the wonder stories that touch upon the supernatural, although in his sentence describing them he refers to "those sacred things to be told only with prayer and purification."[201] It is unclear whether this description applies to the wonder stories or to the sacred myths or to both. Part of the problem is that the centenarian John Ax figures in the discussion of both types of tales. As a boy and young man in the first two decades of the 1800s, Ax was "sometimes admitted" to the "secret rites" that were part of the sacred myths known "only to the professional priests or conjurors," although he claimed to be neither.[202] Furthermore, according to Mooney, Ax had a "poetic and imaginative temperament" and "cared most for the wonder stories."[203]

An additional difficulty in determining the manner and setting in which the stories were told has to do with Mooney's attribution to Swimmer as a source. Swimmer was an adept in Cherokee lore. Born around 1835, three years before the Removal, he was deemed by the Eastern Band to be an authority and had been trained "as priest, doctor, and keeper of tradition." Giving his "recitals" in the Cherokee language, Swimmer had "a happy descriptive style," used a "musical voice for the songs," and mimicked the sounds of birds and beasts.[204] Unfortunately, Mooney is precise only in applying Swimmer's musical voice to songs. Swimmer was the source of three-fourths of Mooney's material. Although his recordings clearly contain literary embellishments, questions remain about whether Mooney applied Swimmer's other characteristics as a storyteller. The difficulty is in creating equivalences in English that might suggest to readers such characteristics and a ceremonial style suitable for the more mythic tales.

Finding Equivalences of Style

Yet many rhetorical devices are available to create a sense of ritual appropriate for stories that partake of a religious nature. Known as *schemes*, these devices constitute deviations in the normal order of words[205] and were part of the study of ancient Greek and Roman rhetoricians. The use of schemes still occurs in modern English, even though the technical names of many of them may not be known to their authors.[206] Some examples from the retellings of the myth "Fire" and the two legends "Ga'na and the Cherokee" and "The Mohawk Warriors" will serve to illustrate how such stylistic manipulations can evoke a feeling of ceremonial significance.

One time-honored way to create ritualistic prose is through parallelism, according to Virginia Tufte's *Artful Sentences: Syntax as Style*.[207] Parallelism is the use of equivalent grammatical constructions to set forth a series of two or more similar items. If the first item is a noun, then the rest of the items must be nouns or function as nouns. If the first is a prepositional phrase, then the remainder must be prepositional phrases. If the first is an adjective, then the others must be adjectives or function as such. In other words, all parts of the series must be similar in structure or coordinate.[208] The key principles are balance and repetition.

One form of parallelism is *anaphora* or repeating at the start of a series of clauses or sentences the same word or words.[209] The repetition creates a dignified cadence to the expression.[210] For example, the adaptation "Fire," which concerns the origin of this divine element, contains parallel constructions in the opening and closing paragraphs to impart a sense of fire's vital importance to the Cherokee in not only their spiritual but also their everyday existence. Through repetition and balance, the sentences of both paragraphs convey an incantatory quality suggesting something mystical. The first paragraph is made to sound like an invocation, and the last, like a benediction. The first repeats the word "fire" at the beginning of four sentences. (Recall that four is a sacred number to the Cherokee.) Two middle sentences have at their beginnings a variation on the word "fire" with the words "Old Fire" and "New Fire," and the last sentence repeats "fire" at its end. The entire introductory paragraph has seven sentences. (Recall again that seven is another sacred number to the Cherokee.) The last paragraph is likewise composed of seven sentences. All but the first sentence begin with the word "fire" or a slight variation as in the last sentence that starts with "The New Fire."

Antithesis is another scheme which juxtaposes opposite ideas and which frequently occurs in the form of parallelism.[211] Once again in the story "Fire," two short sentences within the opening paragraph contrast the old fire of the past with the new fire of the future: "The Old Fire dies. The New Fire kindles." The adjectives "Old" and "New" set up the antithesis. The parallelism here takes an extreme form called *isocolon* in which the exact same number of words is repeated, sometimes even going so far as to repeat an equal number of syllables.[212] In this particular pair of sentences, each has *four* words written in the same grammatical pattern of definite article, descriptive adjective, noun, and verb.

This same paragraph also uses *parenthesis* or an insertion that suspends the expected flow of the sentence.[213] The second sentence of the passage reads "Fire, who with the Sun, gives heat and light and life." The syntactic expectation is for the subject "Fire" to be followed by the verb "gives." This anticipation is interrupted by the phrase "who with the sun." The interrupter creates what Tufte calls a "mid-branching" sentence.[214] Although very short in this example, the use of the interpolation instills a brief suspense by postponing the conclusion of the sentence.[215] Besides *parenthesis*, the second half of the sentence also uses the scheme of *polysyndeton* or the inclusion of many conjunctions to add emphasis.[216] In this instance, the conjunction "and" is repeated between each of the words in the series—"heat and life and light." The repetition of "and" slows the sentence, thus giving it greater solemnity than the opposite device of *asyndeton* which omits all conjunctions[217] and thereby produces a sense of hurry or "emotional haste,"[218] something that seems an inappropriate effect for the religious nature of the story's content.

In each of the instances discussed, the purpose is to convey the sacred nature of fire through ceremonial, religious wording as language distinctly apart from commonplace phrasing. Lest anyone should think the incorporation of these kinds of rhetorical devices an inauthentic affectation on my part for mere mannered prose, Mooney states that the ceremonial numbers four and seven are the same numbers found in "paragraphs or repetitions in the principal formulas" or sacred ritual utterances of Cherokee medicine men.[219] Indeed, in many eighteenth and nineteenth century formal ceremonies as well as in daily living, activities of southeastern Indians were often done in sets of four in association with the four cardinal directions. Anthropologist Robbie Ethridge observes that, when male or female priests gathered bark, they took it from every fourth or seventh tree.[220] In the *Sacred Formulas of the Cherokee*, Mooney notes that conjurors always collected bark from the trunk's east side as it received more healing power because of more prolonged exposure to the sun's rays.[221]

Rhetorical devices can also work effectively not only in Cherokee myths but also in their legends derived from history, especially when these contain sacred elements from the culture. The adaptation "Ga'na and the Cherokee" describes the ceremonies that Indians of the Southeast underwent in preparation for the game of ball play. Among these was the purification ritual of scratching. The following sentence from the story uses the schemes of *anaphora* and *epistrophe*: "Four times the conjuror's helpers scratched each man's upper arms from shoulder to elbow, and four times the helpers scratched each one's lower arms from wrists to elbow." This sentence has two main clauses joined by "and." The second clause begins with the same three words as the first clause, thus using the technique of *anaphora* by repeating identical wording or phrasing at the start of each clause.[222] *Epistrophe* repeats the same word or phrasing at the conclusion of successive sentences.[223] *Epistrophe* occurs here because the word "elbow" ends both clauses. The parallelism that results from the extreme balance and repetition in this compound sentence coordinated by "and" produces a potent emotional effect through both rhythm and emphasis that are the hallmarks of *anaphora* and *epistrophe*.[224] The resulting stylistic effect befits what Mooney describes as complex Cherokee religious theater involved in the ritual of scratching that preceded ball play.[225]

Even when the content of legends is wholly secular, schemes have their uses. For example, "The Mohawk Warriors" describes a torture scene as witnessed by an eighteenth century white trader. This man related the anecdote to fellow Indian trader James Adair who included it in his 1775 *The History of the American Indians*.[226] Consider the following sentence from the story: "And now began the gruesome work." Contained within this short sentence is the scheme of *hyperbaton* or *anastrophe* which distorts the ordinary arrangement of words and functions to add emphasis, thus focusing the reader's attention.[227] The distortion occurs through reversing the normal syntactic order of subject and verb since the verb "began" comes before the subject of "gruesome work." The sentence also serves as the opening topic sentence for its paragraph, and as a short kernel or core sentence, it gives in this particular instance what Tufte calls an "abrupt turn," functioning through "syntactic punctuation"[228] to alert the audience to the horrifying scene that ensues when the two Mohawk warriors endure tortures and are burned alive.

Along with *schemes, tropes* constituted the second subdivision within classical figures of speech, and of these two categories, more than two hundred have been calculated as being available to orators and writers.[229] There is no need here to burden the reader with an exhaustive list. Anyone wanting a more comprehensive discussion can begin with Corbett's *Classical Rhetoric for the Modern Student* or Baker's *The Complete Stylist* referenced in the Notes and Bibliography.

Special Considerations Regarding Simms' and Daniel's Cherokee Legends

The Preface has already broadly given some of the problems in the two legends *about* the Cherokee as developed by nineteenth century South Carolina writers William Gilmore Simms and Reverend James Walter Daniel. Although both authors have more than their fair share of misinformation concerning accurate and authentic background details in their stories, Simms' "Jocassee, a Cherokee Legend" misleads the least.

"Jocassee" is a first person narrative told from the point of view of a traveler visiting the ruins of "Keowee Old Fort," a colonial relic in the "highly picturesque and interesting" Pendleton district of upstate of South Carolina. The traveler informs the reader that he received the story from an unnamed "Col. G_____."[230] With these descriptors and others like "romantic prospect,"[231] Simms is clearly indicating that he is setting forth a romantic tale, which is exactly what he created in this type of Romeo and Juliet tragedy between the two principals Nagoochie and Jocassee, young Cherokee lovers of eighteenth century South Carolina.

"Jocassee" is one of more than a hundred works, including poems, essays, stories, and novels, that the prolific Simms composed just on Native Americans. Simms' scholar John Caldwell Guilds has said that in comparison to other nineteenth century men of American letters, Simms was in his portrayal of Indians the most fair and accurate and "that he constantly sought valid information about the cultural and physical makeup of Native Americans."[232] In his study of Simms as a historian, Sean R. Busick writes that on this subject Simms uniformly averred that his historical romances set in the colonial era were authentic, claiming that his work in this genre to be truer than history. Although he invented characters and motives, Simms felt that he should be careful with background details and fair in his conclusions. His concern was to give attention to the every-day life of the past, something he believed historians often neglected.[233] Busick further states that Simms created complex characters and avoided stereotyping Indians as "the typical brutish or noble savages of American Literature."[234] Of course, while Simms "attempted to be faithful to the *known* history," according to Busick, this attempt "does not mean that his romances are in all respects accurate" and that he "felt free to fill in the gaps in the historical record, provided that he remained within the realm of the believable."[235]

Simms' filling in the gaps of *known* history, however, appears to be a significant problem. In discussing Simms' Indian writings in general, anthropologist Charles Hudson argues that their fidelity to historical accuracy is thin. Simms himself acknowledged that the early history of Native Americans was not well understood in his day and that knowledge of their history prior to European contact was almost nonexistent, giving the writer free rein "to imaginatively fill in the gaps in historical knowledge." Accuracy is thus frequently deficient because it was "not a priority in Simms' historical Indian fiction."[236] Hudson concludes that these works are "myths of place" and says that they contain "hardly any authentic native culture."[237]

Evidence for Hudson's conclusion about Simms' Indian writings is strong in "Jocassee," particularly in the episode of the wolf hunt. The narrator says that "a wolf-hunt was commanded by Moitoy [Moytoy], the great war-chief or generalissimo of the Cherokee nation, to take place, instantly, at Charashilactay, where an immense body of wolves had herded together, and had become troublesome neighbours."[238] According to the story, there was a hollow in the mountains at Charashilactay that had but one entrance so that the wolf pack was trapped within it. In an obvious manipulation of plot, Simms has Moitoy order that the gap be guarded by warriors from the two rival Cherokee clans, the Green Birds and the Brown Vipers. In the Green Birds is Nagoochie, who is Jocassee's lover, and in the Brown Vipers is Cheochee, her brother who is also the sworn enemy of Nagoochie. This command by Moitoy, of course, increases the hatred the two rivals have for each other. Beyond Simms' exploitation of the rivalry between clans and their leaders, however, is the lack of cultural authenticity in the hunt itself. Nagoochie's smaller band of Green Birds, "in proportion to their force," slays more wolves than does a superior number of Cheochee's Brown Vipers.[239] Nagoochie is especially heroic with his knife and hatchet in hand-to-hand combat with the wolves as he engages in heart-stabbing thrills with his knife and skull-crushing chills with his hatchet and thereby fans the flames of Cheochee's wrath against him.

Based on Mooney's research, this great slaughter of wolves appears entirely bogus. In his discussion of animal myths in "The Fourfooted Tribes," Mooney relates that wa'ya, the wolf, is the "hunter and watchdog" of the lord of the game, Kanati, who is the great Cherokee mythical hunter. No ordinary Cherokee would kill a wolf, if at all possible, and would allow the animal to go unharmed if nearby. Mooney describes the belief that a slaughtered wolf's kindred would revenge the death and that the murder weapon would be rendered useless for further hunting until made ritually clean by a medicine man. Only hunters who knew the proper forms of atonement could kill wolves without fear. Other Cherokee hired these individuals if wolves raided fishing traps or attacked livestock.[240] Yet, Simms' episode of the wolf hunt, spurious though it may be, is so integral to his plot that to omit it would be to tell another legend. My judgment, therefore, was to leave it in the adaptation. Though it would be tedious to relate all of them, I have done the same with other inauthentic, yet organic, plot details of "Jocassee." The primary modifications to the story have been to render its prose less ostentatious and its tone less condescending toward Native Americans, two issues on which Hudson has commented in his evaluation of Simms' Indian writings.[241] My elaboration of the text primarily relates to providing information on specific locations that Simms mentions.

In contrast to "Jocassee," omissions of or corrections to historical and cultural inaccuracies in Reverend James Walter Daniel's poem, *Cateechee of Keeowee*, still leave much of the story's essential plot intact. Several versions of the tale and similar narratives, both in prose and poetry, appeared in the 1890s, but the Reverend Daniel "brought the legend to full maturity."[242] He combined two separate stories, one of Issaqueena (often spelled Issaquena) and the other of Cateechee, thus setting his version forever in the public's mind.

Daniel's poem recounts the capture of a Choctaw maiden by King Kuruga, headman of the Lower Cherokee capital of Keowee. She is adopted by Kuruga and his wife and becomes their daughter, having her Choctaw name of Issaqueena changed to the Cherokee name of Cateechee. Upon maturing, she falls in love with the young Allan Francis who had visited the town of Keowee from time to time on trips with his father, a white trader from Ninety Six named James Francis. Daniel's poem opens with Cateechee's long ride from Keowee to the eighteenth century town of Cambridge to warn the adjacent fortified trading post of Ninety Six of an impending Cherokee attack. The attack fails. Afterwards, Cateechee and Allan attempt to settle down to connubial bliss in a humble cabin, but Kuruga kidnaps them and takes them as his prisoners to Keowee. There Allan learns the skills of an expert Cherokee hunter. Longing for freedom after two and a half years of captivity, he and Cateechee escape with their baby. To confuse any pursuing Cherokee warriors sent by Kuruga to recapture them, the couple decides to head west toward the mountains instead of east toward the white settlements around Ninety Six. Despite their attempts to thwart the pursuit of "braves / Led by wily old Saloee,"[243] Allan and Cateechee are almost caught. He, however, hides at the foot of a waterfall on Stumphouse Mountain ready to launch a canoe he has made. She meanwhile is discovered and chased by Saloee and his men on the higher terrain above the cascade until she reaches its ninety foot precipice. Arrows whizzing past her head and with her baby strapped to her back, she leaps over the waterfall, though not to her death. She lands on a ledge just behind the falls where she hides out of sight of her pursuers. Thinking that she has plunged to her death, they leave, hoping to catch Allan back at the couple's shelter atop the mountain. Once he sees the warriors depart, Allan comes from his hiding place and calls Cateechee's name. She appears from behind the waterfall. They then escape by river and land, presumably with their infant still alive and bound behind Cateechee. The poem concludes with their reaching Old Cambridge, where "Like Ruth and Naomi they came, / The great wonder of the people," "gladly welcomed" and "greatly loved." There they live "to a ripe old age / And in great peace lay down in death."[244]

Long have historians and journalists convincingly argued that the legend of Cateechee is the product of fantasy containing no more than a smidgeon of truth.[245] In the words of E. Don Herd, the story "of Cateechee is one of romantic beauty and is certainly worth retelling." Yet he adds that it "is a shame that it cannot withstand the careful scrutiny of history."[246] Herd has amply supported his conclusion in "Cateechee, Issaqueena, and Ninety Six," an essay which traces the development of the legend and its lack of grounding in history. Few aspects of the story are connected to actual events. Cherokee warriors did make two attacks on "the little fort" that South Carolina colonial governor Lyttelton build around Robert Gowdy's barn at the trading post at Ninety Six, and local militia leader James Francis did command the tiny "penned up" garrison in repulsing the assaults.[247] A small attack occurred on February 3, 1760, and a larger one a month later on March 3 and 4.[248] According to Herd's research, Aaron Price, a messenger sent by Captain Francis to the royal governor and his council in Charleston, testified that a "Cherokee Indian Wench" warned the post at Ninety Six of an impending Cherokee attack coming from the Lower towns because "matters were very bad" in the Cherokee nation and that the "instigators of so much mischief" were the young warrior Scaroroski [Seroweh] of Esteroe [Estatoe] and another headman by the name of Round O.[249]

An unknown Cherokee woman advising the fort at Ninety Six of a coming assault is certainly plausible. Besides the testimony of Price, other instances of Cherokee women intervening on behalf of whites occur throughout the eighteenth century. One interesting anecdote that happened in upstate South Carolina is recounted in the third volume of Elizabeth Ellet's *Women of the Revolution* and concerns Barbara McKenny. Her husband having gone to Camden, this woman and her young children were alone at her frontier home near Fishing Creek in the summer of 1761. A party of sixteen Cherokee men and women were in the vicinity in order to hunt and fish. Here is how Ellet describes what happened to Mrs. McKenny:

> One day she saw the Indian women running towards her house in great haste, followed by the men. She had no time to offer resistance: the squaws seized her and the children, pulled them into the house, and shoved them behind the door, where they [the Cherokee women] immediately placed themselves on guard, pushing back the Indians as fast as they as they tried to force their way in, and uttering the most fearful outcries. Mrs. McKenny concluded it was their intention to kill her, and expected her fate every moment. The assistance rendered by the squaws, whether given out of compassion for the lonely mother, or in return for the kindness shown them, proved effectual for her protection until the arrival of one of the chiefs, who drew his long knife and drove off the savages.[250]

Ellet attributes the Cherokee women's help to their compassion or their remembrance of past kindness, yet such assistance to whites may have happened for commercial reasons. Trade on the frontier occurred not only between Indian men and whites but also between Indian women and whites. Exchanges in which Cherokee women were involved often consisted of baskets and foodstuffs. After deer hides, the skillfully crafted and decorated split wood and river cane baskets of Cherokee women were from the outset among some of the trade items of highest value brought to the markets in Charleston.[251] In Ellet's story as well as the legend of Cateechee, economic self-interest rather than either altruism or an affair of the heart may have been a historical reason for warnings about war.

Although the legend of Cateechee possesses a smattering of history, Daniel's story is severely lacking in authenticity regarding Cherokee culture of the middle 1700s. One salient example concerns his division of Native Americans into good Indians and bad Indians. Cateechee or Issaqueena, the Choctaw captive of the Cherokee and heroine of the tale, is brave and noble. A brief reference to another character named Yonah calls him "the good Choctaw prophet." Even though he is not physically present, his supernatural powers work to muffle the hooves of Cateechee's horse "Lest a foot should strike the hard earth," thus drawing "the eagle-eyed / Warriors" to spy the fleeing "damsel"[252] as she rides to Ninety Six to sound her alarm. On the other hand, much of Daniel's attitude toward the Cherokee is that they are bad Indians. As their prisoner, Cateechee is initially a "slave girl to savage masters,"[253] though later she does becomes Kuruga's daughter through her marriage to Allan, once he becomes adopted into the tribe as the chief's son. Of course, the taking of captives to replenish population losses, to serve as slaves, or to enhance a warrior's reputation was a common practice not just by the Cherokee but by other Indians as well.[254] In addition to being savage masters, the Cherokee headmen, warriors, and conjurors gathered in the council house at Keowee are "sly and shrewd"[255] and generally described in vile terms. One is "tall and mordant"; another "Scowled at Issaqueena's baby, /

Scowled and grunted like a fat swine"; another with a "wolfish" face sits and leers; another is "moody / And morose"; and Skiagunsta is an old "wrinkled wizard" whose "skin wigwam" is "painted with hideous / Monsters, emblems of the black arts / Which he practiced."[256] Less forbidding is Old Owasta who is "small and wiry."[257] On the more positive side, Yahoma is a "brave chief," and Corane is a "shrewd chief and a wise Raven," although the "scowl and paint, / On his scarred face lent him terror."[258]

Along with his propensity to engage in cultural stereotypes, Daniel is incorrect in his description of the Cherokee honorific title Raven. Figures having this title play a crucial role in the story. As developed by Daniel, they are characters in Cherokee society whose function is to watch Allan and Cateechee during their captivity in the Lower towns. Besides terms like "wise Raven," he uses the expression "Beloved Raven" several times to depict these leaders.[259] In one of the explanatory notes to the poem, he says that there was a Raven in every town whose duty was to watch and give warning of imminent dangers and to serve as the "great advisors of their people."[260] This depiction is fantasy, having little resemblance to the meaning of the term. Mooney defines it as a war title.[261] In his memoirs of his three months spent among the Overhill Cherokee in 1762, Lieutenant Henry Timberlake, says that Raven was one of two honorary titles "conferred in reward of great action; the first of which is Outacity, or Mankiller; and the second Colona, or the Raven."[262] Contemporary historian Oliphant cites it as one of four war titles, the highest one being "Warrior" or war leader, followed in descending order by "Outacite or Mankiller, the Raven, and the Slave Catcher."[263] Oliphant's information appears to come from William DeBrahm's 1773 *Report of the General Survey of the Southern District of North America*.[264] This document includes maps and other information concerning the colonial Indian frontier of the Southeast.

Related to issues of accuracy and authenticity, a final question to consider in retelling Cateechee is an appropriate form for the legend. As with Daniel's version, several of its antecedents took the form of narrative poems. Plot components regarding a nameless Cherokee maiden are in Francis Muench's "Lover's Leap," a poem that appeared in his 1896 collection *Palmetto Lyrics.* Thwarted in love, she jumps over a waterfall as does Cateechee.[265] Another poem by Muench is titled "Cateechee, the Indian Maiden." It recounts Cateechee's ninety-six mile ride to alert *Frank* Allan, her teacher at Cambridge, of Kuruga's planned assault. No fort exists in this poem, so the settlers decide to build one for protection in the shape of a star.[266] Muench has obviously confused the original Gowdy stockade with the later Revolutionary War star fort of Ninety Six. In 1897 Charles Reid Sloan published *Issaquena, Legend of Upper South Carolina,* yet another story poem containing events that Daniel appropriated for his 1898 rendition.[267]

When considered in relation to setting, the verse narratives by Muench, Sloan, and Daniel seem appropriate for presenting the Cateechee legend. As already noted, the story takes place on the South Carolina colonial frontier in the mid–1700s. Evidence indicates that immigrants from the British Isles were preponderant as settlers in the Southern backcountry.[268] Many of these immigrants had their cultural roots in the south and west of Scotland and in northern England and Wales, with the bulk of those from Scotland and England having settled in Northern Ireland for several generations before coming to the British colonies of North American in the 1600s and 1700s. The area of Northern Ireland in which they had lived was called the Ulster Plantation. They had gone there under the sponsorship of the British government. King James VI of Scotland, who was also King James I of England, thought these Protestant settlers would serve well in controlling rebellions in Catholic Ireland and commissioned the removal of thousands to the Ulster Plantation. A sizeable number of the Ulster Plantation colonists originated in the Border Country between England and Scotland, a place where the enforcement of official laws often did not extend. Sometimes referred to as Borderers, Border Clans, or Border Reivers, even their own compatriots described them as unruly folk, choosing to be English or Scottish whenever convenient. In Lowland Scots dialect, "reiver" signifies "robber."[269]

Upon coming to North America, these new colonists created another border country in southwestern Pennsylvania; in western Maryland, Virginia, and North Carolina; in northwestern South Carolina; and later in northeastern Georgia, eastern Tennessee, and eastern Kentucky. They referred to themselves by the catchall term "Scotch Irish," irrespective of their place of origin.[270] The culture of this group flourished in the mountains and foothills of the southern Appalachians.[271]

Logan's early history of the South Carolina upcountry before the Revolutionary War notes that a man named Andrew Park lived in the area near Newberry and was one of the first settlers there. In 1758, Park traveled among the Indians on the western side of the mountains and told stories of traders of Scottish and Irish origin who had been there for twenty years. Park also said that some had been there for forty to fifty years and that one claimed to have lived in that far distant frontier for sixty years. Logan speculates that this last trader would have been about four hundred miles west of Charleston before the end of the 1690s when the white population of the city extended for only twenty miles outward from the coast. One trader named Daugherty came from Virginia and set up trade with the Cherokee in 1690 before the residents of Charleston had ever heard of the Cherokee.[272] Like other scholars, Logan affirms that these traders were generally lawless men "of vicious practice" who bartered with the Cherokee for "peltries and slaves."[273] This view of traders was common throughout the eighteenth century.[274] In 1756, Captain Raymond Demere, the commandant of Fort Prince George at Keowee lamented in letters to Governor Lyttelton of the "pernicious" effects of rum among the Cherokee. Demere twice mentioned the name of trader Robert Gowdy of Ninety Six as a supplier of rum for the pack horsemen and called for the halt of such "destructive proceedings."[275]

Not all of the settlers of the backcountry who styled themselves as "Scotch-Irish" were of the lawless sort like many of the traders. Nevertheless, these immigrants did bring their culture with them to this new border country, particularly their ballads of love and death.[276] The Carolinas became fertile ground for these narrative poems because of the large numbers of seventeenth and eighteenth century newcomers from the borders of England and Scotland and the Ulster Plantation of Northern Ireland.[277] Writing about a similar frontier in Virginia, the morally earnest nineteenth century historian Samuel Kercheval relates that among the pastimes of the people were "dramatic narrations" of hero tales about Jack the Giant Killer, knights in shining armor, and damsels in distress reunited with their lovers.[278] Moralist that he was, Kercheval also opines that a preference for these "fairy regions of fiction to the august treasures of truth" is "truly a sarcasm on human nature."[279] Apart from his Mrs. Grundyism, Kercheval indicates that a number of the ballads sung by the people were about Robin Hood.[280] As a popular medieval folk figure from England, Robin Hood straddled the law as did many borderers of the southern colonial frontier.

In keeping with some of the early poetic renditions of the Cateechee legend and with the border traditions of the Scots Irish of often recounting stories as ballads, I have used this popular four-line verse form to give the tale an air of greater authenticity. It concerns dramatic episodes of romantic love and physical courage set against a backdrop of war involving common people, all preoccupations of the traditional folk ballad.[281] Although the principal characters of Allan, Cateechee, and Kuruga are fictional, I have attempted, as with the other selections in the anthology, to make the story's background details of time and place accurate, authentic and understandable for contemporary readers. To paraphrase Oscar Wilde, it is for the beholder that pictures are painted or marble sculpted into form and for the reader that books are written.[282]

Guide to the Pronunciation
of Cherokee Words

Vowels:

a is pronounced like *ah* as in *bah*.

e is pronounced like *ay* as in *way*.

i is pronounced like *ee* as in *meet*.

o is pronounced like *o* as in *go*.

u is pronounced like *oo* as in *school*.

v is pronounced like *uh* as in *buh*.

Consonants:

These are generally pronounced as in English except for *k* which in the Eastern Cherokee dialect sounds like *g*. Thus, the ancient Cherokee settlement of *Kituhwa*, though spelled with a *k*, is pronounced as *Giduhwa*. Note that the sounds represented by *t* and *d* in each of these words are allophones, much as in Spanish in which *b* and *v* may represent overlapping sounds or variants of the same sound as in *Cordova* or *Cordoba*.

Origins

THE THREE WORLDS

Long ago This World did not exist as is does today. Everything was water, and there was no earth. All of the animals lived on high in Galunlati—above the mountain tops, beyond the arch of the sky vault. Yet they felt crowded there and wanted more room. When they looked down from the Upper World, they saw the sea of water and wondered among themselves what lay beneath.

At last Dayunisi, who is the little Water Beetle and the Beaver's Grandchild, said to the others, "I will go and see what is there."

Dayunisi darted this way and that over the surface of the water but could find no solid place to rest. Then the little Water Beetle dove below to the bottom where there was soft mud, and taking some, he swam back to the top. The mud started to grow, and it spread in a circle to the north, south, east, and west. The circle became a great island floating on the water and hanging by four cords from the solid rock of the sky vault, each cord suspended from one of the four cardinal directions. Everything happened so long ago that no one knows who hung the earth in this way. The cords, though, kept the island from rocking on the water where it floated.

At first the island was wet, soft, and flat, and the animals could not go there. They decided to send different birds to find out whether the ground had become firm, but these could find no dry place, and they had to return to the Upper World. So the animals waited a while longer until they felt certain that the earth was dry.

Then they sent the Great Buzzard, the father of all buzzards today. All of them have the power to heal, and so they do not fear the dead. The Great Buzzard flew low over the earth and found that the ground was still soft. As he drew near to the center of This World, where the Cherokee now live, he grew tired and began to strike the earth with his wings. Wherever his wings beat upon the ground, a valley formed, and wherever his wings rose, a mountain appeared. The animals on high saw the land change beneath the flapping wings and became afraid that the whole earth would be mountains, so they called for the Buzzard to return. Yet the Cherokee country remained full of mountains.

The earth became dry at last so that the animals could come down, but there was as yet no light. So the conjurors of the World Above, they who had created the Sun, set her path from east to west over the island. At dawn the solid rock bowl of the sky vault rose so that the Sun could pass beneath it and journey from east to west. Then it was day. At dusk the bowl sank so that she could pass over its top and return from west to east. Then it was night, and along the sky vault stretched the Path of Souls, the way that the dead journey when they leave This World for another.

Yet the conjurors of the Upper World had made the Sun travel just above the mountain tops so that This World was too hot. The Red Crawfish, Tsiskagili, got scorched, and his shell became bright red and his meat foul so that the Cherokee refuse to eat it. The conjurors then placed the Sun another hand span higher, but the earth was still too hot. They set her yet a higher span and yet another until finally her path was seven hand spans high, just beneath the sky vault's bowl. The path was now right and is the seventh and highest level of This World.

There is yet another world beneath This World. It is the same and has animals, plants, and people. But the seasons there are different, for in winter the water that comes from below the ground is warmer than the water already here, and in summer the water below is always cooler. The streams that flow from the mountains are trails by which those who live here may travel to reach the World Below, and the heads of the streams are the doors by which to enter. But anyone who goes there must fast and must first be purified with water, and one of the people from the Underworld must guide the way. This World floats on the ocean balanced between the World Above and the World Below. From the center of This World grows the sacred cedar tree, ever green, and the highest branches of the tree connect This World to the World Above, and its lowest roots connect This World to the World Below.

Sometimes horrible creatures from the Underworld visit This World and cause harm. They are ghosts and witches. They are monsters that rise from rivers or lakes or come from behind waterfalls or out of caves in the mountains, for all of these places are doors to the Underworld. They lurk in solitary places like mountain passes or deep gorges and cause great trouble for people. They may be enormous frogs and giant lizards, but the most terrible of all is the Uktena which is unlike any other animal because it is like three kinds of animals. Its body is like a huge snake, scaly and as big as a tree trunk, with many-colored rings that glisten along its length. It is like a bird with wings on its sides. It is like a deer with antlers growing out of its head. On the top of its head is a crest that flashes light from a crystal giving great power to the one who is clever enough to possess it.

All of these things happened so long ago that now no one knows who created the first plants and animals, but they were instructed to stay awake and keep watch for seven nights. To reach the highest level of purity, young men today must also fast and not sleep for seven nights, and seven is the number of directions for the Cherokee—east, west, north, south, up, down, and in the middle or the place where they live on the floating island.

For the first night of their watch, the plants and animals remained awake, but afterwards on each night that followed, some would fall asleep, until by the seventh only the owl and the panther were left. Because these kept sleepless watch as told, they now have the power to see and move in the dark so that they can prey on other animals at night.

As for the trees, only the cedar, pine, spruce, holly, and laurel stayed awake throughout the seventh night, and now they have the gift of being ever green and are powerful for making medicine. Of these, the cedar is the most sacred, for its medicine is the most powerful. Its wood is fragrant and the slowest to decay. Its color is red and comes from the blood of an evil conjuror who once tried to alter the Sun's path, but two warriors stopped his designs. They found him is his secret cave, killed him, and cut off his head. They took it to the people to prove that the wizard was dead, yet his head remained alive. One villager told them it would die if hung from the highest branches of a tree. The warriors tied the head in one tree after another, but at dawn every day they found that the head continued yet alive at the bottom of each tree. The last tree that they hung it from was a cedar, and from this tree the head did not fall, and the wizard's blood slowly drained down the limbs and trunk of the tree and colored its wood red.

From that time forward, the cedar has been a medicine tree. Scalp trophies stretched across their small wooden hoops now decorate trimmed cedar saplings used in war dances, and no one may burn its branches as fuel. Only its green twigs may be tossed into a fire to drive away the harmful ghosts of humans and animals that trouble the sleeper's dreams. They cannot endure its smell. As for the rest of the trees, those that could not keep watch to the end of the seventh night, they now lose their hair when winter comes.

After the plants and animals came people. The first two were a brother and sister. He took a fish and struck his sister with it, and as he struck her, he said, "Multiply."

In seven days, she gave birth to a child, then another child in seven more days, and in seven more days yet another. Soon there were so many people that, if things continued in this way, the earth would not hold all of them. Then the sister began to have only one child a year. And so it is even to this day.

FIRE

Fire is from Galunlati, the Upper World where the Sacred Spirits live. Fire, who with the Sun, gives heat and light and life. The Old Fire dies. The New Fire kindles. Fire purifies all polluted things, consumes all past regrets, and pardons every wrong. Fire brings new hope and gives new life. This story tells of the first fire.

In ancient time, before the beginning of years, This World was without fire and cold. Then from Galunlati, beyond the sky vault's arch, Kanati and his sons sent forth lightning. They are the Thunderers—the Great Thunder and the Thunder Boys. Their home is in the distant west beyond the door of the Sun. They make the thunder, and their robes are lightning and the rainbow.

The Thunderers' lightning fell to earth as fire. When it entered This World, the Thunderers caused it to fall inside a hollow sycamore tree that stood on an island. The animals saw the smoke coming out of the top of the tree, and they knew that now the earth had fire. They wanted the fire, but the water around the island prevented them from having to it. So the animals called a council to determine how they could get to the fire.

The most eager ones were those who could swim or fly. Kalanu, the Raven, first offered to fetch the fire. The animals said to one another, "The Raven is large and powerful. Surely he will be able to get the fire." So the animals decided to send the Raven.

High into the air he flew and crossed over the wide water to the island. There he perched on a limb of the sycamore, but before he could think what he should do next, the heat from the fire in the bottom of the tree scorched his feathers, turning all of them black. The Raven became so frightened that he flew away without getting the fire.

The next to volunteer to bring back the fire was Wahuhu, the little Screech Owl. He reached the sycamore safely, but as he peered down into the hollow tree, a hot blast of air rose from the bottom and almost blinded him, nearly burning out his eyes. He barely managed to fly away, and he was unable to see for a long time. Even today the fire has left his eyes red.

After the Screech Owl, the Hooting Owl, Uguku, and the Horned Owl, Tskili, went to the island. By now, though, the tree was so hot that, before they could alight and look inside, they, too, became almost blind. The ashes blown by the gusting wind from the flames swirled into the air and made white circles around the eyes of the big birds before they could fly away. Like the Raven and the Screech Owl, they had to return without the fire, and even though they rubbed their eyes as often and as hard as they could, the white rings of ash remained.

Now no other birds would volunteer. So the little snake Uksuhi, the Black

Racer, came forward and said that he would swim through the water and get the fire. When he got to the island, he sped through the grass until he reached the sycamore. At the bottom was a tiny hole. He crawled inside, but as with the others who had gone before him, the smoke and heat were too fierce, causing him to dart blindly here and there over the fiery coals. He almost caught on fire himself. If he had not quickly slithered out of the same hole where he had entered, he would have soon burned up. When he got outside, his skin was black, scorched all over from where he had dodged this way and that, turning back on his tracks as if trying to escape the heat and confinement. He still moves so to this day.

After the Black Racer returned without fire, Gulegi, who is the Great Blacksnake, ventured to go. He swam to the island, crossed the grass, and began to crawl up the outside of the sycamore, clinging to the bark as he did so. For this reason, he is called "the Climber." When he reached the top of the tree, he looked down toward the fire that the Thunderers had placed within, but the smoke, billowing from below, nearly choked him, and he fell inside the burning hollow. When he climbed out, he had become as black as the little racer.

The animals still did not have fire, and This World was still cold, so they called a second council to decide what to do. Now no one wanted to go to the island. The birds, the snakes, the four-footed creatures—each in turn gave an excuse, for each was afraid of the burning sycamore.

Finally, Kananeski Amaiyehi volunteered. She is the large Water Spider with stripes and black downy hair on her body, not the tiny one that looks like the Mosquito. The animals knew that she could run across the top of the water or dive below and would be able to get to the island. Yet they wondered whether she would be able to return with fire.

"I have a way," said the Water Spider. Then she began to spin a thread out of her body, and as she spun, she wove the thread into the tusti bowl that has a circle in the bottom with a cross inside it. She next fastened the bowl on the middle of her back and crossed over the water to the island. She went to the tree where the fire still burned. Reaching inside, she took a tiny glowing ember and put it in her bowl. Back across the water she came, and from the one coal that she brought, the rest of This World received fire.

Heat, life, light, and fire—all these came from the Creator God, the Being who created the Sun and her daughter the Moon. Fire—Ancient Red, the Spirit of War that the helper of the red war priest carries to battle in the war chest. Fire—Ancient White, the Spirit of Peace for whom the Uka, the Fire King, wears white robes in the dark council house and lights the new fire of the new year. Fire—the Spirit who is closest to the Cherokee, the principal people, and Smoke who is Fire's messenger, always ready to deliver the people's petitions from This World to the World Above. Fire—over whom parents wave the newborn to protect the child from snakes. Fire—the Spirit who receives the hunter's offerings of meat, the warriors' captives to ensure continued success in battle, and the shaman's gifts of the first ripe corn. The New Fire lit when the Old is extinguished, forever connecting the Cherokee past with the Cherokee future.

CORN AND GAME

In ancient time, not long after the creation of This World, a man and woman lived in what today is Shining Rock Wilderness north of Pilot Knob, one of the tall peaks of the Pisgah National Forest. The two were husband and wife. The man was known as the Lucky Hunter and so was called Kanati, and the woman was known as Corn and thus named Selu. They were an old couple who had only one child, a little boy.

Whenever Kanati went into the forest to hunt, he always returned with a large amount of game for them to eat, usually a deer and sometimes a turkey or two. Selu would take the animals and dress them by cutting up the meat and washing it in the nearby river. There the blood of the animals unfortunately mixed with the water.

Everyday Kanati and Selu's little son would play in the bushes growing beside the river. One morning his parents heard what they thought was another child laughing and talking along with their son. That night, when the boy came home, they questioned, "Who was playing with you today?"

The child answered, "He is a boy who comes from the water, and he says that he is my older brother. He told me that his mother was cruel and tossed him into the river." As the old couple listened, they realized that the strange child had come from wrongful mixing blood and water when Selu had dressed the meat in the river and thus created an impurity. The parents knew that any child from such a union would likely be unruly and hard to control.

After their son had told them about his brother, the older boy continued to join the younger one in play by the water. Yet this mysterious other child always returned to the river at the end of the day so that Kanati and Selu never saw him and considered him wild.

One evening Kanati said to his son, "Tomorrow, when the Wild Boy comes to play with you, the two of you should wrestle. Be sure to hold him tightly in your arms, and do not let go. Then call your mother and me."

The boy promised to do exactly as his father had instructed. So the next morning, when his older brother came out of the water to play, the younger boy challenged him to wrestle. No sooner had the match started than Kanati's son tightened his arms fast around his playmate and began screaming for his parents. They were not far away and instantly ran down to the river.

The Wild Boy saw them coming and fought to free himself, yelling all the while, "You threw me away! Let me go! Let me go!"

His brother, though, squeezed even more tightly until the old folks reached them. They caught the Wild Boy and took him back to the house where they kept him inside and tamed him as much as they could. Yet he remained sly and wild. As for his younger brother, the older boy led him into all kinds of tricks and pranks. Kanati and Selu called him "He Who Grew Up Wild." Not long after they had captured him, they learned that he possessed skill in magic.

Whenever Kanati left to go hunting in the mountains, he always came back with a fat deer and sometimes other game. The Wild Boy observed all of the animals that his father brought back and one day said to his brother, "Where does our father find so much game? The next time he leaves, let's follow him and find out."

A few days passed. Kanati took his bow and some feathers and left toward the west. The boys let him get a head start and then followed him, making sure that he did not see them. After walking for a while, Kanati came to a swamp where he intended to cut some small reeds to make shafts for his arrows.

In the meantime, the Wild Boy had turned himself into a light fluffy bit of bird's down which the breeze lifted into the air. He floated along toward the swamp where he lightly landed on Kanati's shoulder just before the old man entered the swamp. Unaware of the boy's presence, Kanati chopped some slender reeds and attached feathers to them for arrow shafts. The Wild Boy, still in his disguise, wondered what these were for.

After fashioning his arrows, Kanati left the swamp and continued on his way. The breeze blew the down off his shoulder. The Wild Boy, resuming his original form, returned to his brother, who had been waiting all the while, and told him what he had seen. The two then traveled after Kanati, both being sure to stay out of his sight.

The old man came to Mount Mitchell, a high remote summit, and began to climb up its steep slope. Suddenly he stopped. He bent over and rolled away a large rock that covered the entrance to a cave. Out bounded a big buck which he immediately shot. He then rolled the stone back into its place and headed for home.

"Ah," said the boys. "Our father keeps deer in the cave, and when he goes hunting, he comes here and shoots one with the things that he made in the swamp." The two then hurried home, running so fast that they got there ahead of Kanati who was carrying the heavy deer carcass and was none the wiser that the boys had been tracking him during his hunt.

After a few days, the boys took two bows and returned to the swamp and went to where Kanati had entered. They cut some reeds and made seven arrows. Then they set out for the mountain where their father's secret cave was. When they got there, they removed the heavy rock from the entrance and out bounded a deer just as before. They each aimed an arrow, but so many deer began running out that the boys became confused and started shooting everywhere.

At that time, the deer were like other animals and had tails that pointed toward the ground, but when one of the bucks darted past the Wild Boy, he shot it so that its tail stood straight up. His brother shot another deer with such force that its tail arched over its back. They liked this kind of hunting, and every arrow they fired thereafter made the tails curl up and over the hindquarters of the deer. All of the deer's tails still curl up this way even now.

Soon all of the deer had escaped from the cave and gone into the woods. Then other animals came running out. There were rabbits and raccoons and other multitudes of the four-footed tribes scattering in all directions. Only bears were absent because humans had not yet changed into them.

After the four-footed animals came flocks of birds—pigeons, partridges, turkeys. Their numbers were so great that the sky blackened like a huge storm cloud. They created such a violent noise with their flapping wings that Kanati, who was back at home, heard what sounded like the rumble of far off thunder rolling through the mountains. His immediate thought was "My sons have caused trouble. I must go and find out what they are doing."

So he headed for the mountain. When he arrived at the cave where he kept the animals concealed, he saw the boys standing by the rock and knew all the game had escaped. He was beside himself with anger but said nothing and went inside the cave. In a corner were four clay jars. He walked up and kicked them over. Out swarmed all sorts of vermin—bedbugs, fleas, lice, ticks, flies, gnats. At once these covered his sons who screamed loudly in pain and fear and tried to knock the creatures off their skin and hair, but the multitudes of vermin covered them, biting and stinging so fiercely that the two collapsed, almost dead. Kanati watched the boys writhing in pain for a while. After he decided that they had been sufficiently punished, he brushed off the insects and gave the boys a talk.

Their father said, "Your mischief has gone too far. You have broken the boundaries and upset the balance of things. Never have you had to work for the bounty that I provided. Any time you wanted something to eat, I came to this place and got a deer or turkey and brought it home for your mother to cook. Now that has changed, for you have released all of the animals from my cave. From this day forward, if you want a deer or other game, you must search throughout the woods, and even then you may not find any. Go back to your mother. She waits for you at home. I will search for something for our supper."

On hearing Kanati's words, the boys left. When they got home, they asked

Selu for something to eat because they were tired and hungry. Their mother answered, "We have no meat, but if you wait here, I'll find you something."

So saying, she took a basket and left for the *barbacoa* that was close by. This was a small storehouse where she kept food. It was made of logs and raised aloft on tall poles about seven feet above the ground so that nothing could get to the food. It had only one entranceway that Selu reached by climbing up a ladder. Every time she cooked corn and beans, she went there and came back with her basket full. The brothers had never been inside and wondered where their mother got all of the corn and beans that they ate.

As soon as Selu left the house, the Wild Boy whispered, "Let's follow her and see what she is doing."

The boys then slipped out of the house and went to the back of the *barbacoa* so as not to be seen. They climbed up one of the poles and poked out a chink of clay between the logs so that they could peek inside. Selu was there on her knees in the center of the floor. She leaned over and rubbed her stomach. At once corn filled half of the basket. Next she rubbed under her armpits, and beans filled the other half.

The brothers stared wide eyed at each other as if to say "This cannot be. Our mother is a witch and will poison us with the food. We have to kill her." They then ran back to the house and waited for their mother.

After a short while, Selu returned. At once she read their thoughts and said, "You intend to kill me?"

"We must. You are a witch. You know our thoughts and deserve to die."

Selu replied, "When I am dead, prepare a large plot of earth in the shape of a circle outside the house. You must drag my body seven times around the circle and then seven times across it. Do not sleep, and watch throughout the night. By morning, there will be plenty of corn."

Without so much time as it takes to draw a breath, the boys then fell upon the old woman and beat her to death with clubs. They chopped off her head and mounted it on the rooftop, being sure that it faced east, and commanded her to watch for her husband. They next began to prepare the ground, but they cleared only seven small spots in front of the house, not the whole area as Selu had instructed. For this reason, corn thrives in only a few places instead of the whole earth. The brothers did drag their mother's body seven times around the outside of the plots, and in the places where blood stained the ground, corn sprouted. Yet, instead of dragging the body across the plots for seven passes, they dragged it only twice. For this reason, the Cherokee work their crop but two times a season.

After thus preparing the ground, the brothers kept watch throughout the night. When the sun rose the next morning, the corn was fully grown and the ears ripe. Later that day, Kanati returned from his hunt. He looked around the homestead to find Selu but did not see her. So he asked the boys, "Where is your mother?"

"We killed her because she was a witch," the two replied. "Her head is up on the roof."

When Kanati looked up and saw the head of his wife, he was furious and said, "I will stay here no longer. I will be with the Wolf people."

Kanati then left to go to the Wolf people who were his watchdogs and servants, but before he had gotten very far, He Who Grew Up Wild once again turned himself into a puff of bird's down which the wind lifted and let settle on the old man's shoulder. When Kanati arrived outside the townhouse of the Wolf people, he could hear that they were holding a council within. He bent beneath the low door and entered the rotunda where he seated himself near the fire in the center of the floor. The tuft of down was still on his shoulder.

The Wolves recognized the great hunter, and their chief asked, "Why have you traveled to the settlement of the Wolf people?"

Kanati answered, "My two sons are at home. They have done much wrong. In seven days, I want you to play a game of ball with them."

The Wolves understood what Kanati meant. He wanted them to make war on his sons and kill them. The council determined to do his bidding.

At this point, the bird's down lifted off Kanati's shoulder and rose with the smoke of the sacred fire through the hole in the townhouse roof. Outside, the tuft drifted to the earth, and the Wild Boy became himself again. He went back to his brother and revealed to him everything that occurred in the council house. Kanati, though, did not go home. Once he left the Wolf people, he traveled another way.

The brothers meanwhile readied themselves for the Wolves. The older boy, who had the power of magic, instructed his brother in what they were to do. They first trotted in a wide circuit almost completely around the house and made a beaten-down path. They made sure, however, to leave a small gap in the circle on the side from where the Wolves would come. They next fashioned four big bundles of arrows and put them outside the circle, placing each bundle at a point in the four cardinal directions of north, south, east, and west. They then hid in the woods and waited.

Within a day or two, a large war party of Wolves appeared, surrounding the house and intent on killing the boys. The Wolves did not see the path around the house because they had immediately entered the circle through the gap the brothers had left. As soon as the warriors were inside, the path at once grew into a high stockade of brush and closed them in. The boys now grabbed their bows and arrows and began shooting over the brush, and because it was so high, none of the wolves could leap over it and almost all were killed. Only a few got through the gap and took refuge in a large nearby swamp.

Seeing that some of the Wolves had escaped, the boys now ran in a circle around the swamp, and a huge fire blazed up behind their feet. The grass and undergrowth within caught fire and burned up almost all the remaining Wolves, but two or three managed to get out alive. These great Wolves from ancient time are the ancestors of all the wolves today.

Not long after the defeat of the Wolves, some strangers heard about the corn plant that provided Selu and her family grain for making bread. Though the strangers lived a journey of seven days away, they visited the brothers to ask for some of the kernels.

The boys said, "Here are seven grains. On your way home, plant one of these seeds tomorrow night, and keep watch over it until the next morning. Do the same for the rest of your journey, and when you arrive among your people, you will have enough corn to feed all of them."

So the visitors took the seven grains of corn and on their way home planted one each night and kept watch until dawn. Each night a stalk sprouted and grew into a tall corn plant that bore one ripened ear that hardened into seed. The strangers did just as the brothers had instructed for six nights, but on the seventh they became tired because the sun had been hot during their travel that day and they had been without sleep for a long time. They planted the grain of corn but soon became drowsy and fell asleep.

The next morning the kernel had not sprouted. So they took the six ears from the previous nights and planted them when they returned to the settlement. Before then, however, corn would spring up and ripen in a single night. Now it must be cared for and watched for six months.

The brothers remained at home and waited for their father, but Kanati did not return. So they decided to go in search for him. The Wild Boy took a stone disk that he had polished smooth with rocks. The stone was one that he and his brother used to roll when they played the game of chunkey and was about two inches wide and two hands around its outside if a man joined his thumbs and middle fingers together to form a circle. The Wild Boy tossed the chunkey stone so that it rolled to the west to the land where it is always growing dark. The wheel rolled back, signaling that Kanati was not in the Twilight Land. So the boy rolled the wheel two more times, first to the north, then to the south, and both times the wheel returned as before, signaling that Kanati was in neither place. The boy rolled the stone yet a fourth time to the east, and there it remained.

"Our father is in the Sunland," the Wild Boy said to his brother. "Let us search there."

The two then headed east, and after four days, they came upon their father. A little dog walked by his side. He said to his sons, "You bad boys have now come here."

"Yes," they replied. "Whatever we set out to do, we always do it. We are men."

The old man said, "This little dog caught up with me four days ago." He meant the chunkey stone. "So," he continued, "since you have found me, let us walk together, but I will lead the way."

The three went along and went along until they came to a swamp. Kanati said, "Do not go there. Danger lurks within." He kept on walking.

The boys paused. When their father was out of sight, the more disobedient one said, "Let us go into this place and see what is there."

So they entered the swamp together. There in the center lay a huge panther stretched out asleep. The Wild Boy took aim with an arrow and struck the side of the panther's head. The panther turned the other side of his head toward the boy, and again he shot him. The panther then moved his head back to the side where the first arrow struck, and now both boys shot him. Yet the panther gave no heed to their arrows, for he was not hurt. The brothers then left the swamp and came upon their father. He was waiting for them.

"Did you see it?" he asked.

"Yes, but it did not harm us, for we are men."

Kanati was surprised but gave no clue and said nothing. The three continued on their journey. After they had traveled farther, he looked at his sons and said, "You must now take care. We are near the Roaster People. They are cannibals. If they capture you, they will cook you in a pot and eat you." He then left his sons behind.

In a short while, the brothers came to a honey locust tree. Lightning had struck it, but the tree still lived so that its power was great. The Wild Boy told his brother, "Gather some of the splinters from this tree. Put them in the fire when the cannibals begin to cook me."

Soon the boys arrived at the settlement of the Roasters. A troop of them ran out, surrounded the Wild Boy and his brother, and loudly proclaimed, "Here are two plump travelers. They will make us a great feast."

The cannibals then dragged the boys into the council house and called to the others in the settlement to attend the feast. They stoked the fire of the townhouse and filled a big pot with water. When the water began a rolling boil, they threw the Wild Boy into the pot. The younger brother was not afraid in the least of what he saw, and instead of trying to escape, he knelt quietly beside the fire and fed it with the wood splinters to make it burn more fiercely. The cannibals paid him little heed. After a little while, they decided the meat was done and removed the pot from the flames.

At that moment, thunder cracked and lightning flashed, darting throughout the great rotunda of the council house, filling it with blinding light. The blasts struck cannibal after cannibal so that not a single one remained alive.

Then the lightning flew up the smoke hole in the roof, and the brothers found themselves standing outside as if they had never met the Roasters.

The boys left and to their father's surprise soon caught up with him. "What!" he exclaimed. "You two back again?"

"Yes," they thundered. "We are great men. We never give up."

Kanati asked, "What did the Roasters do?"

"They captured us and took us to their townhouse, but they did not hurt us."

Kanati did not reply, and the three continued on their way. Once again he left the boys behind, so they traveled by themselves, at last reaching the Sunrise Place. There, at the end of This World, is the Sun's door where the solid rock of the sky vault is forever moving up and down, and when the sky vault swings up, the door opens between the earth and sky, and the Sun in bright human shape climbs the inside of the arch to bring light to This World.

When the boys reached the sky vault, it was moving down, and the door of the Sun shut. They waited, and then the arch lifted, and the door opened. They entered and ascended the other side of the rocky vault. Kanati and Selu were sitting there and were happy to see their sons and with kindness welcomed them.

The old couple told the children, "Here you may remain for a while, but then you must go to the Twilight Land where the Sun departs."

So the boys stayed with Kanati and Selu for seven days and then left for the Spirit Land of the west where it is always growing dark and where they now live. Their father is the Great Thunderer who is the whirlwind and the hurricane, and they are the Little Men or the Thunder Boys. Today, whenever low thunder rolls out of the west, the two are speaking to each other.

Although the Little Men at first caused problems, as when they let the animals out of Kanati's cave, they will often help humans in their time of need. For example, when all of the game escaped from the cave, people had a hard time in hunting, especially for deer. Hunters would search through the woods for game and not find any so that the people stayed hungry. Then word came that the Thunder Boys had gone to live beyond the Sun's door in the west. The people also heard that the boys could make the game return. So messengers went to the Darkening Land to ask the brothers for help.

When the Little Men arrived, they went to the council house and sat down in the middle. They said to the hunters, "Be ready with your bows and arrows."

Then the two began the first of seven songs. During the first song, the people heard a rumbling noise. It sounded like a heavy wind coming from the northwest. The boys sang more songs, and the wind got closer and became louder. At the beginning of the seventh song, a large herd of deer led by an enormous buck ran out of the woods outside the settlement. By the end of the song, the deer were milling densely around the council house. The hunters went outside and began to shoot into the herd so that they killed enough to feed the people before the deer could run back into the woods.

After the people feasted, the Thunder Boys taught them the seven songs to call the deer. The brothers then returned to the Spirit Land. Everything happened long ago, and only two songs survive today, the rest forgotten. Yet the hunters still sing the remaining two to call up the deer.

Disease and Medicine

Not in recent time but in ancient time, every living thing—plants, beasts, birds, fish, insects, people—could talk, and there was no separation among them. All lived in harmony and worked together to help one another. The early animals of that day were bigger, stronger, and wiser than their offspring today, but after a time humans became more powerful. They multiplied so quickly that their settlements spread over the land, and the animals began to feel that they did not have enough room to live.

As the number of people increased, they created weapons—hooks, blowguns, knives, darts, spears, and bows and arrows. These made them even more powerful, and they began to kill the larger animals as well as the birds and the fish for their fur, feathers, or flesh. But neither were the smaller creatures safe, for the ones like the frogs and worms were often stepped upon and crushed without consideration, either through human disregard or disgust. At last the animals decided to hold a council about what they should do to protect themselves.

The Bears held their council first. In the wildest depths of the Great Smokies are their four townhouses, each beneath a different peak where in winter they gather for their dances before they go to sleep. Near the peak of Kituwha glimmers the enchanted lake of Ataghi, fed by cold springs tumbling from surrounding cliffs but invisible to everyone except the animals and the expert hunter who must pray and fast and keep sleepless watch throughout the night if he is to see its shallow purple water. Innumerable fish swim within it, and enormous flocks of ducks and pigeons nest there and fill the air. Along its shore are the tracks of the Bears going in every direction. If a hunter wounds one, the Bear immediately heads to the lake, plunges beneath its surface, and emerges on the other side completely healed. For this reason, the animals keep the lake invisible to all but themselves.

Deep within the core of Clingmans Dome or Kituwha, the mulberry place, the old White Bear chief makes his home. The Bears now gathered there in the townhouse of their ancient leader who led the council. The White Bear asked all present to air their grievances. Some Bears complained that men killed their friends, especially in winter when they slept in holes, and that men would make fire and smoke to drive them out and shoot them. Others said that humans ate the Bears' flesh and that, out of all the beasts of prey, humans ate only the Bears and never ate the others like the Panthers. Some also said that humans would fry their fat to make sweet oil mixed with sassafras and wild cinnamon. They told how people would eat hot corn fritters fried in the oil with a jelly made of smilax root and honey or use the oil to cure old aches and pains and anoint pierced ear lobes hung with weights and stretched wide. Still others charged people of using their skins to sleep upon, to cover the floors of their houses, or to fashion muffs and hats from the fur of cubs.

When the Bears had finished their accusations, the council cried out for war. Then one of the members asked, "What are the weapons that people use to destroy us?"

Many of the Bears then clamored, "Bows and arrows, of course."

"What are they made of?" was the next question.

Another Bear answered, "The bow is made of wood, and its string comes from our entrails."

At once a council member proposed, "Let us then make a bow and some arrows so that we can use these weapons against our enemy."

As a result, one of the Bears brought to the gathering a good piece of locust wood for the bow, and another offered himself in sacrifice to help the rest so that they might make a string from his entrails. When they had completed their work, a Bear came forward to try the bow. But when he pulled it back to let the arrow fly, his long claws got tangled in the string and ruined the shot. One of the Bears then suggested that the others trim the shooter's claws. They did, and on the second try, when he shot the arrow, it flew straight to the target.

But now the old White Bear chief spoke. "If we cut off our claws," he objected, "we cannot climb trees. One Bear has already given his life for the bowstring. If we give up our claws, we cannot hunt and will starve. Better that we rely on what nature has provided us—our teeth and claws—for the weapons of humans are not meant for us."

No one argued with the old chief's words, so he adjourned the council, and the Bears scattered throughout the wilderness without forming a plan to halt the increasing numbers of people. If only the Bears had been united and sought vengeance for spilled blood, they and humans would be at war with one another. But as things stand now, the hunter does not bother to pray to the Bear's soul for forgiveness after he kills one and is free to take its life without fear of reprisal from its relatives.

Awi Usdi or Little Deer next called a council of his subjects. He is their chief whom no hunter can wound except one who has become a master over many years and has made himself pure through much fasting and many vigils kept through lonely nights. During the council, the other Deer talked for a while as Little Deer presided.

Some of his tribe said that hunters killed and ate them in the belief that the venison would make a man as fleet of foot as the Deer themselves. Others of Little Deer's band described the tricks men used in pursuing them. They spoke of how men conjured them with songs sometimes before or during the hunt. Sung to sweet and slightly sorrowful tunes, these songs tricked the Deer into coming close to the hunter so that he might more easily shoot them. One of the council then sang the following song:

> Close to the trees you stand, O Deer.
> Acorns along the ground you eat.
> The acorns make your spittle sweet.
> O Deer, to me you now are near.

When the council had ended, the Deer decided to make every hunter who killed one of them racked with rheumatism. Only if the hunter asked the Deer's spirit to forgive his deed could the man escape the sentence. They then sent word of their deliberations to the nearest village and warned the people what they must do to receive pardon if they killed a member of Deer tribe. The message also stated that hunters must kill only out of necessity. If any took a life merely for wasteful slaughter, Little Deer would strike him with pain and swelling throughout his body.

When a hunter now shoots a Deer, Little Deer, who is faster than the wind, is aware instantly and is there in the twinkling of an eye. Lowering his head over the blood stains, he asks the spirit of his dead comrade whether the hunter prayed for pardon. If the spirit answers "Yes," Little Deer forgives and departs, but if the spirit answers "No," then this great chief who has branching antlers and is pure white and invisible follows the hunter by the drops of blood left along the trail. When he arrives at the man's house, Little Deer enters unseen and strikes the hunter with tormenting aches and pains, making him a helpless cripple from that time forward to the end of his days.

After the council of the Deer came that of the Fish and Reptiles. They, too, had grievances against humans and determined to revenge themselves by troubling any person who harmed them with dreams of serpents. These would coil around the person and breathe their rotten stinking breath into the victim's mouth and nose. Other dreams might cause the offender to devour raw decaying fish so that on waking the person would not eat, grow weak, and die. For this reason, people will sometimes have nightmares about writhing snakes and unclean fish.

The final council to discuss the human problem was held by the Birds, Insects, and smaller animals. Its chief was the Grub Worm. The council allowed each to have a turn in giving an opinion, and then everyone would vote on the issue of human guilt. Seven votes would be sufficient for a conviction. One by one, the members railed against the suffering and injustice that people inflicted on them.

The Frog came forward to say, "We must halt the spread of humans. They will become so many that there will be no room for the rest of us on the earth. You see how people have abused me because I am ugly. They have kicked me so much that now my back is covered with bruises." Here he paused to show the council the dark splotches on his skin.

No one recalls which one, but one of the Birds rose next to speak and to condemn. "Humans are cruel. After they kill us, they run sharp spits through our bodies and burn away our feathers and our feet, then roast and eat us." Other birds declared the words were true.

Of all the council, only one spoke favorably of people. "Humans hardly ever hurt me because I am so small," said the Ground Squirrel. Scarcely had he uttered these words, however, than the others flew into a rage and attacked him so fiercely that his back even now bears the stripes of their claws.

At this point, the Grub Worm called for the verdict. The judgment was death. The council then began to concoct one disease after another to inflict on the human race. With the mention of each illness, the Grub Worm grew ever more pleased until they seemed to have exhausted the possibilities and were about to conclude. At the very last moment, though, one of the council said, "Let us cause the monthly issue of blood by women to kill them from time to time."

The Grub Worm instantly rose from his seat and rejoiced. "Wadan!" he cried. "Thank you! I am happy to have more of them perish by any means. For they ignorantly destroy the tiny Worms and Insects wholesale, showing no mercy to us, the Tsgaya. We are everywhere in earth and air, and This World now teems with so many humans that, wherever they step, they kill us."

The thought of all the diseases that his council had designed for people filled the Grub Worm with such joy that he began to tremble all over so that tumbled backward. No matter how hard he tried, he could not get up and had to leave the council as he wriggled on his back. He still squirms in this way.

Word of what the animals had plotted now reached the plants. They remained friendly to humans and agreed to defeat the animals' foul schemes which would leave This World unbalanced. From the loftiest Trees down to the lowest Mosses, the plants offered a cure to counteract every disease the animals proposed. Each plant vowed, "When the people call to me in their distress, I will help them."

From this promise came medicine. Every plant has its use as a remedy to fight the diseases that the animals created as retaliation against the multitudes of people and their cruelty. Every weed may serve some good, but people must discover this for themselves. They must listen for guidance from the spirit of each plant.

THE BEAR AND THE BEAR SONGS

Yanu, the Bears, walk on four feet but sometimes on two. Sometimes they eat the same things that humans eat. The Bears can speak if only they would. The Bears are really people. Here is how they came to be.

Long, long ago, the Ani-Tsaguhi were a clan of the Cherokee, and in this clan there was a family who had a son. The boy would sometimes leave home and go into the mountains for most of the day. After a while, he began to start from home at sunrise and would not return until after dark. He would eat most of the time in the woods until at last he would not eat at all inside his house.

He began to behave this way more and more, going out every day before dawn and coming home at night. His mother and father were not happy and scolded him for his behavior, but the boy did not heed their words.

Some time later, his parents began to notice that long brown hair was starting to sprout all over their son's skin. Naturally they were curious about what was happening to him and asked, "Why do you stay so much in the mountains? You are there almost always, and you only eat in the woods."

"I have plenty of good food there," the boy said, "and I like it much better than the beans and corn we eat here. Soon I will be living in the mountains and woods all the time." Then he added, "They are better places than the settlements, and I am different there. You see how I am beginning to change. I can live here no longer."

The boy next invited his parents to go into the wilds with him. "Come away with me to the woods and mountains. All of us will have more than enough. The trees provide acorns and chestnuts; the brambles, berries; the bees, honey; the streams and lakes, fish; the meadows, grass. There is plenty everywhere, and we do not have to work for it, but you must prepare before you can come. You must fast for seven days for a clear vision to guide your purpose."

The father and mother talked over what their son had told them. They then went to the headmen of the clan. These called a council to discuss the matter. After all had been debated, the chief rose to give voice to the decision.

"Here we do not always have enough, and for what we have, we must work hard. The boy says that in the wild there is always enough without work. Let us go into the woods and mountains with him."

So for seven days the Ani-Tsaguhi fasted, and at the end of seven days, they left their settlement for the mountains around Kituwha with the boy leading the way. People in the other towns had heard of their intentions and sent messengers to try to persuade them not to make their home in the woods. When the messengers arrived at the settlement, they discovered it already abandoned, and when they overtook took the clan, they noticed that the people's skin had hair like that of animals beginning to cover it. The Ani-Tsaguhi had not consumed human food for seven days and had eaten only what the wild things of the woods eat. Just as the Cherokee elders had taught, humans who consume only what animals eat will become like them.

The messengers asked the people to return to their homes, but they replied, "We are traveling to a place where food is always plentiful and where no labor is required. From now on, you must call us Yanu, for we are Bears. When you yourselves are hungry, go into the woods and mountains and call to us. We will then offer our flesh for you to eat.

The Ani-Tsaguhi paused and then continued, "The shamans say that all animals have a certain length of life, and no violent death can end it until its appointed time. If we die before our allotted day, death does not last, and from our drops of blood, we return in our own form as Bears. We remain alive until our final end when our spirit is freed. Then it goes to the Darkening Land to reunite with other souls like itself. Do not be afraid to kill us. We will always live.

"But now we go to four high mountains—Tsistu-yi, Kituhwa, Uya-hye, and Gategwa-hi. There we will hold in the fall our festival and dance in our council houses beneath their summits. Then we will sleep for the winter."

When the Ani-Tsaguhi had finished speaking, they gave the messengers the Bear songs to take back to the Cherokee settlements. The messengers were to teach the songs to the people. The Ani-Tsaguhi then resumed their journey, and the messengers left, but before they had gone too far, they turned to look back and saw a large drove of Bears leaving the path for the deep woods.

Here is one of the songs that the messengers brought back. The hunter sings it to draw Bears to him.

> At Tsistu-yi,
> The Rabbit Place,
> You first had life.
>
> At Tsistu-yi,
> The Rabbit Place,
> You first had life.
>
> At Kituhwa,
> Mulberry Place,
> You first had life.

At Kituhwa,
Mulberry Place,
You first had life.

At Uya-hye,
High mountain peak,
You first had life.

At Uya-hye,
High mountain peak,
You first had life.

At Gategwa-hi,
The Thicket Place,
You first had life.

At Gategwa-hi,
The Thicket Place,
You first had life.

Now you, the Bear,
The good black thing that's best,
And I will meet.

The hunter sings this next song during his daily fast when he first leaves camp in the morning, hoping to call a bear to him. When he returns in the evening, he then eats. He repeats the song the next morning when he leaves again. Never, though, does he sing the song twice on the same day.

The Ani-Tsaguhi, I long to stretch them low on the earth.
The Ani-Tsaguhi, I long to stretch them low on the earth.

Yanu, I long to stretch you low on the earth.
Yanu, I long to stretch you low on the earth.

Tobacco

Cutting through the Eastern Continental Divide, Hickory Nut Gorge or Gap is in the Blue Ridge foothills about fifteen miles south of Asheville. Running south southeast, the gorge passes through the communities of Gerton, Bat Cave, and Chimney Rock and ends at Lake Lure. The Rocky Broad River cuts through the gap's lower two-thirds. Nineteenth century travelers found the bare granite outcroppings and perpendicular cliffs of the gorge awe-inspiring, especially the dome known as Chimney Rock, a monolith towering against the sky like the lone tremendous turret of a giant's castle. A long time ago, when the Cherokee ran out of tobacco, they traveled through Hickory Nut Gorge to obtain more of this precious, fragrant weed.

The people originally had tobacco from their earliest days when they first appeared in This World. This tobacco, however, was not the kind cultivated on farms and plantations that later came from the West Indies, but old tobacco that grew wild. An unknown wanderer from the east had made the Cherokee acquainted with its powers. But there came a time when the Cherokee did not have tobacco, and they suffered greatly because of the loss. There was none to sprinkle as incense on the sacred fires of the council houses. There was none to smoke in the large redstone catlinite pipe bowls of the calumet to affirm oaths to take up the hatchet and declare war, and there was none to seal vows to bury the hatchet and guarantee peace. There was none to relieve ailments and none to cure illnesses; none to interpret omens, and none to ward off witches; none to suppress hunger, and none to alter consciousness.

Because of the tribulation, the nation called for a council where would gather the greatest individuals of the different settlements. They assembled in the peace capital of Istati or Chota on the south bank of the Little Tennessee River in the Overhill territory. The townhouse there could accommodate as many as five hundred people. The discussion revealed that tobacco had first come across the mountains to the east from an area near the great salt sea and that the way to this land lay through a rocky gorge which gradually narrowed into a gap between steep cliffs.

At that time the Cherokee had not traveled through this area, but they knew that such places were occupied by countless spirit dwarves or Little People. The various clans of these beings lived in remote locations. One clan dwelt along high mountain ridges, one in high meadows, and one in bushy bottomlands along solitary rivers. Members of another clan made their homes in rhododendron thickets, while those of yet another lived in steep rocky places like the narrow gorge.

The council debated the dangers of journeying through an unexplored land to replenish the supply of tobacco and returning with it in a large deerskin pouch. After some talk, a young warrior boldly stood up and addressed the gathering.

"The tobacco country," he said, "is far to the east near the salt sea. To reach it, one must travel through high mountains where many spirits guard the passes. My father is a very old man. Only tobacco smoke keeps him alive. I do not want him to die. I will go."

With the council's approval, the young man set out the next day, and the hopes of all the Cherokee went with him. He was gone a long time, and the people realized that something had happened and he was not coming back. Because they had not had tobacco for such a long time, their suffering was now greater than ever. So another council was called to determine a new course of action. One speaker after another arose to offer advice. In the midst of the discussion, a celebrated wizard of the Cherokee appeared in the great townhouse and pro-claimed that he would relieve the people of their tribulation.

"Send me to the tobacco country, and your suffering will end," he said.

The wizard left the settlement, and when he arrived at the gorge, he changed himself into a mole and tunneled through to the east beyond the mountains. The Little People were aware of his presence, though, and when he returned through their domain, they pursued him so vigorously that he was unable to bring any tobacco back to the people.

The wizard again vowed to relieve the people. When he reached the gorge this time, he reached into his medicine bundle and took out the skin of a hummingbird. He put this over himself like a dress. Now he became a hummingbird. He flew over the rocky places where the spirits were and came to the far tobacco fields. He then removed the skin and changed back into himself. He pulled some of the leaves and wrapped these in his medicine bundle. Again he placed the hummingbird skin over himself and darted off, flying so fast through the gorge that its guardians could not see him.

Arriving in his own land, the wizard found that many of the people were near death. He put some tobacco in a pipe and blew the fragrant smoke into the nostrils of those who lay sick and dying, and soon they revived.

The wizard now decided that he would return to the unknown land. He would revenge the death of the young warrior who had gone before him, and he alone would possess all of the tobacco that grew there. Immediately he turned into a whirlwind and blew through the gorge. The force of his wind was so fierce that he stripped many of the mountainsides bare and caused huge boulders to tumble into the narrow valley. The Little People were so afraid that they left, and the wizard remained the sole possessor of the route to the tobacco country.

As for the young warrior, the wizard found his bones lying along a stream-bed when he first blew through the gorge. He brought the bones to life again and they changed back into a man. The young man helped the wizard gather both tobacco leaves and this time seeds. Loaded with the precious cargo, the pair returned to the Cherokee, and the people planted the seeds. From that time forward, they always had tobacco.

THE PLEIADES AND THE PINE CONE

Long, long ago, when This World first began, there were seven boys whose only delight was to be in the chunkey yard near the council house. This place was a cleared square, clean and well-kept, with sand strewn along its surface.

Here the boys spent all of their time, for out of all the sports, chunkey was their favorite game to play.

Two of the boys at a time would take their turns playing on a team as the others watched. Both would stand on either side of the chunkey stone. One would cast the smooth round disk along the yard in as straight a line as possible toward the opposite end. Then the players would chase after the stone, and just as it was about to stop, they would slide their long poles, almost ten feet long, toward the slowing disk. They tried to get their chunkey sticks as close as possible to the stone as it came to a halt, and the boy who got nearest would score points based on various marks on his pole.

Day in and day out throughout the whole day, the boys played the game and were of no help in the cornfields. Their mothers grew tired of this constant play and scolded the boys for their addiction to the sport, but nothing could stop them from playing. So one day the boys' mothers gathered some of the chunkey stones and put them in a pot and boiled them with the corn for supper.

That evening, when the boys came home from their game, they were very hungry and wanted to eat, but instead of corn their mothers dipped the stones out of the pot. They said to their sons, "You like chunkey better than tending corn, so here are some stones for your supper."

At these words, the boys became angry and left for the council house. On their way, they began to say to one another, "Our mothers do not treat us right. We should leave and not trouble them ever again."

So saying, the boys began the sacred feather dance and at the same time implored the spirits of the Upper World for aid, especially invoking the great Adawehi who never fail. Before the seven began to dance, they gathered long river canes of six to seven feet and scraped these down to their white surface and adorned one end with white eagle feathers and the other with fresh green sprigs of fragrant pine. The boys laid the rods around the outside of the townhouse in the four cardinal directions and started to dance. They made four circuits around the townhouse. White eagle feathers adorned their heads, and they chanted the name of the Great Spirit Yohewah from time to time. Sometimes they let out loud whoops to call and honor the Bird tribe, and they punctuated these with the war cry of the turkey's gobble.

When the feather dance ended, the boys drank the black tea and went outside the council house to vomit and purify themselves further. They then took damp white clay and painted themselves white to signify purity, and immediately after covering themselves with paint, they went to running water to wash away impurity. Returning to the townhouse, they entered and swept away the old ashes of the sacred Fire and laid four logs in the shape of a cross and lit a new fire. When the flames arose, they sacrificed to the fire four perfect ears of corn. Now they went outside the townhouse and danced four times around it, each time drinking the black drink and purging themselves again four times. At the end, the boys scratched their arms and legs with sharp bone-toothed combs to draw blood and so rid themselves of any remaining offence to the spirits. For the remainder of the night, the boys continued dancing.

Their sons had been gone for so long that the mothers became afraid that something had happened and went to look for them before dawn. The boys were still dancing around the temple. As the sun rose and the women watched, they saw that the feet of the boys began to lift off the ground, and with each circuit of the council house, they climbed higher and higher into the air. The mothers ran toward their sons, but they were too late, for now the boys—except for one—were above the roof of the temple. This boy's mother seized one of the long chunkey sticks to pull him back, but she pulled too hard. Her son hit the earth with such force that he sank beneath it.

As for the other six, they rose higher and higher toward the sky vault until they rested against it. There they became the Pleiades or in Cherokee the Anit-sutsa, meaning "The Boys." The people mourned their loss for a long time. As for the boy who sank into the earth, his mother went every morning and evening to the place where he fell, and there she cried until the spot was wet with her tears. A tiny green shoot eventually sprouted there, and there it grew bigger and bigger each day until it became a tall pine tree. Its essence is just the same as the Pleiades, for both the stars of heaven and the pine of earth contain the same sacred Fire.

Killing the Great Monsters

THE GREAT YELLOW JACKET ULAGU

The blackberry and the raspberry bushes have briars that scratch. Kanugala means "scratcher," and Kanugulayi means "place of briars." There was once a Cherokee settlement of that name, Briar Town. It stood near the mouth of Briartown Creek where it empties into the Nantahala River in present-day Macon County, North Carolina.

In hilahiyu or ancient time, things were not as they are now in recent time. Through rivers, lakes, waterfalls, and caves, monsters sometimes came to This World from the Under World. These creatures often caused much misery.

Long ago the people who lived at Briar Town began to be troubled by Ulagu, an enormous yellow jacket queen. Ulagu was as large as a winter hut, and no one knew where she lived, for her nest was a secret. Sometimes the great insect would suddenly come, darting out of the air, and descend upon the village. If any children were outside at play, Ulagu would snatch them and carry them away. Many had mysteriously disappeared in this way.

No one in Briar Town had ever seen an insect like Ulagu, and no one could track her to her hiding place, for she flew too fast for anyone to follow. The people tried many ways to track her. They first killed a squirrel and tied a white thread to it so that, when Ulagu seized it, they might see the string and follow her, the way bee hunters follow a bee to its tree. Yet, when Ulagu came, she snapped up the squirrel so swiftly and darted away so fast that she disappeared almost as quickly as she came.

After the squirrel, the people decided to kill a turkey and to tie a longer and heavier white string to it. But Ulagu returned before anyone was aware, snatched the turkey, and left so swiftly that no one could tell in what direction she had flown.

The people next took a deer ham, and again they fastened an even longer and heavier string to it. And again the giant yellow jacket queen swooped down and flew away so fast that no one could tell where she went.

At last, the people killed a young deer, and they tied a white cord to it, longer than all the ones before. Ulago returned once again, but this time, when she seized the young deer, she did not dart away immediately, for the yearling was too heavy, and Ulagu had to fly slowly and close to the ground so that the trackers could see where she went.

The hunters followed Ulagu and trailed her along a mountain ridge until they came to where the Cullasaja River meets the Little Tennessee and where the town of Franklin is today. There the hunters gazed across the valley toward the nearby mountains, and on the other side among the rocks they saw a large cave, the secret nest of the monster. Upon seeing her hiding place, they sent up a loud shout, descended the ridge, and made their way across the valley.

When the hunters reached the cave, they saw inside an enormous nest, its countless cells starting from the bottom of the cave and rising in tier upon tier until they reached the roof. And there at the top, was the great yellow jacket queen, Ulagu. Around her and below her swarmed thousands upon thousands of smaller yellow jackets, humming in an almost deafening drone.

At once, the hunters gathered green wood and laid it near the mouth of the cave. They lit fires and fanned the thick smoke that rose from the fires so that it entered the cave and began to smother Ulagu and the innumerable smaller yellow jackets buzzing inside. But not all of them were within, for some had not returned to the nest inside the cave, and these survived the smoke and escaped. And from these smaller insects that did not die, yellow jackets began to breed again and to multiple so that now they are found everywhere, though before they were unknown.

After the destruction of Ulagu and her nest, the people named the cave Tsgagunyi—that is, "insect place" or "where the yellow jacket was." And the ridge west of Franklin from where they first saw the nest, they named Atahita, meaning the "place where they shouted." That place today is called Wayah Gap.

THE LEECH PLACE

But who will reveal to our waking ken
The forms that swim and the shapes that creep
Under the waters of sleep?
And I would I could know what swimmeth below ...
—From "The Marshes of Glynn,"
by Sidney Lanier, 1878

Near the western tip of the North Carolina mountains, the Hiawassee and the Valley rivers converge at what is now the town of Murphy. To the Cherokee, it was Tlanusiyi or the Leech Place. Their Valley settlements were once spread throughout the region. Besides being one of their most populated areas, it was also prized for hunting.

Just above the juncture of the two rivers was a deep hole beneath the water, gouged out over time by the Valley River. Above this hole, a causeway of rock extended across the stream, allowing the Cherokee who journeyed there many years ago to walk from one side to the other. On the high south bank ran a path that looked down at the ledge. According to stories told by the Cherokee, here many of their friends and relatives had vanished mysteriously.

In ancient time, a hunting party traveled down this trail, and as the men glanced toward the ledge below, a huge thing, unknown to any of them, lay curled in its center—slimy, red, and larger than any of their lodges. Ever so slowly, it began to stretch its coils and unroll itself over the rocks, displaying wide stripes of red and white along its enormous length. As soon as it had fully extended itself, it curled into a ball again, only to uncurl once more. Repeating this act several times, it gave one final stretch, crawled down the rock ledge, and disappeared into the dark pool below.

At once the water began to bubble and boil, and a dirty white froth spread over its surface. All of a sudden, a great tower of spray burst into the air. The men scrambled up the trail they had just descended, narrowly avoiding the wall of water that came crashing down where they had stood only seconds before and that would have washed them into the monster's lair. They were the first to witness the giant leech of the Hiawassee and Valley rivers and to live to tell the tale. Some who saw the monster thought that it had wings, making it all the more horrible.

Usually those who encountered the beast were not so fortunate or so nimble as to escape, for the waterspouts made by the creature would sweep them away. Sometimes friends or family would find the remains later, lying on the river bank or floating in the water, often with the ears or nose or other parts of the body devoured. Eventually, the people became too terrified to cross the rock causeway or to go near the trail that led to it.

One day, a young man of the Cherokee heard of the great leech. He scoffed at the story. "I am not afraid," he laughed. "Not of this or anything in the Valley River. And I will show you."

He began to paint his face and dress himself in his finest buckskin made from the whitetail deer. He then headed toward the river. All the people of his village followed him to see what would happen, though they stayed at a safe distance behind him. He came to the steep path and walked down it and over the ledge, the whole time singing a brave song:

Around my legs and shins,
I'll tie the Leech's skins.

And while he sang, before he got halfway across the ledge, the pool below began to boil and foam. A tall, thick column of water spewed high into the air and fell on the young man even as he sang, washing him away before he knew what had happened. No one from the village ever found his body.

There was no sign of the great leech for a long time after the young man's disappearance. So, many years later, two Cherokee women went to the ledge to fish. Others who remembered the young man's fate warned them not to go. One of the women, who carried her baby upon her back, replied, "I am tired of eating the fat meat of the bear. There are many fish in the river below the ledge, and I will have some."

She and her friend then went down the trail, and she placed her infant on the ledge near the bank. She had scarcely turned to prepare her fishing line, when the water churned and foamed and shot high into the air as before, suddenly crashing over the rocks. Yet, this time, because the mother was close to the river's edge, she scooped her baby into her arms and clambered up the bank, barely escaping with her own life and the life of her little child.

Today, the eastern end of Lake Hiawassee covers the pool where the great Leech once lived. The Cherokee of long ago believed that it had always lived there and had never left. And in truth, it still may lurk within the waters near Murphy. For sometimes the surface ripples and grows a yellow foam, while a dark shadow appears to move along the bottom, curling and uncurling itself in the dim depths below.

THE UKTENA AND THE SHAWANO CONJUROR

Long ago, almost before anyone can remember, the people on the earth caused the Sun to grow angry with them. What made her angry was the way they gazed at her. Every time they raised their eyes toward her in the sky dome, they twisted their faces and could never look straight at her.

One day on visiting her daughter the Moon, who lived below her in the middle of the sky, the Sun said, "My grandchildren's faces have grins all over them. They are twisted and ugly when they gaze upon me."

The Moon replied to her mother, "When the people behold my soft light in the night sky, they smile at me, and to me they look beautiful."

The words of the Moon made the Sun jealous and even angrier at the people on earth. So she decided to destroy all of them and sent a terrible sickness to kill them. Each day, when she came near the house of the Moon, the Sun sent such scorching rays to earth that a great fever descended, causing hundreds to die.

Everyone lost friends and relatives, and soon the people began to think that no one would be left alive. So some men went toward the Darkening Land of the west to find the two sons of the lucky hunter Kanati. They are the Little Men or the Thunderers who live in the sky vault of that country.

The Little Men said to the people, "For you to be saved, the Sun must die."

So the Little Men used powerful medicine and changed two of the men who visited them. One they changed into the great Uktena, and the other they changed into the Rattlesnake. The Uktena they made as round as a large tree truck with fiery scales flashing from its coils and having various spots of color along its length. Horns jutted from its crested head which held a clear crystal, faceted like a diamond, with a streak of red running through its center from top to bottom. The stone possessed great power and would impart its magic to anyone who could obtain it. The rattlesnake, however, they made small and quick.

The Little Men then sent the serpents to watch the house of the Moon and destroy the Sun when she came to visit. Everyone thought that the huge Uktena would kill her. The rattlesnake, though, was so eager and fast that he got to the house first and lay coiled just outside the door. Thinking that her mother might arrive at any time, the Moon went to the door to keep a watchful eye. No sooner had she opened it, than the rattlesnake struck and bit her. She instantly fell down dead in the doorway. In his excitement, the rattlesnake had forgotten to wait for the Sun.

Jealous at what had happened, the Uktena became furious and a danger to everyone. If he even glanced at anyone, that person's family would die. After much time had passed in fear, the people gathered for a council and declared that the Uktena, though once a man, was much too terrible to live near them, so they had the Little Men send him on high to Galunlati, the Above World, to dwell with other dangerous things. Yet the first Uktena left others of his race behind, almost as large and as vicious as their father. These lived in remote places, the deep pools of rivers or lonely passes high in the mountains of the Great Smokies, places the Cherokee called "where the Uktena stays." The old mossy rocks of the Nantahala Gorge and the distant Cohutta summit were among the favorite haunts of these monsters. There they would lie in wait to ambush their victims.

Many warriors risked their lives in search of these terrible beasts so that they might obtain the Ulunsuti, the blazing crystal set in the serpent's forehead, for the man who possessed it would become the greatest worker of wonders among his people. To obtain the crystal, though, was no easy task, for flames spewed from the mouth of the Uktena when it moved along. Anyone seen by one of these snakes became dazed by the fiery light of its Ulunsuti so that, instead of fleeing, he would run to it only to be killed. And as with their father, the great Uktena, even to look upon one of these monsters as it slept was to die, not so much for the man who beheld it but for all of his family.

Of all the hunters for the Ulunsuti, only one was successful in his quest—Agan-uni-tsi, the Groundhog's Mother. This warrior was a great conjuror of the Shawnee or Shawano, who fought many wars with the Cherokee but were also allies with them, for both fought on the British side in the Revolutionary War. In the very early days before 1680, the Shawano had lived along the Savannah River, but other tribes had forced them to leave and settle along the Cumberland before they eventually made their home north of the Ohio.

The Cherokee thought that all of the Shawano were conjurors. Their roving life had exposed them to secret magic spells and the religious formulas of many nations and given them powerful medicine to use in sudden raids or to create boundless deceptions in war. Their warriors might signal to each other with the cry of the flying squirrel—"tsu-u! tsu-u!" Or they might imitate with uncanny accuracy the gobble of the turkey as a decoy to draw unwary hunters into an ambush.

The Cherokee and the Shawano engaged in constant warfare. In one of their many battles, the Cherokee took their wizard Agan-uni-tsi prisoner. They bound him at the stake and prepared him for fiery torture, but Groundhog's Mother pled for his life, saying to his captors that he would find and bring to them a glowing stone from the head of an Uktena. The Cherokee knew that the priest who possessed its Ulunsuti would have the power to work marvelous deeds. He could foretell whether the sick would grow sicker and die or whether they would recover and live. He could predict whether a warrior would return safe from battle or whether a youth would attain old age.

But the Cherokee also knew that no one could possess an Ulunsuti, for death was sure for anyone who encountered an Uktena. Even the stench of the serpent's breath would cause a man to die. They told these things to Agan-uni-sti, but the shaman replied that his magic was strong and that he was unafraid. As a result of his claims, they spared his life, and he set out to find one of the Uktena.

Agan-uni-tsi knew the monster's haunts, so he traveled first to a gap in the mountains along the distant northern frontier of the Cherokee lands. As he searched, he discovered an immense blacksnake, bigger than any yet found, but this was not the beast he sought, and the conjuror laughed at the blacksnake as a thing too small for his concern.

He next journeyed south, and in another gap he saw a huge water moccasin, the largest of its kind ever seen. The people there marveled at the creature. Yet, as with the blacksnake, he said, "This is nothing."

He traveled farther. At the next pass, he came across a green snake and called to the people, "Come and look at Silikwayi, the pretty bear grass." He used this name because of the way the snake looked. When the people came, they beheld an enormous green snake coiled along the trail, and they scattered in fear. But once again the green snake was nothing to the powerful conjuror.

He went to other points along the Great Smoky range, where today the border of North Carolina and Tennessee lies. At one gap, he found a large lizard basking in the sun, but it was not one of the Uktena, so Agan-uni-tsi ignored it. Going farther south, he saw a great frog squatting in the pass, and as with the other monsters, when he called for people to come and see it, they fled in terror. The wizard only laughed at their fear and continued his journey. At each place, he found reptiles of a monstrous size, but to him they meant nothing.

Then Groundhog's Mother remembered the great leech and its dwelling in the deep pool where the Hiawasee and Valley rivers join at present-day Murphy. People had seen many strange things there. When he arrived at the pool, the shaman plunged deep beneath its water, and there he saw turtles and water serpents. Two enormous sunfish darted toward him but swam away. He saw nothing else. So he left and went still farther south to other places until at last he came to distant Gahuti, the Cohutta range of the Great Smoky Mountains. There his quest ended.

As soon as Agan-uni-tsi arrived, he came upon one of the great serpents as it slept. The shaman turned silently and ran as fast as he could down the slope almost to the foot of the mountain. When he stopped, he began to pile up pine cones and formed a large circle. Inside, he dug a deep ditch. Then he set the circle ablaze and went back up the mountain.

The serpent was still sleeping. Agan-uni-tsi notched an arrow in his bow and aimed at the seventh ring of color past the snake's head. He fired and the arrow pierced its heart. The Uktena angrily lifted its head—the diamond on its crest shooting flames—and charged straight for the shaman. Groundhog's Mother was too quick, though. He turned immediately and sprinted down the mountainside, jumped over the edge of the blazing circle and into the ditch in a single bound. He lay motionless inside.

The Uktena attempted to give chase, but the arrow soon did its work, and the monster began to writhe in its death throes, spewing its venom in every direction. Yet the poison could not penetrate the fiery circle of the shaman but only hissed and sputtered when it met the flame. Safe in his trench, the wizard remained protected until one tiny drop splashed upon his head as he clutched the ground, but he did not feel the venom. From the serpent's wound, blood also poured forth, as its dark stream flowed down the mountain and into the trench. Although as poisonous as the spray, the thick liquid left the shaman unharmed because of his powerful medicine.

In its final agony, the Uktena began to tumble down the slope, snapping off large trees in its path as if they were twigs, until it reached the bottom. There it breathed its last. The wizard rose from his ditch, stepped across the smoldering ring of fire, and left for the time being. He next summoned every bird of the forest for miles around so that they might feast upon the dead serpent, and their number was so great that, when they had finished, not a single bone of the monster remained.

When seven days had passed, Agan-uni-tsi returned by night to the place of death, and he saw that the body and bones of the snake had been devoured by the birds and that nothing remained. But above the spot where the Uktena had died, he noticed a light glittering through the darkness, and as he walked toward it, he saw that it rested in the fork of a low-hanging limb where a raven had let it fall.

The shaman knew that this was the Ulunsuti, the prized crystal that he had long sought. So he folded the stone carefully inside a soft deerskin and left. When he returned to the settlements, the Cherokee noticed that he was different, for a small snake now hung from Agan-uni-tsi's head at the spot where the droplet of venom had fallen. Yet he was unaware that it was there, and so it remained until the end of his days. On his reappearance, the Cherokee took him into the tribe, and from that moment he became their most powerful conjuror.

The place on the mountain where the Uktena's blood had pooled in the shaman's trench later became a lake, but instead of being clear, the water remained black like blood. Many Cherokee women would come to this lake, and there they would dye their split river canes used to make their baskets.

THE RED MAN AND THE UKTENA

Besides the great transparent crystal located in the forehead of the Uktena, there were also smaller stones of various shapes and hues that came from the monster and were originally from its scales. These, too, possessed magical powers, but their medicine was not as strong as the Ulunsuti. Here is the story of a hunter who received one of the scales of the Uktena.

One day two brothers were hunting for game in a lonely part of the mountains. They came to a place to make camp and built a fire. One brother gathered large pieces of bark to make a shelter for the night, and the other one began to follow a nearby creek to hunt for deer. As he made his way up the creek, he heard something along the top of the ridge. The noise sounded like two large animals fighting each other.

The hunter quietly moved through the underbrush to see what the commotion was, but when he got to the top, instead of two animals, he saw a huge Uktena struggling with a man. The beast had wound its lengthy coils around the man and was strangling him.

As the man fought for his life, he saw the hunter and gasped between breaths, "I am dying, nephew. Help me. He is your enemy also."

Without another thought, the hunter drew back his bow and aimed an arrow at the seventh circle behind the monster's crested head. The aim was true, and the arrow hit the vital spot where the heart was. Blood immediately spurted from the wound. With a loud pop, the snake relaxed its grip, dropping the man from its coils. Writhing to and fro along the ridge, the Uktena quickly lost its balance. As it rolled down toward the valley, it knocked over trees, uprooting some and leaving a path of destruction as if a tornado had passed through the area. The stranger then rose from the ground and brushed himself off. The hunter recognized him as the Red Man of Lightning, called Asga-ya Gi-ga-ge-i.

The Red Man said to the hunter, "Because you helped me, I will give you a gift. With this medicine, you will never lack for game."

When darkness fell, the two walked down to the valley to where the dead Uktena had tumbled. By now, the insects and birds had devoured everything except the bones. In one spot, a shimmering light arose from the earth. The two began to dig there, and beneath the surface, the Red Man noticed one of the serpent's bright scales. He next went to a nearby tree that lightning had struck and gathered splinters, for these held great power, and with them he kindled a fire. He then tossed the scale of the snake into the flames and let it burn.

When it had turned into a coal, the Red Man took it from the fire, wrapped it in a deerskin, and said to the hunter, "As long as you have this, you will always find game. When you return to your camp, hang this medicine bundle on a tree outside your shelter, for like the Uktena it is strong and dangerous. Though its power can aid you, it can also cause harm."

The Red Man added, "When you go into the shelter, your brother will be lying on the ground inside and near death. He could not withstand the power of the Uktena's scale being near to him. Take this piece of cane, and scrape a little into water for your brother to drink. It will make him well again."

The Man of the Lightning then vanished without a trace. When the hunter got back to camp, he hung the bundle on a tree and went inside. His brother was stretched out on the ground and almost dead, just as the Red Man had foretold. So the hunter mixed some cane shavings with water, and the medicine cured his brother. From that day forward, when the hunter searched for game, he found it wherever he went. As for the Red Man, he is Kanati, the Great Thunderer, whose brightest color is lightning, the same color as his clothing.

USTU-TLI, THE GREAT SNAKE
OF THE COHUTTA MOUNTAINS

The peaks of the Blue Ridge Province rise at the farthest end of south and central Pennsylvania. They continue south and west through Virginia, West Virginia, North Carolina, South Carolina, and Tennessee and end in northern Georgia. To the west, a second range of mountains emerges that is more ancient and one of the oldest on earth. It runs through North Carolina, Tennessee, and Georgia. To the north, these mountains are called the Smokies; to the south, the Cohuttas. This southern leg of the range is the gateway to the Blue Ridge, but to the Cherokee, the Cohuttas were "the poles of the shed roof" or the timbers that held up the roof of heaven over their wilderness home.

Located in the center of North Georgia, the Cohuttas have little flat land for farming but many ridges and peaks, with elevations between two thousand and to just under five thousand feet. Known as the Cohutta Wilderness today, this area encompasses thirty-five thousand acres and is part of the Chattahoochee National Forest and Fort Mountain State Park. Here, long ago, the Cherokee liked to hunt black bear, whitetail deer, and wild turkey and would have followed this game without difficulty but for the fact that the serpent Ustu-tli also hunted there.

This monster was not the same as the Uktena, the serpent of the Cohuttas that the Shawano conjuror Agan-uni-tsi had destroyed. For the Ustu-tli had an unusual way of moving. The beast did not crawl upon its belly like other snakes but had two feet on either end of its length. These had three corners and were wide and flat. Once planted on the ground, they held it firmly like huge suckers on a leech. Protected by the armor of its scales, the monster was thick and long like a large pine tree and had a huge head. When it tried to turn in a circle, its great size made it so unwieldy that the width of the circle equaled the length of the snake as it completed its orbit. It moved by rearing up on its hind feet, hurling itself forward with a strong impetus, planting its forefeet upon the ground, and holding itself there by the force of their suction. It would then pitch its back feet forward until these touched near its front, and by this process, it rapidly arched itself along like a giant worm.

Once it had securely anchored its front feet, the serpent could throw its length over rivers and ravines and travel up and down the steep slopes of the Cohutta range. If any hunter saw its footprints, he realized his danger and fled to the safety of home. A sign of the great snake's presence was the bleating of a fawn, for the serpent possessed the uncanny ability to imitate this sound. When it began to pursue its prey, nothing could escape despite all attempts to flee.

Yet the Ustu-tli had one weakness. It was unable to travel with any ease along the side of a ridge. Whenever it threw its front forward, the weight of its large head caused it to slide downward instead of going in a straight line. The snake would thus fall farther and farther behind, and its victim could escape. Yet the Cherokee around the Cohuttas dared not put the matter to a test, and none would venture into the mountains despite the plentiful game.

One summer day, a hunter from a village to the north came to visit relatives in the region. When he arrived, they offered him a meal of corn and beans. "We have no meat," they said, "because we fear the mountains of Cohutta," and when he asked the reason, they told him of the great serpent that haunted the area.

"Do not be afraid, my friends," replied the man, "for tomorrow I will go there and bring you back a deer."

They tried to persuade him against this idea. They described the serpent's size, its skill in pursuing its prey, its cunning through fawn-like bleats to lure the unwary near. All their efforts failed. The hunter had made up his mind. Yet one piece of advice they offered him before he left. If the snake began to chase him, he must get to a ridge as soon as possible and not run down its top but along its side. Only then would he have a chance to survive.

The following morning, the hunter left. He traveled down deep ravines, over rocky ridges, and through dense underbrush. Within a thicket at the bottom of a steep mountainside, he caught the faint sound of a fawn bleating somewhere in front of him. He immediately sensed the monster was near. His first thought was to flee, but keeping his courage, he continued forward.

Suddenly, there before him, the beast reared on its hind feet, its huge head tossing high among the pines, seeking its next meal, whether doe or man. The hunted saw the hunter and attacked at once. It charged in arched strides, each as long as a large tree trunk, and it bleated as it came, with its forked tongue darting in and out of the scaly head held high above the thicket.

Without thinking, the hunter ran up a steep ridge that went from top to bottom of the mountain's side. The serpent followed, tossing itself forward, gaining ground with each thrust of its length. Escape was hopeless.

Then the hunter remembered the advice his relatives gave. He quickly abandoned the top of the ridge and ran along its side. The Ustu-tli pursued him but began to fall behind. Each time it threw its body out, the heavy head dropped lower down the ridge as the monster tired, thus causing the distance from the man to increase.

Reaching the end of the ridge, the hunter swerved toward the top, and the monster disappeared. Cautiously climbing to the summit, he peered below. There, the now-slow snake continued to struggle toward him.

In a flash, the hunter ran down to the foot of the mountain where winter rains had washed leaves and brush. The summer sun had now turned this debris dry and brittle. Taking a hot coal from his fire pouch, he set the leaves on fire.

They smoldered at first but began to blaze and soon ignited the brush. The fire quickly licked up the sides of the mountain.

The Ustu-tli smelled the smoke, saw the on-coming flames, and forgot the man. It turned and began to race toward the summit where a rocky ledge jutted. It pulled itself upon this, but the fire followed fast. The dead pine branches just beneath the ledge burst into flame, their heat causing the serpent's scales to crack and melt.

Grasping the ledge with its back feet, the beast lifted its body and with all its might attempted to arch its length over the fire that engulfed it. But the thick smoke from the pines proved too much. Escape was futile. The serpent began to suffocate. Its hold on the ledge loosened, and it collapsed into the flames. There it thrashed and heaved violently for a few moments and then lay still, burning to ashes.

The hunter returned to his people to bring them the joyous news of the monster's end. That night, instead of feasting on beans and corn, they ate the deer that he had brought from the Cohuttas where the great snake had once roamed and terrified the Cherokee.

THE GREAT HAWKS

In ancient time, not long after creation, enormous hawks called Tlanuwas filled the sky vault of the Blue Ridge Mountains. Even though they soared close to the Upper World, they often threatened the children and dogs of the people below. Woe to the child or animal that strayed too far from the security of home. For then one of the great birds might suddenly swoop down, seize the victim in its powerful talons, and carry it off to become food for its fledglings, safe in their nests high in a cave along some remote and inaccessible cliff side.

A Cherokee hunter was once in the forest when he saw a mother Tlanuwa circling above, and although he tried to escape, she swooped down, stuck her talons into his hunting pouch, and flew off with him. High in the air, the mother bird indicated to the man not to be afraid, for she wanted him to guard her nest of young while she hunted because she had no mate. She came to her cave in a steep cliff. Within, water dripped through the porous rock overhead, and in the back was a nest made of sticks, and in the nest were two fledglings. Setting the hunter down, the old hawk flew off but soon returned with a deer she had freshly killed. Holding it in her claws, with her razor beak, she stripped off pieces of meat which she first fed to the hunter and then to her brood.

Many days passed in this manner, with the young Tlanuwas growing ever larger from the bear or deer meat that the mother brought, always giving some to the hunter first. During this time, he became more and more concerned about his family and made signs to the great hawk that he longed to return home. But she seemed to reassure him that he had nothing to fear and would be able to leave in a little while.

The hunter finally decided that he would escape from his prison. The next morning the mother had flown away to search for game. As soon as she was gone, he ran to the farthest end of the cave, took one of the young hawks from its nest, and dragged it, shrieking and flapping, to the entrance. Taking a leather strip from his hunting pouch, he strapped himself to one of the bird's legs. Then, with his tomahawk, he hit the Tlanuwa on its head several times with the flat side to stun the frantic bird and control it better.

Climbing out on a rocky perch high above the valley below, the hunter sprang into the air and, tied to the hawk's leg, plummeted toward the earth, which rose up to meet the two. Suddenly, a current from below caught the bird's wings as they slapped the thin air in frenzy. The rapid fall ceased so that the pair seemed to be flying. The young hawk revived and now tried to go back to its nest, but again the hunter struck the bird with the flat side of his tomahawk and stunned it once more so that they continued to drop toward the ground.

They soon came to rest in the branches of a tall poplar that rose above the other trees. The hunter untied himself from the dazed bird which flew away as fast as it could, but before it left, he pulled a feather from one of its wings and put it in his pouch. After climbing out of the tree, he headed toward his village. When he got home, however, a strange thing happened. He opened his pack to get his feather, but inside there was only a stone.

Other Tlanuwas were not as friendly as the one the hunter encountered. In what is now Blount County, Tennessee, an immense pair nested in a cave on a steep cliff. Located just below a bend where Citico Creek empties into the Little Tennessee River, the mouth of the cave was halfway between the base and summit. No one could see the opening from below, and no one could see it from above because of the rocks that jutted outward from it.

Trailing down the steep face of the cliff were long white streaks that went from the cave all the way down to the river. These were droppings from the nest of the great hawks. Powerful and strong, with wingspans wider than any bird alive today, this pair ranged, ever seeking prey, often near the settlements along the Little Tennessee.

Sometimes the hawks swooped down on a village in silence, and with their long, sharp talons snagged a dog or a child who had wandered too far away. Swifter than an arrow, they then carried their victim back to the nest. No one could reach the cave to destroy them, and arrows were useless, bouncing off their thick, hard feathers. So large and strong were the birds that occasionally hunters who tried to shoot them were seized and taken away as food to be torn apart and devoured.

Because of the attacks, the people of the area sought the aid of a powerful shaman. This man knew how to achieve a balance in This World between the Upper and Under Worlds. Yet some of the people were afraid of his help. They believed that, if he failed, the Tlanuwas would take a terrible revenge on all of them. The priest vowed, however, that no such thing would happen.

As he spoke, he began to braid the bark of the basswood tree into a long rope, and as he braided, he left loops at intervals for his feet. Taking this rope and a hooked stick, he climbed the back of the mountain until he reached the summit of the cliff and looked down at the river. Then, while the birds were gone, he instructed the people in attendance to lower him until he reached the mouth of the cave. Unfortunately, because of the overhanging rocks, he hung too far out to enter, so he began to swing himself back and forth until he could hook the side of the entrance with his stick. On doing so, he climbed inside and tied his rope to some bushes growing near the opening.

His eyes slowly adjusted to the dim light inside the cave, and there he saw four fledging Tlanuwas in a large nest surrounded by the bones of animals and children that the old ones had brought to eat. Without so much as a pause, as time was of the essence, the shaman took the young birds from their nest, ran to the entrance, and flung them down the cliff into the river below. The priest knew that in the water lurked the deadly enemy of the Tlanuwa. It was one of the giant serpents from the Lower World—an Uktena—that prowled the nearby mountains where it had made its den. As soon as the fledging Tlanuwas hit the water, the serpent swallowed them.

At that moment, the shaman heard in the distance the high-pitched cries of the two great hawks flying toward their nest. So swiftly they came that he barely had time to leave the cave, grab his rope, and climb to the summit above.

When the pair returned and did not find their young, they became frantic, searching the cave's dark corners, all to no purpose. With wings unfurled, they trotted back to the entrance and took to the air, soaring and circling high in the crystal sky, where with keen eyes they spied an object in the water below. There, with its crest flashing, the Uktena emerged from the water. With furious descent, one of the hawks dived straight down, swifter than anything, fastened its powerful talons around the great serpent, and ascended up and up and up. All the while, the other hawk flew beside its mate and slashed the snake with its claws and sharp beak, tearing off pieces bit by bit until finally there was nothing left.

When the hawks had finished, they circled high into the air until they could be seen no more. They never returned to the area. Yet the chunks torn from the serpent were so large that, when they fell to earth, they made great holes in the rocks below on the opposite side of where Citico Creek flows into the Little Tennessee. Although now beneath Tellico Lake, the holes are there still, even to this day.

THE HUNTER IN THE DAKWA

On the south bank of the Little Tennessee, where Toqua Creek once emptied into the river, lay Dakwahi, meaning the "fishing place" or "where the waters race." Also called Toqua, the old Cherokee village of the Overhill settlements now lies beneath the waters of Tellico Lake. Built in 1979, its dam impounds the Little Tennessee and Tellico Rivers. But long ago before the dam, the water ran deep at Toqua. For not only did the creek flow into the Little Tennessee, but the Tellico did as well a few miles upstream from the town.

In those days, the Dakwa lived there, a fish so large that it could easily swallow a man whole. One time a canoe left Toqua to cross the river. The canoe carried many warriors. All of a sudden, the warriors felt something ram their boat hard from below. Before they could do anything, the boat lifted high out of the water and tossed all of the warriors far into the air. As one man fell back into the river, the great fish gulped him down with a single swallow and then plunged with its stunned victim to the bottom of the river.

When the warrior regained his senses, he saw that he was not hurt. But he had trouble breathing, for inside the fish it was so hot, tight, and foul-smelling that he felt he would smother. As he groped through the close and fevered blackness, his hand scraped against the edge of something sharp. He jerked it back quickly, thinking that he had cut himself.

Then the hunter realized that his hand had struck against mussel shells that the fish had swallowed from the river. He carefully pulled one off, for they had stuck to the Dakwa's stomach, and he began to use the shell as a knife, cutting through the inside of the fish to free himself.

Uncomfortable because of the slicing and scrapping inside its stomach, the fish soon headed to the surface of the water and gulped at the air. The man kept cutting with his shell. The Dakwa was now in such pain that it did not know which way to swim, so it swam in all directions—now this way, now that. The pain became so unbearable that it thrashed along the top of the water, churning the surface into foam with its great tail and fins.

At last the hunter had carved an opening so large in the side of the Dakwa that water poured through and nearly drowned the man. Exhausted, the big fish swam toward the shallows and lay on its side, resting beside the riverbank and breathing heavily. Light streamed through the hole. The hunter peered through it. Very carefully, he pulled himself out of the fish's stomach. Then softly stepping along its side so as not to disturb the fish, he slid into the water and waded ashore.

The man returned to the settlement, thinking his ordeal had ended. But when he got back to Toqua, he realized that something was wrong. While he had been inside the Dakwa, trying to cut his way out, the strong juices in the fish's stomach had scalded his head, and all his beautiful hair had been burned off. It would not grow back, and from that day forward, he remained bald.

Supernatural and Animal Adversaries and Helpers

SPEAR-FINGER, THE NANTAHALA OGRESS

Nantahala, Cherokee for "land of the midday sun." There a dense rainforest covers the steep gorge of the Nantahala River, a swift stream that cuts through massive mountains with heights towering above five thousand feet. In parts of the gorge, its perpendicular cliffs rise so high that the sun penetrates its deep floors only at noon. Crystal white waters cascade down numerous cataracts. Along its rocky banks stand ancient trees of oak, poplar, pine, and maple, punctuated by almost impenetrable thickets of lower-growing rhododendron. In spring, the forest fills with delicate pink, white, and red blossoms. In summer, its leaves of emerald green exude a breathless mystery. In autumn, their fiery colors of red and yellow and orange riot through the cool, translucent air. In winter, high somber summits appear through the bare trees, with ice sometimes clinging to the rocky walls.

Here, in this place of deep shadows and perpetual and ever-changing beauty prowled the horrible ogress and shape-shifter Spear-Finger. She could take the form of any forest creature that she choose—a powerful bear, a cunning mountain lion, an innocent little bird—but when she was in her normal shape, she was an old woman. Yet her skin was like rock. No arrow could penetrate it. No blade could cut it. Sometimes the Cherokee called her "Stone-Dress" but most often "Spear-Finger." This last name came from the fact that her right forefinger was of bone and as hard as a flint-tipped spear, and all who came within her reach she stabbed with this finger. Then she would slice open her victims and dine upon their warm raw livers.

As undisputed mistress of the Nantahala Gorge, Spear-Finger ranged throughout its deep hollows and dark passes. She could lift huge boulders and strike them against each other with such force that they fused together. She once built an enormous stone bridge to cross from one mountain to another, but lightening destroyed it and scattered along the ridge line huge fragments, still seen today as evidence of her tremendous powers. The heads of tributary streams were her favorite haunts, and there, by their shadowy pools, ever hungry, she waited to ambush her victims.

Sometimes Spear-Finger used tricks to catch her dinner. She would change her appearance so that she looked like a family member who had left home for a short while. Pretending to be this person, she would enter a house, stab someone, and take her prize. With her movements so skillful and fast, people often never knew that she had speared them and removed their liver, for no gash or blood appeared on their flesh. Yet, when seized by sudden weakness, they fainted to the ground. Some died slow and lingering deaths, and some died quickly, but all suspected in their final moments that the evil ogress had eaten their liver.

At other times, Spear-Finger would watch for little girls gathering berries along paths in the woods or in clearings or playing not far from their villages. Like a kind old grandmother, she would call gently to them, "Dear children, come. Come, dear children. Your granny is here. Let your sweet granny braid your hair."

Then one of the girls, suspecting nothing, would run forward to have her hair combed and braided. She would lay her head lightly in witch's lap, while the old woman would caress the child's head and gently run her fingers through the girl's hair until the little one nodded off at last. Then, drawing her right hand from beneath her robe, the old woman would swiftly take her long gnarled forefinger of bone and pierce the sleeping victim's heart or neck, all the while drooling and chanting to herself:

> The liver of a child is sweet.
> It is my favorite thing to eat.

The fall of the year was especially dangerous for the Cherokee. Then they would fan out over the mountains to burn the leaves in order to gather chestnuts more easily from the forest floor. No one was safe, for the old witch observed everything, and when she smelled the smoke or saw it rise, she knew her prey was near. Like the panther, she glided in silence through the trees and would single out an individual who had strayed a little too far from the others. Sometimes a sensation of being watched by hidden eyes came to the person, but by then Spear-Finger had struck, and life was no more.

The people took precautions to stay close together, but these did not always work. If they made camp in the forest, they suspected any stranger who might approach. If anyone should leave the camp to bring back water from a nearby spring, they feared that the person who returned might be in reality the old woman of the gorge who had assumed the face and form of the friend or relative who had just departed.

Even the bravest hunters were sometimes seized by a sudden terror as they trekked the forest trails. Once a lone hunter told how he had glimpsed the distant figure of an old woman trudging through the woods, half hidden by leaves, softly singing to herself an evil song:

There is no better treat
Than human liver meat.

When he heard the repeated chanting and saw what appeared to be her misshapen right hand, his heart froze in his chest. He realized who the singer was and immediately stole away in silence so that she might not see him.

Finally, the Cherokee decided to hold a great council to determine what to do. If Spear-Finger continued her tricks and marauding, no one would be left alive. Men and women arrived from settlements throughout the region. After many speeches and much debate, the people resolved to make a deep pit by which to trap her. That way, the warriors believed that they could attack her safely.

So the people dug a pit across a path that they knew Spear-Finger traveled, and they cut light limbs to lay across the pit and covered these with earth and grass so that the pit looked like the path itself. They then set fire to fallen leaves and brush near the path, and they hid themselves among the laurels because they knew that she would come once she smelled or saw the smoke from the fire.

And soon enough, down the trail toddled an old woman. She resembled another old woman who lived in a nearby settlement. Some of the warriors wanted to shoot then and there. Others advised waiting, not wanting to harm one of their own.

With her right hand held firmly under her blanket, slowly, ever so slowly came the old woman. Suddenly, the pit collapsed beneath her feet, her blanket dropped, and there before all eyes, she revealed herself. No tottering old woman now, but the fierce ogress of Nantahala, covered with a stony hide and raking her sharp claw through the air to stab anyone she could reach.

The warriors swarmed from the laurel thickets and shot arrow after arrow into the pit, and though their aim was true, their arrows broke or bounced off the thick skin and fell at the witch's feet. Spear-Finger mocked their efforts. She hurled herself against the sides of the pit and tried to leap out.

The warriors kept their distance and fired more furiously, all to no avail. Then a tiny bird began to sing, its chirps sounding like the Cherokee word for heart. They took the bird's calls as a sign and aimed for the heart of the witch. Yet the arrows broke or glanced off her stony chest.

Things stood at a standstill. The warriors could not kill Spear-Finger, and Spear-Finger could not climb out of the pit. Then another bird gave them a sign. It lit on her right hand, the hand with the spear finger. Surely her heart hides there, inside her powerful hand, thought the warriors, the hand that has murdered so many. They altered their aim.

Her secret discovered, Spear-Finger maddened with rage. She doubled her hand into a fist to protect her heart. She rushed now with all her fury against the walls of the pit and made one final effort to vault out. Just as she was about to escape, a fateful arrow struck its target, piercing the vital spot of her heart where the bony forefinger joined the wrist. She at once fell back into the pit, no longer a threat to anyone. The witch's rule was over; her reign of terror, ended.

As for the little bird who told the warriors where her heart lay hidden, he is the cheerful sounding chickadee who always tells the truth. If anyone journeys away from home and if the chickadee comes to the house and sings a song, those who remain know the traveler is always safe and will return to them soon.

THE STONE MAN OF THE MOUNTAINS

During the time when the cruel witch Spear-Finger ravaged the Nantahala Gorge, a similar figure, who may have been her mate, lived in an even more remote part of the mountains. The Cherokee had not yet settled there.

It so happened one summer that all of the people of a neighboring village decided to hunt in this region. One of the men had forged ahead of the rest of the party and had come to the foot of a high ridge. Struggling to its top, he looked down the other side and saw large a river. He then lifted his eyes to gaze across the valley to the next ridge where he beheld an old man walking with what looked like a stick. Yet the stick had an unusual appearance, for it did not seem to be made from a thick sapling but from some type of glistening rock.

As the hunter watched, he noticed that the old man, every now and then, would raise his staff and point it in a different direction each time. Thereafter, he would put its tip to his nose and vigorously sniff like a wild animal. And yet what stirred the hunter's curiosity most was the old man's final act. He pointed his stick toward the Cherokee's hunting camp on the opposite side of the mountain and, when he had sniffed the end, licked his lips in delightful anticipation. He then began to walk slowly and deliberately along the ridge toward the camp.

When the old man came to the end of the ridge, the valley and river blocked his way. Yet he easily overcame these obstacles. Lifting his staff, he cast it into the air over the valley. When it descended, it became a glimmering stone bridge spanning the river. As soon as he crossed the bridge, it became a walking stick again. The old man retrieved it and headed over the mountain in the direction of the camp.

Upon witnessing these events, the hunter became alarmed and hurried back to his camp by a shorter trail to warn the people before the old man arrived. The village shaman was there, a man who knew the mysteries of both earth and sky.

When he heard the hunter's story, he said, "The old man is a wicked wizard and a great cannibal. His name is Dressed-in-Stone, and he abides in these remote regions. He travels ever in search for an unlucky hunter to kill and eat."

The shaman further declared, "The old man is a clever hunter. His stick is his hunting dog, and with it, he tracks his prey. His hide is of rock so solid that no one can kill him with war club, spear, knife, or arrow. When he comes to this camp, Dressed-in-Stone will slay and devour us all. Still there is one way to stop him and save ourselves."

When the people heard these words, they implored, "How? Tell us. Tell us how."

And the shaman replied, "The old man cannot stand to see a woman who bleeds the mysterious moon blood. He dreads its power, for it will draw off his strength."

Knowing that seven was the highest level of sacredness in the World Above, the priest now declared, "If there are seven here who stand before the old man's path when he comes, the sight will kill him."

At once seven women with issues of moon blood came forward, with one whose time had just begun. The shaman said that they must strip themselves, and all did as he commanded. He then sharpened seven stakes from a sourwood tree as the women arrayed themselves along the path where Dressed-in-Stone must pass. No sooner had they done so than they heard his footsteps coming and the clicking of his stone stick.

When Dressed-in-Stone came to the first woman, he cried out, "You are sick, Granddaughter. You are sick." He then hurried by her.

He came to the next woman, and again he cried out, "You are sick, Granddaughter. You are sick." He hurried past her as well, but now he vomited blood.

He continued in this way until he met the third woman, the fourth, the fifth, and the sixth. Again he cried aloud the same words, but with each encounter his cries grew weaker and weaker, and the blood he vomited increased and grew blacker and blacker.

At last, he came to the seventh woman whose time had just begun. Blood gushed from his mouth. At that instant, too weak to walk, he fell.

The shaman immediately drove his seven stakes through the now softened flesh and fastened the helpless wizard against the ground. Night came, and the people threw dried brush and tree trunks over him and with torches set fire to the pile.

No one slept that night but watched the blaze consume the old man. Yet his death was slow, for it took a long time for his powers to ebb because he had eaten many who possessed strong medicine. As the flames grew hotter, the numerous secrets that he had stored inside of himself came out of his mouth, and as he talked, the people learned cures for many sicknesses.

In the middle of the night, the wizard started to sing as more powers flowed from him. He sang the songs of the hunt and chanted charms for attracting bear, deer, wild turkey, and other game of the forest and field. The night waned, the fire became full of hot coals, and Dressed-in-Stone now could hardly be heard, for his voice had grown very weak. Toward dawn, the low voice ceased, a heap of white ashes appeared where he had lain, and the only sounds were those of the half-awakening birds in the trees.

The shaman instructed the people to brush away the ashes. Where the body had been, lay a lump of crimson paint and a large magic stone of the purest crystal quartz. The shaman kept the stone, but he painted the people with the crimson paint. He painted their faces and their chests, and as he painted, in prayer their voices rose and rolled through the forest. They prayed for skill in the hunt, for artful workmanship and crafts, for a long and happy life. Thus from the dead wizard came good for the people, for whatever gift each one prayed for, that gift each one received.

THE RAVEN MOCKERS

Long ago a man of the Cherokee lay sick and dying, alone on a hard pallet in his house. No one would cool his fevered head with water or bring him anything to eat or drink to relieve his hunger or thirst. All were afraid to go inside his house, so the man wasted away and died without anyone to comfort him. His family and friends had abandoned him because they had felt the presence of unseen evil things.

The Cherokee called them the Raven Mockers. The Raven Mockers were a type of witch known as skillies. As witches, they were the essence of evil, and they were beyond forgiveness. They could change their shape, and their in-born wickedness impelled them to kill. They liked to prey upon the old, the feeble, the sick, for these made easy marks.

Feared more than any other witch, the Raven Mockers would come at night to the sick to rob them of life. Assuming the form of a star falling from a cloudless heaven, though the dark sky they streamed, with arms outstretched like wings and with tails of fire trailing behind them. Their sound was like that of rushing wind or water, and as they flew, they would make an intermittent scream like the cry of a raven suddenly diving in mid air. The blood of those hearing these high pitched sounds froze, and they trembled, for they knew that the last spark of a person's life would soon die.

Sometimes the Raven Mockers would hasten the sick person's end through torment. Should the ill toss and thrash upon their bed or groan in pain and foam at the mouth, the Raven Mockers beat or kicked them. Should some victim claw the air and gasp for breath, a Raven Mocker sat astride the person's chest like a great weight encumbering the breathing even more. Should the dying suddenly rise up to walk, only to drop to the ground, the Raven Mockers had flung them out of bed and made them stumble and fall.

No one could see the evil witches' deeds, and as soon as death came, they removed the person's heart and ate it, though no scar appeared upon the body to indicate their grim work. By this means, they increased their days on earth by the same number that their victims had left to live. Because of their murders, the Raven Mockers had added many years to their existence and were thus unusually ancient and withered, if anyone chanced to see them in their everyday appearance. Of course, the only ones who could see these witches possessed strong powers. If such a one remained in the sick person's house, the Raven Mockers feared to enter and withdrew, knowing that, if recognized in their true form, they themselves would die in seven days.

One shaman named Gunskaliski had the necessary medicine to combat the witches. He used to hunt them and was able to kill several. He had obtained his power by drinking a tea made from duck-root, a plant resembling a beetle with a stem growing out of its mouth. In late spring and early summer, a purple fire falls from its stem. The shaman knew that purple was the color of witchery, and the duck-root tea gave him the ability to identify the Raven Mockers and thwart their aims. Other medicine men, who shared Gunshaliski's powers, would help the loved ones of the old and sick. When the end was certain, these men would stay in the house of death and guard the body until buried. Only then was the corpse safe because the witches would not cut out its heart.

Although the other witches of the woods and water envied the Raven Mockers' skill and strength, they dreaded to be near them and refused to go into a dwelling where one had entered or was near. One night a shaman, familiar with the witch medicine, had been tending a sick man and saw some of the other witches lurking about the man's house and looking for an opportunity to come inside and do harm. The cry of a Raven Mocker suddenly screeched though the air, and faster than pigeons scattering from a swooping hawk, the ordinary witches fled and left the man in peace. Because of their great fear, these witches hated the Raven Mockers and, if one eventually died, they would remove the body from its grave and in the dark of night take secret revenge upon it.

The Cherokee were ever alert to the activities of the Raven Mockers as the story of one young hunter proves. Searching for game, he had journeyed far from his settlement, and night had fallen while he was still in the woods. He had heard of an old couple who kept to themselves and lived in a house not far from the trail. So he left the path and headed there. Because it was winter, he hoped to find shelter and a place to sleep until the next morning. As he approached, everything seemed abandoned. He looked in the main house. No one was there. He looked in the asi, the little round winter house that was attached to the larger structure. It, too, was empty. "Perhaps they have gone to get water," he said to himself and entered the warm asi. There he lay down along its dark side to rest.

No sooner had stretched himself out than he heard the sharp cry of a raven nearby. Not long after, an old man came in and, without noticing the hunter, plopped down by the dying fire in one of the earth ovens that was sunk within the floor. Meanwhile, the young man remained quiet along the dark edge of the house. Once again he heard the scream of a second raven outside.

The old man mumbled to himself, "My wife is here," and just as he uttered these words, in came an old woman who sat down beside him. Frightened, the young man stayed silent, for he realized the two were Raven Mockers.

The old man said, "Wife, what did you get tonight?"

"Nothing," she replied. "There was too much strong medicine in the house. What did you get, Husband?"

"I got what I went for," he answered. "The task was not difficult. Unlike you, I had no trouble and came back with what we need. Here, cook this so we can eat."

So the old woman stirred the coals in the oven until the fire was hot. Then she took what the old man had given her, put it on a wooden spit, and held it roasting over the coals. The hungry hunter smelled the aroma of the sweet meat cooking, and his mouth watered. As he began to see more clearly from the glowing coals, he shuddered in horror, for the meat looked like a human heart.

Before the young man could think, the old woman whispered quickly to her husband, "Someone is in the corner."

"It is no one," the old man said.

"Yes, it is," she said. "Do you not hear him snoring?"

She then threw a stick of wood on the fire and stoked it so that it blazed up and lit the sides of the asi. Both now clearly saw the hunter, but he kept still, pretending to sleep. The old man then huffed and puffed, blowing loudly at the fire to try and wake him, but he remained silent and still pretended to sleep. So the old man got up, walked over, and with his foot shook the hunter who then sat up. He rubbed his eyes and acted as if he had been soundly asleep the whole time.

By now, it was almost first light, and the wife had gone to the main house to finish preparing breakfast. As the young man listened, she sounded as if she were weeping.

"Why is she crying?" he asked the old man.

"Oh, some of her friends have died recently, and she feels lonely." The hunter, however, knew the real reason. She wept because she was afraid. He had heard the two talking in the night, and by the dim firelight he had seen what they were roasting. Most important, though, he had seen their true bodies, withered and old.

When he and the old man came outside to eat their breakfast, the husband said, "There is no meat" and offered corn mush which the hunter ate. As he started to leave, the ancient Raven Mocker followed and presented him with fine beadwork and said, "Here is a parting gift. Pay no attention to last night and what you heard and saw. I should not have rebuked my wife. We sometimes quarrel about little things."

The young man accepted the beadwork but tossed it into the first stream that he crossed and watched it disappear into the water. He then hurried to his village and there told of his encounter with the old couple. The people recognized them as Raven Mockers, and the hunter gathered a party of warriors to return to the woods where they might slay them.

Yet the warriors tarried for seven days after the young man first spent the night in the asi so that, when they got to the old couple's dwelling, they found them stretched out on the floor of the winter house already dead. So the warriors took kindling and firewood. And they set the asi ablaze. And the bright flames consumed the house and the witches within.

THE IMMORTALS AND THE WATER CANNIBALS

Not all of the beings whom the Cherokee encountered were monstrous animals or wicked witches and wizards. Some were spirits from invisible realms who often visited the everyday world to assist people in their need.

Among these spirits were the Immortals who lived deep in the remote highlands. They especially liked the bald stone summits where no timber grew, and sometimes they lived near lonely streams. Although they looked and talked the same as the Cherokee and delighted in favorite pastimes like dancing and music, the Immortals revealed themselves only at their own pleasure.

During night or day, a lone hunter in the forest or on some distant path might hear the faint beat of a drum or the song of a dance beckoning him to come near. Yet, when he approached, these sounds would seem to his left or to his right or behind him and never where he thought they should be. Though shy, the Immortals were friends to the Cherokee, and if someone strayed too far from a settlement and became lost, these kind beings would provide food and rest and guide the weary wanderer safely home. Here is how they helped one such man.

A clan of cannibal spirits lived in the mountains and dwelt at the bottom of deep rivers. Little children were their favorite food, but no one in the old days was aware of these beings and their deeds. In earliest dawn, when all was quiet and gray and mist lingered upon the ground, these spirits would enter a village and move among the houses. Armed with invisible bows and arrows, they would select someone and slay the still sleeping victim. Then ever so stealthily, they would lift the dead body and carry it quietly to their dark pools and feast upon the flesh.

Careful to let no one know who they were and what they did, the water cannibals would substitute for the removed body a replica that looked like the dead man, woman, or child. But this was an empty shadow. It would wake, talk, and do what the person had done in life, but there was no life in it, and within seven days, it would die. The living believed that they buried a loved one and had no clue as to the cause of death.

Only much later did people learn about the water cannibals because of a man living in a settlement called Tikwalitsi or Tuckalechee near present-day Bryson City in Swain County, North Carolina. This town lay along the Tuckasegee River. Now this man became sick. His condition worsened, and no medicine could cure him. Thinking he would die, his family and friends left him alone in his house, for they were afraid that witches might come to torment him.

He remained bedridden by himself for several days, until an old woman entered his lodge. She appeared to be one of the women of the settlement, but the dying man could not be sure. As she stood beside his bed, she told him, "You are ill, and your family and friends have abandoned you. If you come with me, I will make you whole again."

The poor man had been so close to death that he had been unable to move, but when he heard these words, he revived. He asked, "Where will you take me?"

The old visitor answered, "I live near your village, but you must follow me, and I will show you everything."

So the old man rose from his bed, and the woman led him toward the river, and when she came to its edge, she walked into the water. He followed, and beneath the river was a road, and the road led to another land like the one they had left. The two traveled for a while and came to a large settlement of many houses.

Things in the world below the water were much like things in the world above. Here women tended gardens, wove baskets, or made clothing. Here children played games and laughed. Here men left to hunt or returned from hunting.

Yet, as the sick man looked more closely, he noticed a party of hunters laden with meat freshly killed. His vision cleared, and what he beheld terrified him. For the men carried not the haunches of bear or the hindquarters of deer. Instead, the hunters bore upon their backs the bodies of people from the surrounding settlements, and two they carried were a man and a child from his own village.

At last the man and the old woman arrived at a house on the outskirts of the town, and the old woman said, "This is my home." She then invited him to enter, laid out a pallet for him to rest upon, and tried to make him comfortable in every way.

By now, he was hungry, for it had been a while since he had eaten. The old woman read his mind and said, "I will bring you some food," and she went outside to the hunting party where she took a long knife and sliced off a piece of roast from the child's carcass and returned.

When he saw what she brought, the man recoiled in terror and shook with fright. The old woman said, "I know now that you cannot eat this meat." She then turned away from him and stretched her hands in front of her stomach, and when she turned back again, they held cornbread and beans and the kind of food that he ate in his world.

Each day the old woman brought beans, bread, corn, and squash and sometimes deer and bear until the sick man recovered his strength and could travel by himself. She told him, "Now you are able to return to your people, but you must tell no one of what you have seen for seven days. If anyone asks where you have been, signal that your throat is sore and be silent."

The old woman took the man back along the same path to the river's edge and pointed him in the direction of home. Then she turned, and the water closed above her head. The man went to his village, and when the people saw him, they were astonished, for they thought he had wandered into the forest and died.

"Where have you been?" they asked, but he made signs that his throat was swollen and that he could not speak. And thus he remained silent for seven days, and thinking that he was still sick, his friends and family left him alone.

When seven days had passed, the man spoke and told them everything. He told them of the old woman and the village beneath the water. He spoke of the human flesh that the hunters had gathered and how he had fed, not on this, but on the food of his own land and how the old woman had cared for him. He told of his recovery and how she had guided him home.

When he finished, the people marveled at his tale. They said that the old woman was one of the Immortals and that she had saved him from the cannibals who lived beneath the water. They said that his adventure was a warning to them and said from that day forward they would rise before the first light and tell their children, "Awake, for the hunters walk among us."

THE MAN WHO TRAVELED
TO THE WORLD BELOW

The Tallulah River is only forty-eight miles long. It begins in western North Carolina and travels south through northeastern Georgia. Its famous falls are just twelve miles south of Clayton in Rabun County. Joining the Chattooga, its waters eventually empty into the Tugaloo, a tributary of the Savannah River. Today a hydroelectric power dam has reduced the Tallulah to a trickle. Considered the Niagara of the South, it was once a mighty stream that rushed and roared through the depths of its narrow gorge where, over the eons of time, it had cut its way for two miles through a high dome of sandstone and other rock created from the collision of continental plates. Numerous crevices and crannies dot the steep vertical walls that tower as high as a thousand feet. Before the dam, the waterfalls thundered and echoed through Tallulah Gorge, beginning with the uppermost Ladore, from the French *L'Eau d'Or*, meaning "water of gold," then continuing with Tempesta, Hurricane, Oceana, Bridal Veil, and ending with Sweet Sixteen which empties into the smooth water at the bottom.

The origin of the name Tallulah comes from an incident that occurred at the height of the falls. According to a Cherokee woman, a child fell over the steep sides and disappeared into the rushing waters. In the calm water below, the body was unexpectedly seen. From this occurrence, Tallulah means "There lies your child." Because of the dam, the falls today are not as spectacular as when the Cherokee lived in the mountains. Yet in the old days, the people rarely ventured to go there to hunt or fish, for they considered the gorge haunted by another race of beings.

Known as the Little People, they were fairy spirits, handsome to look upon. They wore long hair that hung to the ground and were as high as a grown man's knees. They enjoyed music and wiled away half their days in dancing and drumming, and depending on their mood or how others behaved, they could be good or bad. Sometimes helpful and kind, they would aid the lost find their way home, especially children who had wandered too far away from their parents. Yet sometimes the Little People, if unexpectedly disturbed, would cast a spell over the unlucky traveler who strayed too near their dwelling places so that he became lost. Should he be so fortunate as to find his way home, he remained dazed and confused thereafter. The Little People always warned anyone whom they helped never to speak of their kindnesses.

Once in winter, a deep snow lay on the ground, and a lost hunter found tiny tracks like those of little children in the woods. He followed the footprints until he came to a cave, and inside the cave were many Little People of all sorts—ancient grandfathers and grandmothers, young men and women, and children of all sizes and ages. They invited the hunter in, were good to him and fed him, and allowed him to stay with them for a while, but when his time came to leave, they cautioned him to tell no one about their deeds or where they lived. He then returned to his village and at first obeyed the Little People, but when his friends pressed him to say where he had been, he told them. Not too many days later, he died.

Another time, many generations ago, a band of hunters was searching for game near the headwaters of the Savannah River. They never returned to their camp. Their disappearance caused much concern among their people back home. Several medicine men were sent into this area to find the hunters. The priests searched for a whole month without any luck. When they came back to the settlement, they told that they had come upon a terrible fissure in the cliff of one of the mountains in an unknown country and that from this fissure gushed a torrent making a deafening uproar. The medicine men said that they had seen other people in that wild place and that they were tiny men and women who lived among the rocky crevices behind the waterfalls. None of these Little People would come to a council with the priests, however, despite their best efforts to draw them out. They only would shriek loudly and make signs to indicate their hostility to the intruders of their domain. From these actions, the medicine men believed that the lost hunters had been lured to their deaths among the rocks.

Other beings, too, lived in the Tallulah Gorge. They were not like the Little People at all and were the thunder spirits whose roar is heard in the great waterfalls there. The Cherokee did not know about them until a strange event occurred in a settlement near the source of the Chattahoochee. The longest river in Georgia, the Chattahoochee begins in high mountain springs of northeastern Georgia and travels for 436 miles before it empties into the Gulf of Mexico. Just above its headwaters flows the Tallulah.

In the old days, the people often liked to dance throughout the night until dawn, and in this particular settlement, a dance had begun one evening. When it was well underway, two young and beautiful women, who appeared to be sisters, quietly entered the village. No one had ever seen them before, and no one knew where they were from. The two danced first with one and then with another.

A young warrior could not take his gaze off one of the women because of her long and beautiful hair. As was the custom among the Cherokee, he sent a message to her through an old man of the village and asked her to marry him. Through the old man, she replied that she first had to consult her brother who was at home. She said that she would return in seven days and give an answer at the next dance. She also said that, while the warrior waited for her, he must prove his devotion by not eating during that time. He quickly agreed. By morning, the dancing ceased, and she and her sister had mysteriously disappeared.

The warrior kept his fast, and on the seventh night, another dance began.

He arrived early, eagerly awaiting his love. Later that night, she and her sister again appeared as suddenly as they had before. She told the young man that her brother had agreed to the marriage and that, once the dance was over, she and her sister would take him to their home. However, she added a warning. He must tell no one where he went or what he saw. Otherwise, he would die.

The three danced until dawn and then quietly left without notice. The young man followed the sisters through the woods along a path that he had never seen before. They came to a small creek with a deep pool which the women entered without hesitation, but the young man paused, unwilling to step into the water.

Knowing his thoughts, as if he had spoken aloud, the women looked at him and said, "What you see is not water. It is the path to our house." Still he paused, but after much persuasion, he entered the pool. As the water closed above his head, he began to walk along a smooth trail covered with tender grass.

The three traveled farther until they came to a larger stream rushing through a steep gorge. The man immediately recognized the Tallulah River, a place where his people seldom fished or hunted because of the mysterious beings rumored to live there. Again the sisters stepped into the water, and again the man hesitated, saying to himself, "The water here is deep and wild. If I enter, I must surely drown."

And again the women read his mind and looked at him and said, "Do not believe what you see, for it is not water. It is the path to our home. We are close now. Come and follow us." So the warrior entered as before, and instead of water, a trail opened between high grass that waved above his head and closed over it as the sisters led him onward.

After a short while, they came to a cave in the rock, scooped out by one of the waterfalls in the river. The sisters entered, but again the warrior hesitated, pausing in front of its mouth. Reading his thoughts, they turned to him and said, "Come in. This is our home. Soon our brother will arrive. He is coming even as we speak." Then a low rumble of distant thunder echoed through the gorge.

The young man entered and stood inside the opening, where a strange sight greeted his eyes. For the women removed their long hair and hung it from a rock jutting from the side of the cave. Their heads were completely bald, smoother than two pumpkins. The warrior's fears so far had been mild, but now grew rapidly.

The younger sister, the one he was to marry, took his hand, sat down, and asked him to do likewise. But when he looked, instead of a seat covered with hides and furs, it began to rise on its legs from the cave floor, stretched, and showed its clawed feet. These it extended angrily. The young man saw that it was a huge turtle, an animal that like the frog crossed the edge of two worlds.

Like the four-footed tribes, they lived among humans in This World, but like the vermin they also could dwell under water in the World Below. So the young man refused to sit on the giant beast. Yet the woman knew his mind and insisted that it was, in fact, a seat. As she did, a loud clap of thunder rolled up the gorge. "Our brother is almost here," she said.

The two women continued to urge the man to sit. Still he refused and would not leave his place near the doorway. Another peal of thunder suddenly sounded as if just outside. The warrior spun round, and there in the entrance a man stood before him. One of the sisters said, "Our brother is home."

He came into the cave, walked past the warrior, and seated himself on the turtle. Again it lifted itself on its legs and stretched forth its claws. The young man remained beside the door. Without any ceremony, the brother declared that he was on his way to a council. "Will you go with me?" he abruptly asked.

The warrior replied, "Yes, if I have a horse to ride, for I have traveled far this day." So the brother told the younger sister to bring a horse. She went outside and soon returned. But no horse did she lead. Instead, what appeared to be a great snake as thick as a tree truck crawled behind her. It had a pair of wings along its back, two horns upon its head, and between them a large crest that fanned up and down, sparkling like a bright diamond. Its scales shot flames like fire, dazzling the eyes. Coils of many colors ran round its length which curled in every direction along the floor of the cave.

The beast was one of the Uktena, terrible because, though it had horns like a deer, it was not four-footed and thus not from the earthly realm of This World. Though it had wings, it was not a bird from the Upper World of air. And so like a serpent that can swim in the water below or crawl here on the land, or hang in the air from a tree, it possessed no set place in any world.

Fear seized the young man's heart, and his legs trembled, yet he managed to whisper, "I cannot ride a snake." The brother and his sisters, however, insisted that the beast was no snake at all but their favorite riding horse. Still the man refused his mount.

Growing impatient, the brother told his sisters, "Perhaps he will ride if he has a saddle and some finery. Bring him a saddle, and fetch bracelets for his arms and wrists."

So the two left and came back with arm bands, richly decorated, and a saddle of fine leather, and they fastened the saddle to the serpent's back. Yet the saddle was another turtle, and the arm bands more slithering snakes, only much smaller than the first. These the sisters made ready to twist around the young man's arms and wrists.

At this point, nearly dead from fear, he cried in a loud voice, "What is this den of horror? What man could live here, among writhing snakes and crawling things?"

With these words, the brother's eyes flashed fire as though of lightening. "Coward!" his voice boomed, and he struck the young man across the face. Knocked unconscious, he fell to the ground as thunder crashed once more, sounding now as if were inside the cave itself.

When he came to his senses, he was standing in water on the edge of the tumultuous Tallulah River. Above the narrow gorge, a black cloud hung low as the wind howled and lightening flashed and thunder reverberated through its steep, rocky walls. If the warrior's hands had not held tightly to a laurel bush growing from the side of the bank, the surging water would have swept him away.

He struggled out of the river along its slippery edge, and when he looked around, he saw no sign of the cave or its inhabitants. Heavy sheets of rain descended as he made his way home through the lonely woods. When he arrived at his village, the people were astounded to see him, for he had been gone for so long that they thought he had wandered off and died. Yet to the young man, only a day had passed.

His friends came to him to offer comfort, and when they asked him where he had been and what he had seen, he was silent, causing them to question him all the more. As they crowded round in eagerness to hear of his adventures, he began to speak, forgetting the sister's warning on the night of the dance—that he must tell no one where he went or what he saw. He told them about what had happened and about the strange Thunder People of the Tallulah Gorge.

When he had finished, an uneasy feeling came over the warrior, and he said, "I am sick and must rest." His friends took him to a house where he lay down, but he never got up again. For no one can go the Underworld and return to tell about it, and in seven days, the young man died.

JUDACULLA, THE SLANT-EYED GIANT OF TANASEE BALD

Before the Cherokee made contact with whites, the old town of Kanuga lay on the western fork of the Pigeon River, a few miles to the east of present-day Waynesville, North Carolina. The name means "a scratcher," and comes from the bone-toothed combs used to draw blood in purification rituals. The Cherokee abandoned Kanuga long ago. Yet a widow once lived there with her only daughter.

When this girl came of age to marry, her mother advised her to find a husband who was a good hunter. That way, the old woman and her daughter would always have someone to provide plenty to eat. The girl said to her mother that finding such a husband might be difficult. The mother, however, insisted to her daughter that she should not marry the first man who wanted her for a wife but that she should wait until the right one came along

Now where the pair lived, they had a house and an asi, the latter being a little round hot house or sweat lodge. The mother would sleep in the house and the daughter in the asi. Unknown to the mother, one dark and moonless night, a stranger arrived, went to the little house, awoke the daughter, and told her that he would like to make her his wife. Remembering her mother's earlier advice, she said that she could marry no one except a great hunter. The stranger replied, "You have found him."

So the girl let him enter, and he remained all night. Just before the sun rose the next day, he said, "I must return to my home, but I have some deer meat outside for you and your mother."

The hunter then left, and when the girl went outside, she found the meat. She immediately took it into the house to show to her mother and told her that it was a present from an admirer who had come to court her. The gift pleased the old woman, for they had had no meat for a long time.

The following night, the hunter returned and departed before dawn as he had on the previous visit, but this time, instead of deer steaks, he left two whole deer outside. Although these pleased the mother even more, she said to her daughter, "I had hoped that he would bring us wood as well."

The stranger, although he was far away by that time, could hear the widow and even read her thoughts. In reality, he was the giant Tsulkalu or Judaculla, whose name means "he has them slanting," a reference to his misshapen eyes, which made him horrible to look upon. Despite his appearance, he was a mighty lord of game animals and could control wind, thunder, rain, and lightning.

Judaculla visited again on the third night, and having heeded the old woman's last wish, he told the daughter before he left, "I have brought wood for you and your mother."

When the girl went outside at first light, not only did she find deer, but piled in front of the house were several large trees—trunks, branches, roots and all. As soon as the mother saw the sight, she angrily said, "How can we use this? We can't chop whole trees into firewood."

Of course, the hunter heard her words from afar, and the next night he brought nothing so that the old woman had to go and gather her own wood. Still he came almost every night to visit, and still, after each departure before earliest light, he left a gift of deer or other game.

By this time, Judaculla and the daughter were more than sweethearts and had become husband and wife, and the widow was growing more and more curious about this stranger who had become her son-in-law, for she had never laid eyes on him. So one morning she finally said, "Your husband never stays past the night. Why does he leave? I want to see this man you have married." The girl, too, had never seen her husband because he always came after dusk and left before dawn.

Of course, Judaculla had already heard what the old woman had demanded, so he was not surprised to hear his wife repeat her mother's words on the following night. He replied, "For her to look upon me would frighten her."

Yet the girl persisted, telling him that her mother wanted to see him anyway. She then began to shed a great many tears whereupon her husband consented but warned, "Your mother must not say that I am horrible to look upon."

When morning came, Judaculla did not leave as before but stayed in the sweat lodge. So the daughter brought her mother to see the stranger, and when she looked inside, what did she behold? There, lying inside the asi, doubled up on the floor, with his head in one corner and his feet in the other and both ends touching the rafters was a huge giant who had long slanting eyes that drooped down his tremendous face. The widow gave one glance and at once ran back toward her house, screaming, "Usgasetiyu! Usgasetiyu! How horrible! How dangerous!"

On hearing the woman's cries, Judaculla at once became very angry. He undoubled himself, crawled out of the little hothouse, bade his wife farewell, and declared that she and her mother would never see him more. Off he headed south to his home country in the Balsam Mountains. There he had a farm of one hundred acres of cleared land on the south and west slope of Richland Balsam Mountain. To the southeast of his farm lay Tanasee Bald, which means "the place of Judaculla." Slightly to the northeast of it was a peak supposedly inhabited by an evil spirit, perhaps Satan himself, and thus forbidden to the Cherokee. Aware of where the giant had headed, his wife thought that she would never be able to see him again.

Because she had been with her husband for several nights, the woman suspected that she was with child, but soon after he left, her moon blood returned, and she thought no more about the matter. In fact, she began to have such a great issue of blood that her mother collected it and tossed it into the nearby river, forgetting that she should not mix blood and water.

One night soon thereafter, the wife was asleep in the asi when Judaculla returned and woke her. He said, "You appear to be alone. Where is our child?"

She replied, "There is no child."

Judaculla next asked what had happened to the issue of blood, and she answered, "My mother threw it into the river" and then described exactly where so that he could find the place. He went there and in the water found a tiny worm. He put this in his hand and took it back toward the asi. As he was walking, the worm began to grow and change into a definite shape so that, in the short time that it took him to return, it had become a baby girl.

He said to his wife, "Your mother fears me, and she has abused our child. Now let us leave and go to my land."

The woman wished to be with him. After all, he was her husband. So she told her mother goodbye, took the child in her arms, and followed Judaculla as he headed south. They went along the trail beside the West Fork of the Pigeon River toward the giant's home in the Balsam Mountains At times they stopped to rest but always continued toward Tanasee Bald. It lies just north of Tanasee Creek, the headwaters of the Tuckaseegee River. Inside a cavern of the mountain, the giant had a spacious council house.

Now in another settlement of the Cherokee lived the widow's son who had a wife. He was the older brother of the woman who had married Judaculla. When he heard about his sister's marriage, he decided that he would travel to Kanuga for a visit, but when he arrived, the old woman said that her daughter had left with Judaculla for a country not well known. Because the widow was now by herself and seemed sad, her son told her that he would try to find his sister and bring her home to Kanuga.

The brother had no trouble in tracking her and her husband because of Judaculla's gigantic footprints. So the brother went along the path beside the river until he came to where the couple had stopped to rest. The grass all around lay flattened, and there were signs indicating that a child had been born.

The young man picked up their trail and went along until he came to a second place where they had stopped. Here were more signs, but this time there were two sets of tracks, one of a child walking and another of a child crawling.

Again the young man followed the trail and went along until he came to a third spot where they had rested. The signs now showed one child running and a second walking. From here, the tracks went beside a stream and into the mountains. So he followed along this trail and came to yet another resting place. The footprints here revealed two children, both running about everywhere.

Two more times the brother found signs of resting places, where at the last one the tracks led up the slope of Tanasee Bald. As he climbed higher, faint echoes began to play about his ears until they resembled drumming and voices coming from within the mountain, the kinds of sounds people make when dancing. He continued and saw above his head what appeared to be the entrance to a cave. Yet the mountainside here was so steep and the rocks so smooth that he could not get a toehold or handhold that would allow him to reach it.

Just as he was about to climb back down, the young man noticed above him a narrow ledge that led toward the cave opening. He made his way around and up toward this ledge and inched himself along it until he could peer over the side of the entrance and into the cave itself. There he beheld numerous people dancing and his sister among them. When he called to her, she turned toward his voice, and he motioned for her to come to him, whereupon she did, leading her two children by the hand. None of them had the least difficulty climbing out of the cave, over the rocks, and onto the ledge. She was most happy to see her brother and talked with him for quite a while, yet she did not invite him inside. The two parted, without the brother ever seeing his sister's husband.

The brother returned several additional times to the mountain to visit his sister, but she always met him by herself outside the cave so that he never saw her husband. Four years passed in this way until one day the girl went back to her mother's house. As her brother happened to be there, she told him and her mother that her husband was hunting nearby.

"He and I will leave for the mountain tomorrow, but if you come to our camp early in the morning, you may both see him. If you come after we leave, you will find for yourselves plenty of game to take home with you." With these words, the daughter turned and disappeared into the woods.

The following morning, the old woman and her son headed toward the camp, but they arrived too late, for the giant and his wife were already gone. However, drying poles stood all around. On these hung the meat of freshly killed deer, just as promised. In fact, there was so much of it that the mother and her son went back to the settlement and invited their friends to help them carry it. That night, all of Kanuga feasted.

Having missed seeing Judaculla made the brother all the more eager to find out what he was like. Again he went to the cave, and again his sister came out to see him. This time, though, when he asked to see her husband, she invited him inside. Instead of climbing down through the mouth of the cave, however, they entered through a hidden doorway that appeared beside the ledge.

A marvelous sight greeted the brother's eyes, for inside the cave was an enormous council house where a huge clan might gather for feasting and dancing. The two seemed to be completely alone when suddenly the sister cried out, "My brother is here to see you!"

A mighty voice echoed though the cave in reply, "I must first put on new clothes, and then you may see me!"

When the brother indicated that he willingly accepted these terms, the voice again thundered through the cave, "Go back and tell all of Kanuga that they, too, may see me, but first they must enter my townhouse. Here they must fast for seven days and not leave, nor may they raise the war cry. After seven days, I will clothe all of them in new clothes so that each may behold me."

When the young man returned to Kanuga and told everyone what he had witnessed, they clamored loudly to go the mountain, for they longed to see the giant who was lord of all the game there. So the people left the village and went to fast in the great townhouse of Tanassee Bald. Among them, though, was a man who was not from Kanuga, and while the people fasted throughout the seven days, he would leave at night to eat in secret and return in the dark when no one watched.

The morning of the seventh day came. The sun rose a glowing red. All at once, a loud noise thundered as if a rock slide tumbled down the side of the mountain. Inside the townhouse, the people huddled together in fear, and no one dared to speak. Louder and closer came the noise as it crescendoed into a terrifying roar. All held their breath and shook, except for the stranger. Fear overmastered his mind. He fled in terror from the cavern and screamed a blood-curdling war whoop.

The roar ceased, and the cave was silent. Then another war cry arose but fainter and farther off, and then another but fainter and farther still, until finally in the distant mountains, it died completely. In the silence, the people cautiously came out of the townhouse. Nothing had changed, and all was as it had been seven days before, with no sign of the giant. The people returned to Kanuga.

For many years, the brother never wavered in his attempts to see his sister's husband. He came again and again to visit her, and she would take him inside the mountain. One time he asked her why the giant had not given the people the promised clothes, and as he did, a low and deep voice whispered through the cave, "I brought them, but you did not keep your word. You did not fast for seven days, and the war cry sounded."

The brother answered, "A stranger to our village broke the fast and raised the war whoop, but our people obeyed. Promise us to return so that we may see you, and we will surely do as you tell us."

Again the voice whispered through the air, this time more softly and slowly, as though tinged with sadness. "It is impossible. Now you will never see me." In awed silence, the young man left his sister and went back to Kanuga and to their mother. He never came again to see his sister.

In the Great Balsam Mountains lies Cold Mountain, a summit between the east and west forks of the Pigeon River in Haywood County, North Carolina. The mountain today is part of Pisgah National Forest and is about fifteen miles southeast of Waynesville and about thirty-five southwest of Asheville. A rock at its base contains impressions that, according to the Cherokee, are the footprints made long ago by the children of Judaculla when he and his wife stopped to rest before arriving at his townhouse within Tanasee Bald.

LEGENDS OF PILOT KNOB

Pilot Knob is about halfway between Waynesville and Brevard, North Carolina, and is one of the bald mountains, so-called because at one time no timber grew on their tops. Before the removal of the Cherokee to Oklahoma, a clan of mountain spirits, were said to live inside Pilot Knob. There they had a settlement with a large council house for meetings and social occasions. They were relatives of the Cherokee who lived in neighboring settlements. The mountain spirits claimed that they did not live forever like the Immortals or Nunnehi, but circumstances seem to indicate otherwise.

One time two strangers came to a Cherokee settlement named Kanasta on the French Broad River. They told the chief that they were related to his people and invited him and his village to escape from their world of wars and sicknesses. The strangers said that they lived within Pilot Knob and that they were happy. They said that they always had peace and that they did not have to fear danger. They even prophesied to the chief that a day would come when he and his people would meet an enemy so strong that they would lose their whole country. So the chief and all of Kanasta left to live with the mountain people and were never heard from again.

Many believed Pilot Knob was haunted because of strange events that occurred there. Some years after the people of Kanasta vanished, a party of hunters made camp one night at the mountain. As they ate their supper beside the fire, they spoke about the former settlement and began to joke and laugh about what had become of its inhabitants. Later that night, when the hunters were sleeping, they were awakened by the sound of stones being thrown into the camp. They searched among the surrounding trees but could find nothing. Alarmed, the men decided not to wait until morning. They immediately gathered their guns and hunting pouches and left.

An event similar to the Kanasta episode happened later to the people of Kanuga. The old settlement lay to the north of Pilot Knob and was the same place where the giant Judaculla met his bride.

A young man once lived there who had a reputation for being lazy. He would go from the house of one relative to another, always asking for food, Even though he stayed most of the time in the woods, he never bothered to offer game to anyone. This stingy behavior irritated his relatives so much that they finally got tired of him and refused to keep him up.

The fellow told his relatives that, if they would fix some parched corn for his hunting pouch, he would kill a deer for them and that, if he did not, he would trouble them no more. So they prepared enough to supply a short hunting trip, and off he headed for the mountains below Kanuga. Day followed day. After a while, he ran out of parched corn and had eaten nothing for the last seven days of his absence. His relatives thought he was gone for good. Then at the end of two weeks or so, he reappeared but without so much as a rabbit. However, he did bring back a tale of wonder.

As his friends gathered round to listen to his adventures, he told them that, no sooner had he left the village and began to climb one of the ridges, he met a stranger who, by his speech and appearance, seemed to be a Cherokee from another settlement. This stranger had asked him where he was traveling, and he had replied that he had promised his relatives to bring them a deer or return never again to Kanuga to bother them for food.

On hearing the young man's words, the stranger said, "My town is near this very spot, and we who live there are your relatives. Will you not come with me?"

The invitation pleased the young man, for he knew that he was a poor hunter, who was unlikely to bring back the promised game, and he did not enjoy the thought of going back to Kanuga empty-handed. So he went with the stranger toward Pilot Knob, and when they had climbed nearly halfway up the mountain, they came to a cave which they entered.

As they went deeper and deeper, the cave became wider and wider and seemed to run to the very heart of the mountain. There it opened into a rich and spacious countryside with a great town having hundreds of inhabitants. With gladness, the people welcomed the hunter as though he were a relative or an old friend. They took him to their chief, who invited the young man into his house and offered him a seat beside the fire. But when he sat down, the seat started to move, and when he looked at it, it was a huge turtle poking its head out of its shell.

The hunter bolted up, but the chief reassured him by saying, "The turtle only wants to see you and will not harm you." So the young man resumed his seat, although this time very carefully, as the turtle pulled its head back into its shell.

The people brought food, like the kind the hunter ate in Kanuga, and when he had satisfied his hunger, the chief kindly escorted him through the town so that he saw more of the houses and the big townhouse. He also talked further with the people, but after several days of hospitality, the young man grew anxious to return home. So the chief took him back to the cave door and led him to the path that would take him to Kanuga.

As the two parted, the chief said, "You have seen our land and our way of life, and when you return to your village, you can be happy there no longer. Come back to us whenever you wish. You now know the trail." Then the chief turned back toward the cave, and the young man walked down the mountainside.

When he arrived home and told what had happened, no one believed him, and everyone laughed him to scorn. Thereafter, he had little to do with the people of Kanuga and would stay away for days on end. Yet each time he returned, he spoke of the great settlement in the mountain and its people until another man finally believed him and offered to go there with him on his next visit.

When the time came, the two headed for Pilot Knob and made a camp in the woods. The young man said that he would go to the mountain and told his friend to wait and hunt close to the camp. After two nights, he returned, and although he was by himself, he appeared to be speaking to someone. As he got nearer to the camp, his friend heard the voices of girls but could not see anyone. When the hunter stood by the fire, he said, ""Here are two friends. They tell me that their town will hold a dance in two nights. At that time, if you want to go, they will come again and take you there."

His friend immediately agreed. The young man turned toward some trees and, as if speaking to someone not far from camp, called out, "He will go with us." Then turning back to his friend, he said, "I see you have killed a deer. Our sisters are hungry and would like some venison."

Taking the drying rack away from the fire, the other hunter said, "What portion do they want?"

The invisible sisters replied, "Our mother would like some ribs."

So he removed some of the ribs off the rack and handed them to the young man who took them and paused, saying to his friend, "We will return for you in two days." And with that, he disappeared into the dark forest, as his voice and the others grew fainter and fainter until all was quiet.

As promised, in two days the hunter and the girls came back to the camp, but this time the girls were visible. As they drew close to the fire, the friend observed that the girls' feet were round and short, somewhat like the pads of a dog's paws. When they noticed that he was staring, they plopped down by the fire and covered their feet. After a savory supper of venison, they all left the camp and walked beside a creek toward Pilot Knob.

They entered the cave and followed it toward the heart of the mountain. As they went along, the cave opened wider, as it had before, to reveal the spreading countryside until at last the party saw the great town ahead. All of a sudden, the hunter who had never been inside the mountain collapsed, his legs feeling as if they were dead. Then the others of his party realized that, before coming to this land, he had not prepared his spirit by fasting for seven days. They lifted him up, but still he staggered and fell to the ground. They sent for the medicine man, and he brought the ancient tobacco that originally grew in the land and that held great healing power. The priest took the old tobacco, and he rubbed it on the man's legs and made him breathe the smoke from it so that he sneezed and became whole again. He now stood up, and he and the others entered the town.

The dance had not yet started, so they went into the townhouse where the people had gathered. The young man told his friend to take a seat by the fire, but the seat had been fashioned of honey locust, and the thorns of the tree were still on it so that his friend was afraid to sit. However, the young man told him to have no fear, so he sat in the chair, and the locust thorns were like feathers and did not prick him.

The drummer and the dancers now made their entrance, and the walls of the great townhouse soon echoed with the dance and the drum. Yet the voice of a man sounded above all other sounds. Though he did not dance, he trailed the dancers at the end of the line, and his voice rose with the cry of "Ku! Ku!" The hunters could not guess the reason for his call, so the people near them said, "He was once lost in the mountains, and he called through the forest so that his friends might find him. Yet his voice at last failed him so that he could only utter in soft tones "Ku! Ku!" until we saved him and brought him here to live with us."

When the dance ended, the two men left the cave and went back to Kanuga. There, at the next dance, they told of what had occurred in the mountain—of the town and of the dance in the townhouse and of the people's kindness. This time, because two people told the story, all in Kanuga believed it, and many in the settlement wanted to go to see for themselves this land in the heart of Pilot Knob.

But the first hunter told them that they must fast for seven days and that he would go ahead of them to arrange a place for them and that at the end of seven days he would return to take them with him. So he left, while they stayed behind and fasted, and when the seven days had passed, he returned. And those who had fasted went with him into the mountain. And those who remained in Kanuga never saw their friends again. And yet on some days, when there was a certain slant of light on the face of the mountain's cliffs, those who had stayed in Kanuga would look at the layers of rock on the bald summit and saw, or thought that they saw, windows and doors and the roofs of houses where their friends now lived with the mountain spirits.

YAHULA

The small town of Dahlonega is surrounded by the peaks and summits of the mountains of northern Georgia and is the seat of Lumpkin County. The name comes from a Cherokee word meaning "yellow." Gold was discovered there in 1828, and miners flocked into the area for the "yellow money" as part of the first great gold rush in the United States.

In colonial days, Creeks and Cherokees mingled in Dahlonega, and it was a place of trade and considered part of the traditional Cherokee lands of the southern Appalachians. Some descendants of the Creek and Cherokee still live there today. Yahoola Creek is nearby, and its reservoir of Lake Zwerner supplies water for the residents and is a center of recreation. Here is how the creek got its name.

Many years before the Revolutionary War, there lived among Cherokee a well-to-do stock trader called Yahula. His name meant "the black drink" and may have related to the song that the Creek sang in their rituals associated with this liquid. Yahula would load up each of his horses with about 150 pounds of trade goods and bring into the interior coffee, sugar, kettles, and cloth that came from England through the ports of Charleston and Savannah. In return for these items, the Indians would swap deerskins, furs, hides, tallow, oils, and honey. He then would sell these and return with more supplies. Everyone knew when Yahula was coming to trade because of his singing and the bells of his pack-train. These dangled from the necks of his horses and jingled brightly as they walked along the mountain trails from place to place. When not traveling, he lived among the Indians of Dahlonega.

One day there was a great hunt in the mountains, and all the men for miles around were out. Yahula had gone with them. When the hunt ended, the warriors prepared to return to their homes, but Yahula was nowhere to be seen. The hunters waited for a while and then began to search for him, but no one could find him. So they decided to go back without him. When his family and friends heard that he was missing, they mourned for him as if he had died.

After a period of time had lapsed, his wife, children, and brother were having supper one evening when into the house walked Yahula and sat down among them. They were surprised and overjoyed to see him, and at once they began to ask, "What happened to you? Where have you been?"

To their questions, Yahula replied, "During the hunt, I became lost in the mountains. Then the Nunnehi, Those-Who-Always-Live-Anywhere and who are the Immortals, found me. They took me to their town beneath a mountain and cared for me with kindness. I have been living with them from the time I became lost. But I longed to see my old friends again, and so I came back."

Yahula's family invited him to stay for supper, but he said, "I cannot. For me, it is now too late. I have tasted the food of the Nunnehi and can never eat again with my own kind. Neither can I stay with you, my family, but must go back to the Immortals."

They begged him not to return and said, "You must stay with us. This is your home."

Yahula answered, "If I stay, I die. If I go back, I live."

He spoke with his family a little more, then rose to leave. All the time he had been talking with them, they could see him clearly, and they saw him when he stood and walked to the door. As soon as he stepped through the doorway, however, he disappeared as though he had never been among them.

Thereafter, Yahula would return from time to time to visit his family. He appeared to them as soon as he came through the door, and all the while he sat and spoke, he seemed like himself in every way. Yet the moment he walked across the threshold, he vanished no matter how many eyes might have been watching him. Yahula continued to visit his people often, but at last their pleas to remain with them became so strong that the Immortals may have become angry and refused to let him return, for one day he did not go back.

About ten miles above the town of Dahlonega is a mountain where lies the head of the creek. A small enclosure is there made of uncut stones. It has no roof and no entrance and is the place where Yahula lived with the Nunnehi, according to the Cherokee They named it Yahula-yi and gave the creek the same name after the songs of the vanished trader. In the old days, people used to say that, if travelers came along the creek trail late at night, they often would hear the cracking whip and jingling bells intermingled with the voice of a man singing, urging his pack train forward. Yet no one had ever seen the man and his horses, even though their sounds seemed nearby.

After Yahula had disappeared for good, a man who was his friend continued his songs for a while, but this man died all of a sudden for no apparent cause. Upon his death, the Cherokee became afraid to sing Yahula's songs. At last, no one heard any of his songs, and the people began to think that the trader had left for the Indian Territory out west where many of the Cherokee had gone already.

The stone house is no more, but people in the old days saw it and heard the songs and the bells. After their removal in 1838 from Georgia to Oklahoma, the Cherokee thought that they might hear Yahula sing once again in the new place, but no one has heard him since.

THE UNSEEN HELPERS

On lands west of the Hudson River and throughout the Finger Lake district of New York lived the powerful Hodenosaunee, "the people of the longhouse," also known as the Iroquois. To the British, they were the Five Nations because their members included the Mohawk, Oneida, Onondaga, Cayuga, and Seneca peoples. Long before Europeans came to North American, they had united under their Great Law of Peace to put an end to warring among one another and for protection and mutual aid against outsiders.

According to Iroquois tradition, Deganawidah, originally a Huron, proposed an end to intertribal fighting. Known as the Peace Maker, he spoke of casting away self-interest and taught that the people should act for the good of everyone. A leader of the Onondaga named Hiawatha heard the Peace Maker's message and took it to the sachems and sagamores of the Iroquois. These leaders agreed to follow the Great Law of Peace. Even the angry war priest Thadodaho agreed. His hair looked like writhing snakes; his hands, like the claws of a turtle;

and his feet, like the paws of a bear. He had always fomented conflict and disunity among the Five Nations, but once he accepted the Peace Maker's teachings, Thadodaho lost his horrible appearance and looked like a man. To commemorate the new order of things, the Peace Maker planted a great white pine as the Tree of Peace under which the Five Nations might flourish, united like the tree's bundles of five needles.

By the time of their contact with whites, the Hodenosaunee had formed the Iroquois Confederacy to strengthen their political and diplomatic unity, for their league was not only one of peace but also one of power. As many as two thousand people lived in their large, well-fortified towns that the Europeans called "castles." These had double and sometimes triple wooden palisades and other sophisticated defenses. Through their dominance of the fur trade in seventeenth and eighteenth centuries, the Iroquois had become one of the most powerful forces in the English colonies of the Northeast and throughout the region of the Great Lakes.

From approximately 1670 to 1710, the Five Nations expanded their territories southward throughout the western part of Virginia to as far as the Ohio River valley—where West Virginia is now—north to Hudson Bay, and south to lands claimed by the Cherokee and had made contact with the Tuscarora of eastern North Carolina. Before migrating south, the Tuscarora had originally lived in the area of New York near the Iroquois and were connected to them by similarities of language. After many of the Tuscarora were driven out of North Carolina around 1715, the Iroquois became known as the Six Nations, accepting their linguistic cousins into their membership.

Sometime in the 1680s, the Cherokee and the Hodenosaunee began to war with each other. No one knows who started the hostilities. Two accounts from the Iroquois indicate that the Cherokee were the initial aggressors. One story says that a band of Cherokee attacked and robbed a hunting party of Seneca in the west where they had expanded. Another tradition claims that the Cherokee broke the peace by killing ambassadors of the Iroquois. The subsequent wars were not between large armies fighting great battles, but small encounters so that the warriors of each side could practice their skills and gain prestige.

From the country of the Hodenosaunee, a journey to the northern frontier of the Cherokee took five days for a swiftly moving war party that might be as large as twenty to forty men or as small as one or two. Because of the distance, the raids were frequently made by only one warrior. No matter which side attacked, the other was certain to take to the warpath to retaliate quickly. Because the Iroquois and the Cherokee were evenly matched, neither side could gain a lasting advantage over the other. Both nations took captives, and, if these were young enough, they were adopted into the tribe to replenish the individuals lost in war. If a captive were too old or if he were of fighting age, his fate was usually death by burning. Not until 1768 did a permanent peace break out between the two sides through the diplomacy of the British Indian agent, Sir William Johnson. With the Cherokee delegation headed by Oconostota, the Great Warrior of Chota, representatives from both sides met in New York to ratify the treaty that set the Tennessee River as the boundary between them. However, even as late as the middle of the 1800s, there were descendants of Cherokee prisoners, who had been captured by the Seneca, still living among them after the earlier decades of long warfare had passed.

The Seneca, who were the most numerous and warlike of the Iroquois, referred to the Cherokee as Oyadage-onon—that is, "the cave people," and the Cherokee called the Seneca Nundawegi from Nundawa-ono, meaning "the people of the great hills." One of the war chiefs of the Seneca named Ganogwioeon decided that he would take the warpath against the Cherokee. His war party consisted of ten men. When they arrived in the territory of the cave people, the Seneca found them on the lookout for raiders and could do nothing.

Thinking that it would be safer if he went by himself, Ganogwioeon decided to leave his warriors behind, hidden in the forest. When he arrived at one of the Cherokee settlements, he entered the village. At the first cabin that he came to, he saw an old woman and her granddaughter named Odju, but they did not see him. He slipped into the asi, and there, in the little hot house, he hid under some wood.

The people of the settlement knew that the Seneca were on the warpath. As the light began to fade more, the chief heard the grandmother say, "Ganogwioeon may be near. I'll shut the door before we go to bed." He heard her and continued to wait.

After a while, Odju said, "I'm going to sleep."

The chief heard her words also and waited until he could hear the girl climbing up the ladder to the sleeping loft above while she spoke to her grandmother below. He decided to wait a while longer. Then he heard the old woman fasten the door of the asi with tough strips of green braided elm bark. He remained quiet. At last, when he thought the two had fallen asleep, he removed the braided fasteners of the asi and went into the cabin. Even though the old woman had shut the door, she had forgotten to latch it from the inside, and he entered silently.

The fire had burned down low, but the coals were still alive so that the chief could see the ladder to the loft. He climbed up to where the girl was, but Odju was still awake and could make out the warrior from the glowing coals. Just as she was about to scream, he whispered, "I am Ganogwioeon. Scream and I'll cut off your head. Be quiet and I won't hurt you." He then said, "The chief of this town has a daughter. Have her to go into the woods with you in the morning, and you will be safe."

Fearing for her life, Odju promised to do as the Seneca commanded and told him where to wait for her in the woods. Just before dawn, while the grand-mother was still asleep, he left the house but turned and said to Odju, "Betray me and I will come back and kill you."

A little later, after the grass had dried, the girl went to her chief's house and said to his daughter, "Let's go and gather firewood."

So the daughter went with Odju, who led the girl to where Ganogwioeon was waiting in the woods. Suddenly, he sprang from behind a tree, grabbed the girl, and killed her before she could cry out. Yet he was true to his word and did not harm Odju. Terrified, she ran back toward the village, screaming as she went.

Ganogwioeon quickly took his knife and scalped the dead girl. He then gave a war whoop so loud that everyone in the town could hear him. Cherokee warriors rushed out of their houses and raced toward the woods. The Seneca chief shook the bloody scalp at them and turned to run. One of warriors was faster than the others and began to gain on him. When Ganogwioeon saw his pursuer getting closer, he ran into a deep ravine for cover. The warrior followed after, but Ganogwioeon turned and shot the man with an arrow as he ran up the ravine. The chief quickly took the man's scalp and shook it at the approaching Cherokee warriors. He then darted away.

As the Seneca came to a second ravine, another man ran after him and was ahead of the rest. So the chief notched another arrow, but this time, as he pulled back the string, the bow broke, and the Cherokee warrior was upon him before he knew it. The rest of the warriors ran up rapidly and captured him. They tied his arms behind him, put a rope around his neck, and took him back to the village.

There, two women of the tribe, who were War Women or Pretty Women and held the title of Beloved, would decide his fate. These women had two snakes tattooed across their mouths. The upper jaw of each snake was on the top lip, and the lower jaw of the other snake was on the same side of the bottom lip so that, when the women opened their mouths, the snakes seemed to open theirs.

When Ganogwioeon appeared before them, the women said to everyone present, "Here is how to torment him. Tie him near a fire, and burn the soles of his feet. When they are blistered, let the water out. Then put grains of hard-ened corn under the skin, and chase and beat him with clubs until he dies." All the while, the snaky jaws of their tattooed mouths opened and closed as they pronounced their verdict.

So the Cherokee stripped their prisoner and burned his feet until they were blistered. They put the corn under the skin and tied a bark rope around his waist. The War Women were to hold the end of the rope while he ran between two lines of people with sticks and clubs. Before he started, though, an old man said, "Let me hold the end of the rope." So the women gave the rope to the old man.

When the signal was given, the Seneca chief ran so fast that he jerked the rope out of the old man's hands. Then plunging to one side, he broke through the line and escaped into the woods before the Cherokee knew what had happened. He ran with such speed that he was able to evade his captors. When night fell, he crawled into a hollow log and hid. He was naked and unarmed, and his feet were so raw that he thought he would never get back to his own people. Later that night, he heard footsteps on the leaves outside the log and thought his enemies were nearby and would soon find him.

Beside the log, a voice whispered to someone, "This is our friend." Then two voices said directly to Ganogwioeon, "You think you will die, but you will not. We will take care of you. Stick out your feet."

The chief did as he was told and felt something begin to lick his feet. After a little while, the voices said, "We have licked his feet long enough. Now let us crawl inside on either side of him and keep him warm."

So, whatever they were, they crawled inside the log on each side of Ganogwioeon and kept him warm throughout the night. Before daybreak, they crawled out and told him to stick his feet out again, and again they licked them and soothed them. Then one of the strange voices said to him, "We have done everything that we can so far. Now you must leave and go to the place where you once built a shelter of bark when you came into this country a long time ago. When you get there, look under a piece of bark lying beneath the roof, and you will find some things beneath it to help you."

When the chief came out of the fallen log, his feet were much better, and he could walk more easily, but his friends were nowhere to be seen. He traveled until about midday, when he came to the old bark shelter, and there under the roof lay a large piece of bark on the ground. He lifted this up, and, just as the voice had said, he found a knife, an awl, and a piece of flint. Then he remembered that his men had hidden those things there when they were on the warpath some years before. He took the objects and left.

After he had traveled for some hours, it began to grow dark, so Ganogwioeon looked for a place to sleep for the night. He saw a hollow tree and crawled inside. In the middle of the night, he again heard footsteps rustling through the dry leaves, and a voice whispered, "Our friend is here." Then the voice said, "Put your feet outside the tree."

He did as the voice told him, and again tongues began to lick the bottom of his feet. Then, as if talking to another, the voice said, "Enough. We will lie next to our friend and keep him warm." So they entered the hollow tree and lay down. Before daylight, the two crept out and licked the Seneca's feet once more, and they said to him, "About noon, you will find food." Then they disappeared.

Ganogwioeon continued his journey. When it was nearly midday, he came upon a bear in the woods that had been freshly killed as it was still warm. He skinned the bear with the knife that he had found under the bark. He gathered dry wood and leaves and started a fire with the flint that he had uncovered. As the fire blazed and grew hotter, he cut the bear meat into small strips and roasted them on sticks over the flame. Some he ate, and other pieces he saved to take with him the next day. While the meat was cooking, he rubbed wood dust from decayed branches on the underside of the bearskin to clean it. Then he stretched the skin over sticks beside the fire to let it cure.

When it was finally dark, he lay down to sleep. As on the previous two nights, he heard the leaves rustle. A voice now said, "Our friend is resting. He will not die, for he has had plenty to eat. We will lick his feet again."

When they had finished, the voices said, "Nothing is going to happen to you. You will reach your home safely." Before the first light, the two disappeared as before.

That morning, Ganogwioeon put the bearskin around his shoulders like a blanket. He took as much of the meat as he could carry and headed north toward home.

On the fourth night, his friends returned just as they had previously. In the dark, the unknown voices said to him, "Your feet are well now, but you will be cold, so we will lie on either side of you again tonight."

Just before dawn, the voices spoke to him, saying, "Today at noon, you will find more to eat and to wear." Then the two were gone.

The chief walked that day until the sun shone directly overhead, and there in the woods he saw in front of him a pair of young bears that had just been killed. As on the day before, he started a fire with his flint, skinned the bears, and roasted as much of the meat as he could carry. While it was cooking, he tanned the hides beside the fire. Then he lay down to rest because he was very tired.

Early the next morning, he used the cured skins to make leggings. With the awl, he punched holes in them through which he threaded leather strings so that he could tie them around his legs to keep warmer. Then he took the meat that he had roasted and started once again on his journey.

That night, his friends came to him as before. They told him that the next day he would find something to put on his feet.

And just as they said, the next day at noon, as Ganogwioeon walked through the woods, he came upon two fawns recently killed. He skinned them with his knife, as he had the bears, and that night he started a fire with his flint. While some of the meat was cooking, he dried the skins beside the flames, and from the skins he cut out moccasins. With his awl, he punched holes in these and threaded them with leather strings so that the moccasins would fit comfortably on his feet. Then he ate and lay down to sleep.

No sooner had he stretched out, when he heard the familiar voices whisper, "Our friend, tomorrow you will reach your home where your warriors are safe and are waiting for your return. Now we will tell you why we healed your feet and took care of you. In the past, whenever you went hunting, you always left something for us to eat in the woods. You kept only the smallest part of the animal for yourself but left the best meat for us. We are thankful for your kindness. Tomorrow, when you leave, you will see us and know who we are."

Early the next morning, before the sun had risen, Ganogwioeon woke up. His helpers were still there—two men as he thought. As soon as he got to his feet, they said goodbye to him and started to leave as did he. The dawn light began to filter through the trees. As it did, the chief turned to look at his friends for as long as he could while they were leaving. Then, in the twinkling of an eye, he saw that one was a white wolf and the other a black one. That very day, he reached his home among the Iroquois just as his friends, the wolves, had promised.

Legends from History
by or About the Cherokee

THE LOST CHEROKEE

In the late seventeenth and early eighteenth centuries, the lands claimed by the Cherokee amounted to around 120,000 square miles and included territory in the present-day states of Virginia, West Virginia, Kentucky, Tennessee, Alabama, Georgia, South Carolina, and North Carolina. These lands were also part of the territory that the rival European colonial powers of France and England hoped to dominate in their struggle for the North American continent.

The French controlled the Mississippi River, and in 1717 had established Fort Toulouse on the Coosa River in Alabama. They began to make inroads among the Cherokee, many of whom in the Overhill settlements on the western side of the mountains preferred to trade with the French rather than the English. To bind the Cherokee more closely to the interests of the English and the colony of South Carolina, its first royal governor, Francis Nicholson, invited their representatives to come to a conference in Charleston. In 1721, he negotiated a treaty with Cherokee headmen from thirty-seven towns of their fifty-three settlements at that time. The treaty altered trade regulations, set a boundary between Cherokee and English lands, established an agent to oversee matters of commerce, provided the Cherokee with presents, and designated a paramount chief named Wrosetasatow. He held the prestigious war title of Outacite or Mankiller. As a result of the treaty, he now had the power to punish all crimes, murder included, and to represent the Cherokee in their dealings with the government of South Carolina.

The Treaty of 1721 also included a cession of land to the colony of approximately 2,623 square miles between the Santee, Saluda, and Edisto Rivers. This territory was the first land ceded by the Cherokee. A little over one hundred years later, all of their land was gone.

Part of the tribe opposed selling the land. They believed that the whites would not be satisfied but would want more and more until the Cherokee would be without any territory. Yet this party could not stop the sale. Bitterly disappointed, they decided to leave their homes and never return. They would go west across the Great River, where there were no whites.

When the rest of the Cherokee heard about this plan, they were grief-stricken at the thought of losing family and friends and begged their loved ones to stay. Yet their minds were made up, and they began preparations for the long journey. Seeing their determination to leave, the others accepted the decision and worked to make the march west less difficult. They loaded up pack horses with all kinds of food—acorns, hickory nuts and chestnuts, honey, dried persimmons and beans, smoked venison and bear, parched corn, bear's oil and hickory nut oil, and other necessities for travel.

With everything ready, the company left under the leadership of their chief. A band of the nation's best warriors went as well to help the travelers cross the Mississippi. Each night, until they reached the Great River, messengers returned home to let those who remained behind know how the journey progressed. Other runners headed west to bring news from the Cherokee back home.

After many days, the travelers reached the Mississippi and crossed it with the aid of the accompanying warriors. These then returned to the Cherokee lands in the east, while the rest continued to the west. All communication now ceased, and the wanderers were heard from no more. As time passed, their friends and relatives back home forgot them and believed that their story was an old tale without any truth.

In the meantime, after the Cherokee ceded territory to South Carolina in 1721, inroads continued onto their lands, and the nation sold one tract after another in an additional series of twenty-one treaties. Some of the land tracts were small, and some, large. Some were made voluntarily, and some, forcibly. The smallest was to Tennessee in 1805 and was one square mile. The largest was a private cession in 1775 to Richard Henderson of the Transylvania Company. This tract was 27,050 square miles and included territory in present-day Kentucky, Tennessee, and Virginia. The Kentucky section of the purchase was at that time called "the Bloody Ground," thus named because of the constant skirmishes and contests between Indian hunting parties from various tribes, each one claiming sole ownership of the land for killing game.

Known as "Carolina Dick," Colonel Henderson and others of his enterprise met with Cherokee headmen at Sycamore Shoals on the Watauga River, now Elizabethton, Tennessee. Some twelve hundred Cherokee men, women, and children were in attendance. Henderson used generous amounts of liquor to facilitate negotiations with Attakullakulla, the Peace Chief, and Oconostota, the War Chief, along with other leaders of an older generation. Their signatures to the agreement transferred vast amounts of the Cherokee's traditional hunting grounds to the whites, lands that the Indians relied upon to sustain themselves and to obtain hides and other raw materials for trade with the British colonies. In return, the Cherokee received wagon loads of goods worth about fifty thousand dollars, including firearms, shot and powder, mirrors, clothes, hatchets, knives, blankets, beads, trinkets, and other presents.

The treaty was, of course, completely illegal, for the Proclamation of 1763 forbade white settlement west of the eastern Appalachian watershed. Its purpose was to keep peace on the frontier through benevolent British protection of Indian rights and thus prevent further colonial encroachment and the sale by Indians of their lands. The negotiations with Henderson illustrate the futility of the crown's attempts to control the immigration of settlers onto Indian territories after 1763. Other whites who were traders with the Cherokee and who had married Indian wives sometimes claimed large blocks of land for their half-blood sons, often in collusion with headmen like Oconostota, the Great Warrior of Chota.

Of course, great numbers of the Cherokee were against the deal with Henderson. The son of Attakullakulla, Dragging Canoe, vehemently opposed the land sale. He angrily warned his people that whole Indian nations had vanished like snowballs and that the whites would not be satisfied until they possessed his nation's entire territory without even a distant wilderness to claim until the Cherokee were utterly destroyed. In the final negotiations, Dragging Canoe spoke of Henderson's greed. He ominously warned that the land had a cloud over it and declared that its settlement would be dark and bloody. He punctuated his speech with a stomp of his foot and left, refusing to sign. Many of the younger headmen and warriors followed him.

Before Dragging Canoe, the old Cherokee of earlier days had prophesied that the Indians would be driven west and finally conquered because they had no lands left to take. History ultimately proved their prophecy and the later words of Dragging Canoe to be true. The encroachment continued unabated until the Indian Removal Act of 1830 and the Treaty of New Echota in 1835 when the nation ceded all its remaining lands east of the Mississippi to the United States.

Yet before the Trail of Tears in 1838 forced the great majority of the tribe from their homeland, many of the Cherokee began to leave for lands west of the Mississippi. Small parties of warriors crossed the Great River to discover what lay beyond. One of these bands is said to have crossed the wide plains and traveled to the edge of the Rocky Mountains. There they came upon a tribe who spoke the same language and still lived as in the old days before the Cherokee had ever encountered the whites or knew their ways. Perhaps these people were the Cherokees who had migrated west after the Treaty of 1721 and who had lost all contact with those who remained back east.

GA'NA AND THE CHEROKEE

Of all the nations of the Hodenosaunee, the Seneca were the most populous. Living along the Genesee River below Lake Ontario, they guarded the western door of the longhouse or Iroquois Confederacy and protected it from enemies that might come from the north, south, and west.

Ga'na, or Arrow, was a mighty war chief of the Seneca. He called a council one day to discuss making peace with their long-time enemies, the Cherokee. "We must go the Cherokee," he said, "and see if we cannot agree to live together in friendship and peace."

His people approved, and a party of warriors agreed to accompany him to their enemy's lands. Together with Ga'na, their number was twelve. Before they began their journey, they had to purify themselves so that their mission would be successful.

Ga'na told his warriors, "We must go to water first," and they nodded in approval of the cleansing.

So he and his men went deep into the woods where there was a river, and for ten days they bathed in the cold water every morning. And each morning after they had bathed, they drank the black drink of hot water, holly berries, and button snakeroot. And each morning, after they had drunk the black tea, Ga'na and his warriors would vomit the impurities from their bodies, and throughout the day and night, they would pray and fast to insure the success of their journey.

Then Ga'na told his men, "We must now gather eagle feathers."

So they went to a high hill and made a trench as long as a man is tall, and they put a man within the trench and spread green boughs over the top of the trench so that he could not be seen. On these, they laid a fresh deer carcass. Then the warriors left the pit so that they could not be seen, and they began to call out, inviting the great eagle to descend from his home in the clouds and to come down to them.

Soon the warrior under the boughs heard a sound, and an eagle came to the deer, ate a little, and flew away, but this was an ordinary eagle and not the great bald eagle of peace. It came back after a while, ate more of the deer, and flew away again in another direction. This time, it told other birds about the deer, and these came to feed on it, but the warrior shook the boughs and frightened them away so that they were unable to eat the food set out for the great eagle.

After a while, the man heard a loud noise, like the rush of a mighty wind, descending through the air, and he knew that Cloud Dweller, Shadagea, the great eagle was coming. After he had touched the ground, Shadagea looked around cautiously and would not touch the deer for some time. When he thought it safe, he began to eat. As the Cloud Dweller became comfortable, the man carefully raised his hand through the branches where Shadegea stood, suddenly grabbing the eagle's tail and holding on as tight as he could. Shadagea flapped his large wings and rose up quickly toward the clouds.

Only one feather had pulled loose from the tail. The Seneca warriors came out of hiding and brought a soft deerskin and wrapped it around the sacred feather. For two winters—for winter is the season of the eagle and the time when the snake is in his den—they gathered feathers in this way, not wanting to offend the snake whose season is summer. At last they left, ready with a full offering of twelve tail feathers, and started for the country of the Cherokee.

After Ga'na and his men had traveled for five days, they arrived in the land of the Overhill Cherokee who lived on the western side of the Appalachians. Not far away was their capital of Chota, lying along the East Tennessee River some twenty-five miles above its mouth. Tall mountains protected the town from behind, palisades twelve feet high fenced in its other sides, and dozens of war canoes that could hold as many as twenty men rested on the bank of the river. No one could enter the town except through its gates. Here resided the Uka, the Fire King or supreme chief of the Cherokee.

As the Seneca drew closer to the town, two of Ga'na's warriors, who had painted their bodies a milky white, began to dance, all the while singing songs of peace and shaking the twelve white tail feathers of the great eagle. Hearing the commotion outside their protective stockade and thinking they were about to be attacked, the Cherokee warriors streamed together to the center of the town. Through the gate, however, they could see the dance of the painted Seneca and the flash of their eagle feathers signifying peace.

The chief of the town said to the people, "These men have come to us for an important purpose. Let us hear what they have to say."

So the people opened the gate, and the two Seneca who were holding the eagle feathers came forward and said, "We have a message for your people and have come to talk to you in your council house."

The Chota chief then signaled that a council be held, and all the people turned and walked toward the townhouse. The two Seneca warriors came next, continuing their dance, while Ga'na and the rest of his men followed, singing as they went. Inside, the council house was so dark that nothing could be seen until the Cherokee brought bundles of canes. These they placed in the center of the floor and lit them, and the dim light revealed that the council house was full, humming with the murmurs of the people. As they entered, bending under the low lintel, the Seneca kept dancing and singing until finally they became tired and stopped. None of the Cherokee danced.

Once the dancing ceased, Ga'na stepped forward to speak. "Now you will hear my message and learn why we have journeyed such a great distance through the woods to come to you. Our people have thought that fighting should end. For a long time the Cherokee and the Seneca have looked for any chance to kill one another. We believe it is time for peace. As a sign that I tell you the truth, we have brought a belt of white wampum and twelve white feathers of the great eagle. If the Cherokee want to be friends with the Seneca, take these offerings."

The Fire King took the feathers and the belt made of white beads that was the length of a warrior, and he raised the gifts aloft in his hands before the people and said to Ga'na, "I will hold these until tomorrow when we will give you our decision."

The Uka then turned to the people and asked them to go to their houses and bring food, and, when they returned, they carried the servings in small flat baskets of split river cane and passed these around to all present. For meat, they had venison, bear, and buffalo. They also had potatoes, pumpkins, beans, and peas. In the dim twilight of the council house, everyone groped with their hands from dish to dish and ate. Along with water, the people drank hominy or boiled cracked corn mixed with wood ash and slightly fermented, and with gourds they dipped this soup from large earthen jars and passed it around for all to enjoy. That night, such was the abundance at the feast that the Cherokee and their guests could not finish all of the food.

On the next day, everyone again ate together. When they had finished, the Uka said to Ga'na, "We have agreed to be friends with the Seneca and to bury our weapons of war   our knives and our tomahawks—that no one may take them up again."

Ga'na answered, "We are happy that you also want peace. We will pile our weapons here before you so that you may destroy them. The white wampum belt signifies the friendship between us as long as the grass grows and the rivers run."

The Fire King now turned to his people and said, "The Seneca are our friends. Except for Ga'na, select any man from among them to adopt as one of your relatives."

Some of the women walked up to a warrior and said, "You are now our uncle."

Other women took another warrior and said, "You will be our brother."

And so the adoptions continued until only Ga'na remained. A young man stood next to the Cherokee chief, who announced to all assembled, "This young man beside me will now make his claim."

The young man immediately walked up to Ga'na and said, "Father, I am happy to see you again. Let us go home."

Then he led the Seneca chief to the house where he had slept the night before, the same house where the young man's mother lived. When Ga'na came to the house, he embraced the young man as his son and the mother as his wife, for both had been captured and adopted many years before by the Cherokee, and Ga'na had known all along that they were his wife and child.

While the family was in the house, a messenger entered the village and announced that he came from the Santee who lived to the east beside the great salt sea. He was dressed in skins of all kinds sewn together, and his garment was so long that the raccoon tails fringing it trailed along the ground. As he delivered his message, he danced the dance of peace, leaping and at the same time singing that the Santee challenged the Cherokee to a ball game and that his people were now on their way to the town and would arrive in seven days.

Throughout the early summer, the men of Chota had prepared for the matches that took place from midsummer until the weather became too cold to play, and they trained the same as they would for war. They competed in fierce foot races, and they abstained from certain foods. Because the rabbit scares easily and becomes confused, they ate no rabbit. Because the frog has brittle bones that readily break, they ate no frog. Because the sucker fish moves sluggishly, they did not eat it. And for similar reasons, the men could not eat the spinach-like leaves of the goosefoot, nor could they eat salt and hot food, and for the seven days before the arrival of the Santee, they could not touch any woman. Also, if a player touched one of the racquets used for ball play before a game began, the stick could not be used, and, if his wife were with child, he could not participate, for he would not be at his full strength since he had lost some of it in creating the baby.

On the evening before the day of the ball game, the people of Chota held a festival in anticipation of the event. At around nine o'clock, they gathered in the great rotunda of the council house. A small fire burned near the tall post in the center, and a thin smoke overspread the dimly lit interior. Between a ring of wooden columns and the outside wall, the Cherokee and their Seneca relatives sat on three successively higher steps arranged like the tiers of a theater. Over the seats were mats woven of thin strips of ash and oak. Near the center of the building, close to the central column, were musicians who beat drums, played flutes, and shook rattles made of dried gourds, and around the musicians were gyrating dancers. Once the rotunda was filled and the people seated, an ancient headman arose and stood in the middle to address the assembly of hundreds of men, women, and children.

"The Santee will come tomorrow. They will challenge Chota in ball play, the game much beloved by us, our men and our women, with our women playing often. The ball game is so old among us that no one can remember when it began. Tomorrow our young men will conquer the Santee as our old men now sitting in the council house have done in games long past. When young, I often caught the ball with my stick and tossed it to make points and to win the game for my fellow players."

The old man paused and then continued, "Chota is famed for its victories over the other towns of the Overhills and over the Valley, Middle, and Lower towns as well, and we will conquer the Santee just as we have conquered others of our nation and of other nations."

When the headman had delivered his speech and inspired the young men gathered in the townhouse, the musicians began. Some sang and some played their instruments. A troop of young women presently entered through the low door of the rotunda. They wore clean deerskin robes of the softest white and had ornamented themselves with beads of all colors and with bracelets, and they had decorated their flowing black hair with bright ribbons. When all had assembled, they made two semicircles of twelve each, back to back, and each girl held hands with the ones beside her in the same line. Then all sang in low, sweet, and gentle voices to the onlookers as the two lines moved slowly round and round the floor.

Suddenly, a loud and high-pitched whoop interrupted the soft singing, and a company of twelve young men entered briskly, one behind the other. In his hand, each carried a ball stick about two feet long, with the handle made of hickory and one end bent into a loop like a large spoon woven with deerskin thongs for catching and tossing the ball during the game. Feathers from purple martins and crested flycatchers dangled from the sticks to make them swift, accurate, and misleading to opponents. The players had painted themselves, and some wore bracelets twisted from brass, and others wore brass or silver armbands engraved with swans. Around their necks hung necklaces fashioned from tubes of brass and neck collars of brass and silver or gorgets of silver or shell. Beaded moccasins adorned their feet, and tall waving plumes crowned their heads.

The young men now formed a semicircle in front of the young women whose formation changed into a single semicircle as well, and both lines began to sing, each responding to the other as two files danced together. Along each line, the dancers rose and fell, alternating from tiptoe to heel so that, as one was on tiptoe, the next one started to raise the heel, with the men and women moving around the rotunda as a pair of undulating arcs, up and down, up and down, all the while their voices fluidly rising or falling in song in sympathy with their movements. Occasionally a shrill whoop punctuated the song and the dance.

At last, Dalala, the Woodpecker, stood up and left the audience. He took a few steps toward the east, where the Santee lived, and put his hand to his mouth yelling four times, the last one quivering for a long time like the cry of a woodpecker. The men in the ball game dance echoed the cry with a series of yelps like barking puppies. Without warning, Dalala turned, leapt toward the dancers, and shouted, "They are already beaten."

At this signal, the dancers tossed boughs of green pine on the fire, thus smothering the flames and causing thick clouds of smoke to billow and render everyone nearly invisible. By such means, the players concealed themselves from the magic of Santee conjurors who had likewise cast spells to make the Cherokee ill or perhaps die, just as the Chota medicine men had done to their opponents.

The Santee arrived at the town early the next morning, yet the Cherokee team and their Seneca relatives were nowhere to be seen. Dressed in their everyday clothes accompanied by their conjurors and conjurors' helpers, they had left Chota at sunrise and had started in a roundabout way for the ball field. Four times, they stopped and went to water, submerging and washing themselves each time in the river, and for the first three times, the medicine men performed protective rituals over each man. They warned him not to sit on a stone or fallen tree but only on the earth itself, and no one must lean on anything except another man's back. If a man failed to do these things, his team would lose to the Santee or a rattlesnake would bite him.

Before going to water the fourth time, the players paused, and the chief priest uttered in a rapid, staccato style, "The signs favor victory. Play with all your effort. Play with all your skill. Chota will give you praise."

The men immersed themselves in the river for a fourth time and then headed for the ball ground. As they drew near, the Woodpecker, Dalala, went before them and uttered four yells, the final one a long quavering whoop like that on the previous night. The Seneca and Cherokee responded with a loud shout and suddenly left the trail and sought a secret place to complete their preparations. There the chief conjuror marked off a small plot to resemble the ball field. Next he pulled from a bundle twelve sharpened stakes, each a foot long, and stuck them in the plot to show the men their positions when the game started.

And now the final part of the ritual commenced—the ordeal of scratching. The men stripped themselves so that they wore only loincloths. In his hair, each wore an eagle feather for keen sight, a deer's tail for swiftness of foot, and a snake's rattle to strike fear in the Santee. They had painted their skin red and black—black from the charred embers of a honey locust struck by lightning yet remaining alive. A shaman's apprentice now came forward, bringing the kanuga, a large sharpened comb. The conjurors had fashioned it from long leg-bone splints of the wild turkey, the fierce bird of war. The splints formed the comb's teeth and were bound together in a frame, with the sharpened ends of the bones jutting through one end.

Four times the conjurors' helpers scratched each man's upper arms from shoulder to elbow, and four times they scratched each one's lower arm from wrist to elbow. Then the helpers scratched each man four times above the knee and four times below. And after that, they made an X across each one's chest and joined the upper legs of the X with a long horizontal mark across the top of the chest, and they scratched the same figure across the back from shoulder to shoulder. With the ordeal completed, the bloody marks numbered three hundred on every player.

Then the chief shaman came forward and gave the men a root to chew, and they spat its juice into their wounds and massaged it in. Once they had rubbed it over their bodies, they went to water again and washed themselves to remove the blood. They then oiled themselves with bear grease to be able to slip away more easily from their rivals when the game commenced.

For the last time, the players went to water. They entered at a bend in the river so that they could look upstream toward the east. Gazing down into the stream and holding their ball sticks across their chests, they stood in a row, side by side. Behind them stood the head shaman. A helper laid one cloth of red and one of black along the bank, and he put twelve beads of red on the red cloth and twelve beads of black on the black cloth. Each red bead signified a Cherokee ball player, and each black bead a Santee opponent. The priest then grasped a red bead in his right palm and a black one in his left. Raising these aloft, he praised Long Man, the river, he who could hurl huge logs in his foaming current.

The shaman looked at the first player and then prayed to the river, "Give this man the power to toss the Santee about as you toss about the trees." He prayed the same prayer for each.

Next the priest called up the red animal spirits of victory and prayed that they grant the powers that they possessed in the greatest abundance. He prayed that each man in his turn receive a gift.

To the Red Bat, he prayed, "Let this man dart about as you dart through the night."

To the Red Deer, he called, "Let this man run with your swiftness over the field."

To the Red Hawk, he appealed, "Let this man have your keen vision."

To the Red Rattlesnake, he beseeched, "Let this man be terrible as you are terrible."

And so the shaman continued until each player received his gifts from the red spirits. Then he called upon the swift creatures of flight to grant their speed—to the dragonfly, to the wood pewee, to the great hawk, to the martin, and to the crested flycatcher.

"Now they are coming to join their spirits to you," said the shaman.

As soon as he had spoken these words, he lifted each man to the seventh heaven, where the gods dwell, so that the Cherokee and Seneca might meet with the utmost success in the ball games.

Once the priest had raised the players to the heights, he asked each who was his most hated rival, and all whispered to him in turn, "the Santee."

Now the shaman laid a curse of great medicine upon each of the Santee ball players so as to cast them beneath the earth. He first invoked the Black Fog and then the Black Rattlesnake. Lastly, he prayed to the most powerful, the Black Spider. For each black bead, he called to the Black Spider, "Let your black thread descend, and let it spin round the soul of each Santee. Once he is wrapped in your thread, drag his soul to the west. Put it in a coffin of black, and there in the Darkening Land, bury it beneath black clay."

When the conjuror had completed his curse, the Cherokee and their Seneca brothers shouted, for they knew that the medicine of the priest would carry them to victory just as surely as the Long Man sweeps uprooted trees along his flooded path.

By now, it was midday. The men formed a single file and went toward the ball field. Hundreds of spectators from Chota and neighboring Cherokee towns stood round as did the attending guests from the Santee country. The game would be played on a stretch of cleared bottomland along the Little Tennessee. The field was about one hundred yards long, and at each end were goal posts three yards apart at the base but wider at the top where a crosspiece rested upon two forks. The teams would try to toss the ball through the goals or hit one of its posts to score a point, and the side that first scored twelve points would win.

As was the custom, the opponents furnished the ball. Its surface was of scraped deerskin, moistened to make it dry hard when stuffed with deer and squirrel hair and tightly sewn together with deer sinews. Since the Santee had challenged the Cherokee, the host team examined the ball closely. They did not want the ball to be so small as to slip through the webbing of their racquets.

The ball passed muster. Now the wagers began, with both spectators and players betting as to who would win the game. Both sides laid heavy bets, with the Santee staking two expensive robes along with personal ornaments. Some of the Cherokee removed their clothes and bet these.

With the wagers made, the teams marched onto the field, all the while yelling and whooping, as they formed two lines of twelve facing each other from opposite ends. All laid their sticks on the ground and pointed them toward the other side to ensure both were evenly matched. An ancient Cherokee, whose title was Beloved, came forward and stood between the teams and began to speak.

"Remember that the Apportioner, the Sun, she who divides day and night, looks down upon you. She sees all that we do. Follow the rules and break none. After the game, those who win and those who lose must travel the white trail that ever ends at the white house of peace."

Then the old man shouted, "Now for the twelve," and he tossed the ball high into the air, the signal for the game to begin.

At once, there was a clatter as the players scrambled for their sticks, each eager to take possession of the ball. One of the Santee got the ball in his basket, spun around with his stick for greater impetus, and hurled the ball toward the goal as another Santee raced down the field and threw it between the poles for a point. The Beloved Old Man returned the ball to the center, tossed the ball into the air, and the game began anew. The players bumped and jostled one another, and no one on either team worked together. Everyone played for individual glory.

From one end of the field to the other, the match shifted to and fro. The Santee were close to winning when one of their men and a Cherokee became entangled—arms, legs, and sticks—and fell to the ground where they began to roll around and fight, kicking and choking each other. From the sides of the ball field, Santee and Cherokee drivers quickly ran toward them. With long hickory switches, the drivers whipped the two players until they separated and returned to the game. At one point, a man on the Cherokee side dropped his stick and tried to score a point by running with the ball in his mouth, but the drivers stopped him, returned his stick, and forced him to follow the rules of the game. After a short time, the Santee won. For the most part, the teams played fairly, and no one was so unmanly as to lose his temper to any great degree.

After the first match, the Seneca said, "Now let us play the Santee."

Each side made heavy wagers once more, some staking their clothes and others betting many of the fine ornaments they wore. The game began. After some running up and down the field, a Seneca scored the first point. Within the space of an hour, the Seneca had made all twelve of the points and beaten the Santee.

The Santee proposed a third game to reclaim their lost wagers, and the stakes were even higher, with some on both sides who had lost their clothes and various precious objects now betting their very selves so that they would become the slaves of whichever team might win. Everyone was laughing and having a good time. The Seneca won the third match.

Throughout the ball play, the conjurors of both sides had removed themselves to secluded areas and continued to work their magic to ensure victory for their side. Receiving advice from seven councilors, who were wise in the skill of ball play, the helper of the chief priest of the Cherokee watched the matches and told him from time to time how the games progressed. Depending upon the news, the shaman adjusted his conjurations to affect the outcome. Because the Seneca defeated the Santee in each match, the priest of the Cherokee seemed to have the stronger medicine.

None of the players drank any water throughout the ball play. Yet all could drink the sour liquid crushed from the juice of scuppernongs, wild crabapples, and other plants.

After their last defeat at ball play, the Santee leader proposed to the victors, "Instead of ball play, let us have a foot race. The track is very level here, and the space is wide. We will pick our runner, and you pick yours."

So each side selected a runner, and the Cherokee chose one of the Seneca. The first race would be a trial run, and no one would bet, everyone agreeing to make wagers on the second race. The two runners ran the first race. As they neared the post, the Santee crossed five and a half feet, his body length, ahead of the Seneca.

Afterwards, Ga'na and his people asked their runner whether he had given his best. He answered so that only they could hear, "No, I did not."

Everyone began to make bets for the second race, the one that counted. At the signal of the Beloved Old Man, it began. The two men were neck and neck. As they approached the middle of the course, the Seneca said to the Santee runner, "Try your hardest, and I will try mine." As soon as he said these words, he spurted ahead, leaving the Santee far behind, and won the race.

Not to be outdone, the Santee said to the Cherokee and their Seneca brothers, "There is yet another race to run—the long race. Let us make it twice as far as the first two. We will run from one goal to the other and back."

The Fire King and Ga'na agreed to the long race, but when they were apart and among themselves, so that the Santee could not hear them, the Uka said to Ga'na, "Our side has won everything from the Santee. We would be wise to give them one race, for if they lose all they have, even to their freedom, they may cause trouble. This way, their wagers can redeem their kindred."

Ga'na agreed with this thinking. So the two leaders selected a Cherokee runner not as fast as the Seneca who had won before. The race began, and the Cherokee made a good race at the beginning, but the Santee runner handily won at the end by two lengths of his height.

Now that the ball play and races had ended, the athletes went to water, and they bathed themselves in the river to wash away the blood and the dust. They put on their clothes, and the people brought food, and the men of both teams ate for the first time since the night before. After the meal, the Santee returned the next day to their country near the great salt water.

After a few days had passed, they sent a message to the Cherokee, and the message challenged them to meet in battle at a halfway point between the two sides. The council of Chota debated and accepted the challenge.

Before the council had ended, however, the Cherokee turned to their brother Ga'na and the other men of the Seneca and said, "There are too few of you here. We do not want any of you to die in this fight. We think you should go back to your country in the north." So Ga'na and his warriors returned to their own land.

The council had determined that Kalanu, the Raven, would lead the war party. As they had prepared for the ball play, so the people of Chota now prepared for war. The Raven went to his asi, and at the low winter house, he planted a war pole with a red flag streaked with large strokes of black announcing the conflict of blood and death. He then marched around the asi three times while he made the war whoop and beat a drum as volunteers answered to these sounds. They brought with them a small bag of wissactaw or parched corn beaten into meal as nourishment for the campaign. This they would mix with water to sustain them on the warpath, and no other food did they take.

To the gathering crowd, the Raven rapidly spoke in a commanding voice between short pauses. "The Santee came as our guests. We fed them. Now they call for war with the Cherokee. The white path has become the red path, and it will flow with their blood."

The next day, the warriors began to drink the warm black tea, and they drank for three nights and three days to purify themselves and to protect them from harm. No other nourishment did they take until after sunset, and only after sunset could they sit. Throughout this time, they avoided all contact with the women and so denied themselves to ensure the success of the war. The older warriors watched the younger ones so that no one might break the taboos and bring them into danger, and the older men told the younger men stories of great deeds during wars past so that they might be encouraged. All the warriors sang their death songs and danced.

When the purification and fasting had ended, the men painted themselves red and black to signify war and death. One-half of their faces, they painted red, and one-half they painted black. They painted large white circles around their eyes. The warriors painted their bodies various colors as well, and they mixed with the moist paint on their bodies the down of feathers and the clipped fur of different beasts so that the fur and feathers remained fastened to their skin. When the men had finished, they could not be recognized by their enemies and were almost unknown to one another, and all seemed like demons who had taken bodily form.

On leaving the settlement, the war party fired their weapons, shouted war whoops, and sang war songs. The Raven went before them and carried on his back a small medicine chest of great power in war. It measured a foot and a half on all sides and contained sacred objects and vessels that the old women had made. The warriors followed the Raven in a single column, each man three or four steps one after another. As the Raven led the procession out of the town, he sang a song used only for the occasion to strengthen their hearts for battle:

> Where shines the sun by day
> Or glows the moon by night,
> Where grows the grass
> Or waters flow,
> Let all men know
> We travel far
> And bring the curse of war.

We go to find
Our nation's foes,
Who woman-like
Shall flee our blows.
They are like women,
Who see the shining scales
Of writhing snakes
In thick canebrakes,
And jumping back,
They stare and quake
In wild-eyed fear,
Then, panting, breathless fly.

Like trembling deer,
Our foes will run
And throw their weapons down.
Through thickets they will crash,
At every turn
Torn by sharp thorns
Until they reach their town,
Its shame and scorn.
When winter's winds
And snows shall come
And barren woods
Deny them food,
They'll sit and weep
And in their tears
Wish war had never come.

And as a sign
That we were there,
We'll leave war clubs
Upon their earth,
And, if they dare
Come back to us,
Their painted scalps,
Hung from our poles
Shall tell our name
As signs of Chota's fame.
If any of our foes we spare,
We bring them home
To torture there
With slow and fiery death.

No one can tell
When life will end,
For with each day
New dangers come.
And so to little ones,
We say, "Goodbye."

We say, "Goodbye"
To wives and friends.
Cry not for us.
We love our lives.
And, if our quest
Ends not in death,
We shall return again.

But, if we fall,
Let Chota vengeance bring,
And with the tomahawk
Spill blood for blood
So that our spirits rest.
And on some nearby tree,
Signal with bloody paint
The red sign to our foes
You brought them death.

As soon as the warriors were out of sight of the town, they ceased their song and in silence entered the solemn woods. With eyes as sharp as an eagle or a lynx, the men looked for signs of danger everywhere, and they walked with the care of a panther in stalking its prey.

They traveled lightly, dressed only in loincloths and moccasins. Their packs held only an old blanket, a small pouch of corn meal, a wooden cup, and pieces of leather and strands of cord to mend their moccasins. Bows and arrows were the chief weapons because of their silence, but in their belts they carried hatchets or knives, although some had brought small war clubs carved from dense wood. One or two had rusty swords obtained from the white traders, and a few carried muskets, although these were too noisy for surprise raids.

While on the move, they looked for ill omens. If any evil dream should come at night to disturb the sleep of a warrior and suggest that the battle might end in a death or defeat, he could return to Chota, and no one would question his decision. If the small wagtail or pipit, known to the open fields and the coasts but rare to the woodlands, should chirp its ill-omened oracle near the war camp, the men might grow faint in their purpose, disband, and go home.

The warriors also observed all the required rituals for success. The Raven had selected one member of the troop to be the waiter to him and the rest. None of them would consume anything unless served from the hand of the waiter at designated times, and then they ate and drank very little. Neither would any lean against a tree, whether he stood or sat, nor would he sit directly upon the ground but only on rocks and logs. The same held true for the medicine bundle. The Raven never set it upon the earth but placed it always upon a platform of stone or wood. And no one could touch the sacred bundle except the Raven and the waiter. Throughout their journey to the Santee, the men did these things to obtain the good will of heaven for victory in battle and a safe return to their families.

Three years passed, and the Ga'na and the Seneca returned to visit their Cherokee relatives. The Fire King told him and his warriors that the Raven and the Cherokee had lost their battle with the Santee.

The Uka then said to Ga'na, "The Raven tells us that the enemy chief wants to fight the Seneca, for their chief says that he is a double man."

Not long after, the Santee learned that the Seneca had come to visit, and they sent a messenger to challenge them to a battle.

Ga'na replied, "We must answer their challenge."

So to satisfy the Santee, Ga'na and his men, once they had purified and prepared themselves, set forth for the land of the Santee. Led by Cherokee guides, they traveled across rivers and through forests until they came to a clearing in the woods and halted. They were one day's distance from the first Santee settlement.

Ga'na said to the Cherokee, "We will send two messengers to tell the enemy that we are here."

But the guides answered Ga'na by saying "Send your messengers, but have them remove the paint from their faces and send them so that they arrive at the village near sundown when the light will soon fade. That way, your men can surprise the Santee."

Ga'na had the messengers do as the guides had said. When the two Seneca came close to the town, they remained concealed along the line of trees and saw the people outside playing on the ball field. The men went to the other side of the area and drew closer. As they approached some of the Santee, the Seneca began throwing darts. These were larger than arrows and tipped with buffalo horn, and the men threw the darts as if they played a game to see who could cast them the farthest. In this manner, the two got closer to the Santee who paid little heed and thought the Seneca were from their own village.

When the warriors were near enough, they aimed their darts at one of the enemy who was standing by himself and killed him. Before the others were aware, they scalped him quickly, working so fast that they removed the top of the skull with the skin and hair. Then springing up and giving the scalp yell as their message, the Seneca raised the war trophy.

Darting into the woods, they rushed back in the direction of their friends, all the while saying to each other, "Be strong! Be strong!"

In the meantime, some of the Santee had gathered their horses and given chase. The Seneca, though, had come to a dry stream. There they saw a washed-out hollow place underneath the bank over which hung tree roots. The two hid within, and their enemies passed by without seeing them.

They stayed beneath the bank all night, and with the first gray streaks of dawn, they headed toward a secret place where Ga'na and their comrades had arranged to wait for their return. The Santee, though, had been out all the while, mounted and still searching. The two Seneca warriors soon saw behind them dust rising from the hooves of the enemy's horses.

As the distance narrowed rapidly, the Santee began shooting arrows, but by now the Seneca had entered the woods where there was a clearing. Ga'na and his warriors lay hidden on either side of the opening. As the Santee rushed in pursuit, Ga'na blew his war whistle. His warriors sounded their shrill death cries and attacked from each side, first firing their guns and bows or throwing swift darts with great accuracy. They then dashed into the clearing and with sure blows tomahawked their foes, leaving them dead or disabled. By the end of the battle, Ga'na and his men had killed or captured all of their opponents.

The Seneca hurriedly scalped and dismembered the dead. Because of the distance back to Chota, they did not take time to cut off arms or legs, for these would be too heavy to carry. Yet, in order to return home with war trophies, some removed the noses and ears of the enemy, while others knocked out their teeth.

The Seneca immediately departed for the mountains. When they arrived in Chota, the people tormented those who had been taken captive with fire until they died. The Seneca then fasted for three days under the direction of their war priest Ga'na and thus purified themselves for spilling human blood. When a month had passed, they returned to their own country.

The Fire King later sent a message to his northern brothers and told them, "The people near the great salt water believe that the Seneca are dangerous. Yet, even though the enemy's conjurors are powerful and can foretell another's actions, they cannot say what you will do. For the medicine of Ga'na and his men is mightier than theirs."

THE MOHAWK WARRIORS

Before and after the arrival of the European colonists, the Indians of eastern North America often pursued war for the sake of vengeance. Anyone who killed another had to be killed—a life for a life. Spilled blood cried out for spilled blood, and only blood could quench the crying blood of the dead. If not revenged, the ghosts of slain relatives or fellow tribe members would haunt the living. Yet, once vengeance was exacted, the spirits became satisfied and flew away.

To revenge the dead, warriors would endure extremes of heat and cold and of hunger and thirst. They might travel as far as a thousand miles through pathless woods and dismal swamps, over hills and mountains, across swift-flowing rivers, wide lakes, and deep gorges. Distance, starvation, and the dangers of travel did not matter as long as there was a skirmish with the enemy. The aim was to scalp or murder, often slashing and mutilating dead foes. If the killing occurred near the homeland of the warriors seeking retaliation, they would dismember arms, legs, and other body parts and carry these back as evidence that the enemy had been punished and revenge obtained. Although the size of the war parties varied, they usually numbered between twenty and forty members, but they could be as small as two or three. Ever cautious, when they set out, they were always on the lookout for enemies and moved as stealthily as wild cats or panthers in seeking their prey. If an enemy were captured, what often awaited him were the indescribable horrors and torments of being tortured and burned alive.

The Cherokee were no different in these matters than any other tribe. In answer to calls for peace with the Tuscarora of eastern North Carolina with whom they fought in the early eighteenth century, they reportedly responded, "We cannot live without war. Should we make peace with the Tuscarora with whom we are at war, we must look for some other with whom we can engage in our beloved occupation."

Once in 1747, seeking revenge for slain relatives, two Mohawk warriors came from the north to the Lower Cherokee towns in upper South Carolina where Oconee and Pickens counties now are. Throughout the spring and summer of that year, before being discovered, the warriors ambushed and killed over twenty Cherokee in various episodes throughout the area. The two possessed a thorough knowledge of the terrain and were so long-winded that they could run swiftly for great distances in order to escape if they killed or scalped anyone. They would hide in the nearby mountains and run over rocky ridges, sometimes backwards, to conceal their tracks. One time, when a large party of Cherokee chased them, the warriors ran around a steep hill near the headwaters of a branch of the Savannah River and lay in wait for their pursuers. When most of the Cherokee had passed by them, the Mohawks ambushed, killed, and scalped several in the rear of the company. They then eluded the Cherokee and hid near the main town of Keowee, where the Cherokee lived who had been in pursuit. The Mohawk warriors were such clever enemies that the Cherokee began to think that they were wizards. Baffling their foes and striking fear in their hearts, they lived for four months off whatever game they could catch and whatever other food they could obtain in the wild.

Having revenged their relatives and signaled their prowess as warriors by killing many and taking a large number of scalps, the two now decided to kidnap one of the Cherokee from Keowee and return home with their captive as undeniable proof that they had made war upon their enemies. The Mohawk warriors approached the town with the usual caution required for such occasions. One crawled along the ground for about a hundred yards to keep himself concealed. The other moved quickly from tree to tree, sharply looking in every direction to make certain that no one saw him.

In the evening, however, while there was still light, one of the old men of Keowee who had been honored with the title of Beloved glimpsed the Mohawks from his perch on the top of a nearby hill overlooking the town. From his vantage point, he could see by the cut of their hair, closely trimmed for running, and by the way they behaved, attempting to conceal themselves, that they must be the warriors who had caused so much misery to his people. He immediately left and entered the village, where he stopped at the first house that he came to, the home of one of the white traders who lived there. He told the man of the two warriors lurking just across the Keowee River on the outskirts of the town. He asked the trader to tell no one as yet, until a party could be formed to track the enemy and have a better chance of killing or capturing them.

Supposedly neutral, the traders were enemies neither of the Cherokee nor the Mohawk nation but conducted business with both. Therefore, this trader should have said nothing, but he informed the headmen of the town what the old man had told him. They then told the youth of Keowee to go about their normal activities, making the usual noises that were part of their evening routines. That way, the Mohawk warriors would think that the Cherokee suspected nothing of danger. The headmen then instructed runners to leave in secret for nearby towns and request help in capturing the enemy. The runners departed, and warriors from other Cherokee towns soon arrived as silently as ghosts. Meanwhile, the people of Keowee appeared to be about their business as though nothing out of the ordinary were occurring.

Unknown to the Mohawk warriors, the Cherokee war party formed a large semicircle near the place where they believed their enemies had hidden and advanced toward them. During this operation, the tips of the formation moved forward with greater speed than the rest and gradually enclosed the Mohawks, tightening around them like a noose. At last the Cherokee found the two men lying beneath the tops of some small pine trees that had fallen where they had attempted to conceal themselves. The troop sounded the war cry. The Mohawks jumped to their feet and echoed the cry. However, because of the closeness of their surroundings, they could make no defense with their firearms and resolved to kill or be killed in hand-to-hand fighting. One of the Cherokee braves, a young man noted for his courage and strength, immediately set upon them but was knocked down, his sword taken, and he almost killed with his own blade. Yet, superior numbers ruled the day, with the Mohawks being captured and knowing full-well what awaited them, having done the same to their own prisoners of war.

The Cherokee entered Keowee in single file, each warrior following a few yards behind the one before, whooping and firing their muskets, all the while insulting the captives. That night, the war party camped near the town within a large square plot of ground designed for such purposes. In the middle of the square stood tall war-poles or stakes, where they secured their prisoners. On rising the next morning, the company went to the dwelling of the king of Keowee and gathered in the front around his red-painted war-pole. Here they determined their captives' fate. They decreed that the Mohawks should suffer the usual punishment of death by fire. The Cherokee then took the two back to the square beyond the town. Their only hope of salvation lay in a reprieve that might be granted by one of the Ghighau or War Women of the Cherokee. These Beloved Women, sometimes called Pretty Women, possessed such power that, with no more than the wave of a swan's wing, they could save a victim even though he had already been bound to the stake to be burned. Yet no pardon was forthcoming for the Mohawks.

Knowing the torments that awaited him, the younger warrior, upon seeing one of the white traders among the gathered crowd, spoke to the man in English and earnestly pled with him to intervene and save their lives. The elder warrior immediately spoke to the younger in his own language, telling him to stop, whereupon the young man calmed himself, becoming quiet and appearing unconcerned as to whether he lived or died. Soon thereafter the white traders left the scene as was their custom, for they did not have the authority to save the victims' lives.

And now began the gruesome work. The captors first stripped the Mohawks naked and put on their feet a pair of moccasins made of bearskin with the hairy part on the outside. Then they bound the warriors' arms behind their backs. At the top of two tall and heavy stakes were affixed strong ropes of braided grapevine with the other ends knotted into a noose to secure the prisoners' necks. Also tied to the top of each pole was a torch just beyond the reach of their heads.

The women now took complete charge of the ceremony, which they eagerly conducted before the gazing spectators. As the two were led to the stakes, the women began to chant in joy as they beat the men with long bundles of dry cane or sticks full of pine fat. At this point, it would have been an act of mercy to dispatch the captives by sinking a tomahawk into their heads. Yet no such kindness occurred as the grapevine nooses were tightened round their necks. The ropes measured approximately fifteen yards each, allowing that much distance for the men to circle each pole. The women then placed tough caps of wet clay on each man's head to prevent any flame from singeing his hair or setting it on fire. Throughout these preparations, the onlookers hooted in delight and mocked the Mohawks, who sang their war songs in a manner that insulted their captors, telling them that they would suffer a similar revenge when opportunity presented itself.

The women next filled the circle and set upon the prisoners with burning brands as each stood beside his stake. Suddenly, the two rushed forward toward the outskirts of the circle, and like maddened, savage beasts of prey, extended the grapevine ropes until they were taut, enabling the Mohawks to sweep around the circumference as they pulled down their tormentors, while at the same time biting, kicking, and trampling them with the utmost ferocity, all to no avail.

The crowd quickly surrounded the captives and again attacked them with fire, forcing the warriors to run to their stakes for safety. Yet retreat was useless, for the women followed closely behind burning them all the while. Once more the warriors ran to the outer edge and cleared the circle of the women. This pattern repeated itself time and again until the flames had burned the victims' tender parts and they fell exhausted, halting the spectacle. To revive them, the women took cool water and poured it over each man, allowing him to recover sufficiently so that the ritual could begin anew.

Finally insensible to pain, both at last collapsed. At this point, they were scalped, the procedure taking no more than two minutes. Two Cherokee warriors stepped forward, each seizing the head of a disabled Mohawk and placing a foot on his neck. Then with one hand, they twisted the hair and pulled it as far out as possible, while with the other they used a sharp knife and cut cleanly around the top of the skull. With a few quick scoops of the blade, off came the trophy of war. As a final act, the Cherokee dismembered the bodies of the Mohawks and sliced off their arms, legs, ears, noses, and private parts to display around the town.

As to the scalps, to prevent them from rotting, the Cherokee stretched them over a hoop five to six inches wide and painted the underside a bright red to signify the shedding of enemy blood. After letting the scalps cure in this manner, the victors cut them into strips, attached them to small branches of green-needled pine, and placed them atop the conical winter huts of their fellow tribe members whom the Mohawks had killed during their depredations in the vicinity of the Lower settlements.

During this ceremony, the women chanted softly, singing a grateful song of triumph to the Creator, Yohewah, while the warriors echoed their rejoicing. For days and nights, all danced, in movements like those of a wild cat that cunningly stalks its prey, their minds happily at peace that their fallen dead would haunt the eaves of their houses no more. Only now did the Cherokee consider their slain relatives properly revenged so that their ghosts might depart for rest. After a proper interval had passed, their spirits would return to live forever in the lands they loved best.

THE FALSE WARRIORS

Chilhowee was one of the major settlements among the Overhill Cherokee and lay along the more western reaches of Little Tennessee River opposite its confluence with Abrams Creek. The Great Smoky Mountains were to its northeast, and the Unicoi Mountains were to its south. Neighboring villages were Settico and Tallasee.

Having 110 warriors at its disposal, Chilhowee was third in military importance among the Overhill towns, which often leaned toward the French in their struggle with the British for dominance in North America during the mid–1700s. In fact, the Overhill Cherokee at one point considered relocating their settlements to be closer to where the Little Tennessee enters the larger Tennessee River so that vessels from the French in Louisiana could more readily reach them for trade.

Conflicts sometimes developed between the inhabitants of the Overhill settlements and those of the Middle towns, which were located to the south and east also along the Little Tennessee. The people there spoke a different dialect and tended to be more disposed to trade with the British and to support their colonies of Virginia, the Carolinas, and Georgia.

The Cherokee town of Cowee or Kawi-yi, shortened to Kawi, may mean "the place of the Deer clan." It was an important Middle settlement, one of the oldest and largest, and was located where Cowee Creek enters the Little Tennessee about ten miles down the river from the present city of Franklin, North Carolina. At the beginning of the American Revolution in 1776, the town had more than a hundred houses.

After the northern Indians, the Shawnee or Shawano, had made peace with the Cherokee, one of their warriors, who had once been held as a captive in Cowee, returned there and from a hill called out to some of its inhabitants who stood on another hill nearby, "Is Cowee still yours?"

The people called back to him, "Yes, it is still ours."

In response, he shouted, "Hold on to it for as long as you can. It is the best town you have and is in a good country."

In the eighteenth century, when the Cherokee still warred with the Shawano, some of the men of Chilhowee pretended to form a war party to fight against them and to head north where they lived along the Ohio and Cumberland Rivers. Like members of the Iroquois League, the Shawano had long been traditional enemies of the Cherokee. So the Chilhowee warriors started along a leg of the Great Indian War Path that led toward the Cumberland Gap and from there to the lands of the Shawano. When the company got to the Tennessee River, the warriors headed northeast and followed it until they came to the French Broad and traveled along its course until they reached the confluence of the Pigeon River. At that point, they changed their direction. Instead of continuing toward the Shawano country, as the Chilhowee men had claimed were their intentions, they headed east through the valley of the Pigeon so as to approach the town of Cowee from the north.

When the war party got close, the men hid along a path leading into the settlement. They waited until a small group of three or four of its inhabitants came along the trail. The warriors immediately jumped out and killed and scalped the unsuspecting villagers. The attackers also took a gun that one of the victims had been carrying. His name was Gunskali-ski. Taking the same trail by which they had come, they hurriedly returned to Chilhowee. There they displayed the gun and the scalps and boasted that they had not lost a single man in capturing these trophies from their victory over their Shawano foes to the north.

After the war party had arrived home, Chilhowee made the customary preparations for a great scalp dance to celebrate the defeat of the Shawano. Everyone gathered in the townhouse, and the wives and sweethearts of the men brought into its dimly lit rotunda the scalps recently taken. The women carried these attached to poles, each scalp's fleshy side now painted a bright vermillion and stretched over a small hoop for display. As the drummer drummed, the people sang, and when they paused, one of the warriors would rise from his seat and give the drummer a phrase of a few well-chosen words that summarized his exploits. The drummer then improvised a song recounting the man's deeds, and the two sang together.

During the festivities, one of the onlookers was a gunsmith from Cowee. He was a gunstocker and highly esteemed. The stocks of rifles often broke because they were made of wood and consequently were the weakest of the three basic parts of the lock, stock, and barrel. The Cherokee called him Gulsadihi. He had learned the trade of repairing, carving, and decorating gun stocks and was very skilled at his craft. Seeing the captured gun, he could not help but notice that it was one that he had repaired for the now dead Gunskali-ski back home in Cowee. Though the gunstocker kept his thoughts to himself, he was curious as to how Shawano enemy warriors had come to possess it.

The dance ended that night, but another one was set to take place in seven days to allow the rest of the warriors an opportunity to boast of their deeds, as was the custom. In the meantime, Gulsadihi the gunstocker had gone back to Cowee and to his Cherokee wife. He had been away when the Chilhowee warriors had made their attack under the pretense of being a raiding party against the Shawano. When he arrived home, he heard about the recent raid and the killing and scalping. The people of Cowee believed that the Shawano had attacked them. He also heard about the gun that they thought the Shawano had stolen.

Gulsadihi now began to piece together what had really happened. So he went to the headman of Cowee. Gulsadihi related what he had seen at the scalp dance in the Overhill settlement of Chilhowee.

The chief could hardly believe his ears and said, "Such a false deed is not possible."

Gulsadihi replied, "The gun I saw is the one that I repaired for our warrior who was killed and scalped. I am sure it is his."

Finally the chief was convinced that the men of Chilhowee were guilty of the treacherous attack and called together the men and women of Cowee for a council. He convinced them of the truth of what had occurred, and everyone clamored for revenge.

The plan was to send ten of their best fighting men to the upcoming scalp dance in Chilhowee. Gulsadihi would lead them in taking revenge for the crime. Many men volunteered to go, but Gulsadihi selected the ten he thought were the best. The war party set out so as to arrive close to the time when the dance would begin. As they neared the town that night, they had to ford a stream. There they met a pregnant woman walking down to it to get water, and their first act of vengeance was to split her head with a tomahawk before she could sound an alarm. The woman died instantly from the silent, swift blow, and they left her body in the water.

The Cowee men moved closer. From their place of concealment, they could see the people of Chilhowee—men, women, and children—all going to their townhouse. So the warriors bided their time and remained hidden.

As with the former dance, a warrior would recite in song some action that he had performed during the raid. He would whisper a few words to the drummer, who would then pause momentarily and then resume his drumming as he sang along with the man. Usually the recitation was a serious matter, and the participants would often anoint themselves with new war names. Once in a while, though, a man would make a joke and exaggerate his accomplishments to such a ridiculous extent that the audience would start to laugh at its improbability.

The Chilhowee warriors who had not recounted their deeds at the previous dance now took their turns in singing as one by one they stepped into the circle of firelight in the center of the council house. Toward the end of the dance, one of the men left his seat and whispered to the drummer what he had done to the enemy. The drummer, who had been one of the war party, now sang about the raid on Cowee—the people slain, the scalps, and the gun.

All the while, the warrior carried the stolen gun as he sang with the drummer and pantomimed the events throughout the performance. These antics caused the chief of Chilhowee and his people to cackle with laughter. They had no idea as to what had really occurred. They thought everything was a big joke.

For they believed the war party had attacked their enemies, the Shawano, not another Cherokee town.

During all this time, the gunstocker and the other men from Cowee had been waiting outside the townhouse. When the festivities within had reached a fever pitch, he stripped himself of his breechcloth, scrambled through the low door, and ran inside naked. No one recognized him in the smoke-filled, dim light and thought he was part of the celebration.

Stepping up double-quick to the treacherous drummer, Gulsadihi bent down and whispered the words of his war deeds. He then straightened up and loudly sang as he began to dance.

"Hi! Who did this?"

The drummer beat rapidly, so the song was fast. Round the floor of the rotunda Gulsadihi went, cavorting and making insulting signs to all present. After he circled a second time, he again leaned over the drummer and whispered, and again he straightened up, this time singing, "Yu! I just killed a woman and her unborn child. Her body lies in the stream below."

At these words, some warriors looked uneasily at one another, but the Chilhowee headman said, "It is a joke. Enjoy the dance."

The drummer beat more fiercely than before. Gulsadihi circled another round, whispered again, and sang louder still, "Our foes live in the north! Yet they are here within!"

The drummer now knew exactly what he meant and drummed more slowly. Everyone watching grew restless. Breaking the beat of the drummer, Gulsadihi no longer sang but suddenly cried out, "Cowee will give you a ball play."

All of Chilhowee knew that these words meant war. The audience paused, and Gulsadihi in a loud voice said, "But we are ready to fight you now and die here."

As the people murmured among themselves, Gulsadihi left the council house before anyone could move. The dancers uneasily glanced at one another, and some stood up to leave. The chief was still unaware of what his warriors had done and urged them to continue the dance, but his words were useless. The men left the council house. Outside they saw the Cowee war party. Everyone was armed with guns and tomahawks, but neither group said a word or did anything to provoke a fight. Each side, though, knew the grim contest that would come.

Gulsadihi and his men left. When they arrived home, they gathered a large party of warriors from Cowee and all of the Middle towns. They intended to take vengeance on Chilhowee and Kituwa or the Mulberry Place, a town at Clingmans Dome, for it, too, had participated in the attack. Only the blood of those places, a life for a life, would satisfy the spirits of the dead and give them peace.

The warriors from Cowee and the other Middle towns headed down the river toward their enemies and passed through the mountains. Yet when they got to the Overhill territory around Chilhowee, there was a strange silence, for the people had abandoned the settlement. Every house was empty. All had taken flight for more remote villages in the mountains or sought refuge to the north among their foes, the Shawano.

JOCASSEE

In northwestern South Carolina, the Keowee and Jocassee Rivers once flowed without interruption through their respective valleys. Here, on the eastern side of the Blue Ridge escarpment, the clans of the Lower Cherokee of the eighteenth century had many settlements. Among them were Toxaway, Eastatoee or Estatoe, Tomassee, Tugaloo, Oconee, Seneca, Coonasastchee or Sugar Town, Brass Town, and Keowee, the principal town. There were also numerous smaller villages. Today the valleys of the Keowee and Jocassee are covered by two lakes named after the same streams. Both bodies of water are situated between Pickens and Oconee Counties. The lower, Lake Keowee, was created in 1971, and the upper, Lake Jocassee, in 1973. They are part of Duke Energy's Keowee-Toxaway complex for generating electric power.

Centuries before the lakes were completed, however, two rival clans of the Cherokee lived on the banks of the Keowee. The Eastatoees, whose totem was the green bird or Carolina parrot, occupied the east bank, now part of Pickens County. The Oconees lived on the west side, where Oconee County is today. Their emblem was the brown viper.

The cause of the rivalry was many years old and supposedly dated to an indeterminate time when Chatuga, a leader of the Oconees, lost his bid to become supreme chief of all the Cherokee—that is, the people of the Overhill, the Middle and Valley, and the Lower settlements. Instead of Chatuga, the nation chose Toxaway, a mighty warrior and the war chief of the Eastatoees.

As a result of his failed election, Chatuga's bitterness knew no end, and he fomented resentment within his own clan against his neighbors. In war, he said they were women, and in all other daily doings, he called them dogs and devils. Although the clans did not resort to full-scale war with each other, a cold and sometimes turbulent peace prevailed between them, and both sides took care not to purposely trespass into the territory of the other. Only when the Cherokee had to attend to matters that concerned the nation as a whole did the Eastatoees and Oconees mingle uneasily together. However, if hunting parties from either group accidentally crossed paths, then quarrels, scuffles, and occasional minor bloodshed often ensued, though not to the extremes of scalping and killing.

Yet Nagoochee, a young warrior of the Eastatoees, did not heed the unspoken rule of boundaries that the clans had established, and without fear of consequence, he would cross the river and freely hunt throughout the land of the Oconees. They were not particularly pleased with his incursions, but because he was not boastful or proud and because he had the reputation of being a brave warrior and hunter, they made no effort to stop him.

During one of his forays across the Keowee, Nagoochee journeyed northward into the Sarratay Valley which the whites would later call Jocassee. His hunt so far that day had been without success. Then late toward evening, he sprung a buck into a clearing in the woods and attempted to bring it down with an arrow. Although normally he was a skillful archer, the arrow missed and fell wide of its mark.

Off bounded the deer with Nagoochee in fast pursuit. But the animal began to behave strangely. It would run some distance from the hunter and then allow him to get within bowshot. Once within range, Nagoochee would fire and miss, while the buck would again bound away. This pattern repeated itself several times, and the hunter began to think that the deer might be an Oconee wizard or shape shifter attempting to lure him into a trap.

Although somewhat afraid, his confidence in his skill as a hunter would not allow him to give up the chase. He vowed to the spirit that protected his clan that, if he killed the buck or overcame the wizard, whatever the case might be, he would sacrifice a green parrot as a gift of thanksgiving for his success. And so he continued his pursuit.

As he stood on an outcropping of rock, he saw the deer nibbling on tender grass in a lower part of the valley, downwind and almost within range. Nagoochee quickly tried to jump off the ledge to get a better shot, but in his haste his foot caught a root from a small tree growing out of the rock. Unfortunately, he tripped and tumbled down, breaking his leg in the fall. The deer trotted off, glancing back from time to time, seemingly unconcerned and giving the impression that everything had been planned.

Now convinced that he had fallen victim to a wizard's trap, Nagoochee expected a party of Oconee warriors to come out of the tree line and take him prisoner for having violated their hunting grounds. He prepared himself for whatever might happen and decided to fight and die rather than be taken and face the possibility of being burned alive, a torture that the Cherokee frequently inflicted on the enemies they captured.

But as he steeled his mind for death, he heard a soft voice singing in the distance. It floated up the valley toward him and sounded like that of a young woman. As he listened, Nagoochee thought to himself that he had never heard a sweeter voice. The singer came closer and, in the daydream of her song, almost stumbled over him where he lay stretched upon the grass.

Startled, she asked, "Who are you?"

Knowing that she must be an Oconee and bravely wishing to conceal nothing, Nagoochee pulled back the deerskin shirt which covered his chest and said "Look!"

There, on the left side, was a tattoo of the green Carolina parrot, symbol of the Eastatoees and of a possible enemy. Yet the young woman showed no sign of fear, for the warrior did not appear hostile, and she saw that he had broken his leg. Because she was kindhearted, she had compassion for him and told him that she would return with help. She then turned and ran swiftly back the way she had come in the direction of the Oconee settlement.

She had been gone for quite a while, and the shadows in the valley soon began to lengthen, and the air to grow colder as night came on. In the distance, Nagoochee could hear a solitary wolf howling somewhere in the surrounding hills. "Surely, she will return," he said to himself, wanting to believe her words as he imperceptibly dropped into a restless sleep.

Later, the lights from torches and the sounds of voices woke him in the darkness as the young woman, surrounded by several men from her village, stood over him. She took care to make sure that his shirt covered the green bird stamped on his chest. She then had the men lift him on a litter of saplings woven together with vines and padded with leaves. As they placed him there, he heard one of them call her by the name of Jocassee.

Within a few hours, they arrived at the lodge of her father, Attakulla, a man of high esteem among the members of his clan and a peace chief. Here Jocassee herself washed the young man's cuts, applied herbal balms to sooth his bruises, and made a splint to set his broken leg. She remained his sole nurse during the weeks it took for his fracture to mend, and during that time the two fell in love with each other. Fortunately for Nagoochee, Jocassee's father bore no grudge against the Eastatoees and willingly provided shelter to the wounded warrior even after the old man discovered his origin. In fact, soon after Nagoochee's arrival, Attakulla had taken his hand and called him "son," a gesture which tended to strengthen the young man's initial attraction and growing affection for the old chief's daughter.

After several weeks, the leg had healed, and though Nagoochee was well enough to return to his own village, he lingered. One evening, as Jocassee stood among the trees beside her house, he asked her to marry him. She consented, provided her father approve the match to which Attakulla readily gave his consent. As was the custom of the Cherokees and other Indian nations, Nagoochee offered to give the father a sufficient number of presents to make the ceremony almost complete.

The final act, though, that would fulfill all the usual requirements for marriage would be to obtain the acceptance of Jocassee's brother, Cheochee. Yet he been away for a long time at a remote hunting camp beside the White Water River near its upper falls, a high cascade that churns to a milky color as it descends a little over four hundred feet down its steep gorge. Although Jocassee hoped for her brother's approval of Nagoochee to be her husband, she knew that he was not gentle like his father but was hot-tempered and considered the Estatoees enemies. So while she longed for her brother's return, she dreaded it as well because she feared his likely reaction to the proposal would be one of anger.

In the meantime, Nagoochee had gone back to his village to prepare the wedding gifts for his new family. Jocassee continued to wait, but there was still no sign of her brother. Then, not too many days after she had accepted Nagoochee, a runner suddenly appeared. In his right hand he carried a stick, and on the stick were strips of skin torn from the hide of a wolf. He ran to the council house, and the Oconees gathered there to hear the news he brought.

The messenger declared that the Great Warrior Moytoy of Tellico—he whom Sir Alexander Cumming in 1730 had proclaimed emperor of the Cherokee at Nequassee and crowned with the opossum wig or crown of Tannassy and to whom the headmen, warriors, conjurors, and Beloved Men swore allegiance as their supreme leader—had called for a great wolf hunt, the event to take place as soon as possible on the upper falls of the White Water River. The messenger further added that a large number of wolves had gathered in the region and that Moytoy requested that the Lower Cherokee towns send hunters to destroy them. However, all the inhabitants were welcome to attend—male and female, young and old.

Young men, longing for adventure and glory, and others, seeking curiosity or a change of pace, immediately set out for the falls. Individual hunters, bands of hunters, and their followers from the Lower towns began to converge in a large party threading its way through the forested valleys toward the higher elevations. Though old, Attakulla left the Oconee village as did his daughter Jocassee. Nagoochee, whose fame as a hunter was widespread, had not yet joined the small band of thirteen of his fellow Eastatoees who had answered Moytoy's call.

Warriors, old men, and women and children of all ages at last coalesced in a large hunting camp at the height of the cascades that form Upper White Water Falls. Representatives from each settlement bivouacked together and raised on long poles the totems of their affiliation. Stuffed with moss, the emblems of a green Carolina parrot reached above the camp of the Eastatoees while those of a brown viper above that of the Oconees.

Members of this later group had turned out in superior numbers, larger in fact than any other of the Cherokee present, and the Oconees' pride in their numbers and in their prowess as hunters displayed itself for all to see. Unfortunately, the Eastatoees could view these displays more easily than any of the other Cherokee because their camp stood hard by their rivals who never lost an opportunity to insult the Green Bird hunters. And proudest and most scornful of all in the Oconee camp was Cheochee, Jocassee brother.

Not long after the Eastatoees had come to the falls, Nagoochee arrived, and his people rejoiced to see him. The hunters shouted and danced, and the women danced and sang. The noise of the celebration could not help but reach the neighboring Oconees and their leader. Cheochee called out in mockery, "Why do the painted birds squawk so loudly in the ears of the Brown Vipers?"

Because the Eastatoees could not hear him above their rejoicing, no one from their camp responded. Yet Jocassee heard her brother's words and said, "The great hunter Nagochee comes, so the Green Birds dance and sing."

Detecting the note of admiration in her words and the look of tenderness in her eyes, Cheochee replied, "What do you know of this man, and why does his coming cause thanksgiving among our enemies?"

Seeing his attitude of bitterness and hate, she said no more of Nagoochee and the Green Birds and went about her business in the camp, but her brother pondered her words and wondered what they might mean. He could not bear the thought that his sister might have a secret fondness for a hunter and warrior of the Eastatoees, especially one as brave and handsome as Nagoochee. Cheochee's resentment was great indeed.

Yet his anger festered even more when his father, Attakulla, told him of Nagoochee's accident and how Jocassee had brought him back to their settlement and tended his injuries. The old chief recounted these details approvingly. But what made Cheochee's bile even more bitter was when his father said that he had come to see Nagoochee as a second son, a sure sign to his blood son of the marriage blessing.

All the while, Jocassee tried to soften her brother's heart by humbling herself before him. She fetched cool water for him to drink. She made wissactaw for him to sip by mixing parched cornmeal with water sweetened with honey. She brought thin slabs of smoked venison for him to eat. But throughout the day, Cheochee remained unmoved and nursed his wrath toward Nagoochee.

Early the next morning, well before dawn, the Cherokee were up and active, preparing for the wolf hunt that was soon to begin. Scouts had reported that the wolves were in the hollow of some nearby hills. Hunters, stationed on the slopes, were to descend, driving the animals toward the narrow opening. Across this gap, other hunters were positioned. Noting the rivalry between the Green Birds and the Brown Vipers and hoping to take advantage of their competition in the hunt, Moytoy had placed them beside each other along the outlet, a strategy bound to bring the two parties into contact with each other.

The day advanced. From the surrounding hills and down the hollow, the drivers ran the wolves ever closer to its opening. Eyes flashing, lips snarling, teeth and jaws snapping, they came down a narrow defile toward the Eastatoees and Oconees. In the wild melee that followed, both sides mingled in united action, their banners often raised above warriors of the opposite party. With bow and arrow, knife, hatchet, and spear, they slaughtered the trapped and infuriated beasts and confirmed their reputations as fearless hunters.

Without dispute, however, Nagoochee proved to be the bravest of the brave. Before he could wield his knife, a big male wolf, with teeth gnashing and claws flailing, threw itself at the young warrior. Barely avoiding the biting jaws, Nagoochee nimbly leapt aside and, in doing so, thrust a short dart, tipped with deer horn, down the gaping mouth of the maddened animal. Almost before the wolf landed on the ground, Nagoochee pounced with his blade ready and dispatched the beast while it lay writhing in its death throes.

Another attacked, and in the wink of an eye, the hunter split its skull with his hatchet and killed it in one fatal stroke. The Eastatoees cheered his deeds with a resounding war whoop, and witnessing all, his foe Cheochee both admired and hated their brave and skillful leader.

The day closed. Moytoy signaled for the various bands to come to his camp to tally the hides taken by each. The greatest number of wolf skins belonged to the smallest contingent of hunters, the Green Birds and their sachem, Nagoochee. The Great Warrior bestowed upon the young man the acknowledgement of having been first in the hunt and signed for the women to sing of his exploits. The Eastatoees lifted him high as the song of praise rose beside the White Water River and mingled with the sounds of evening and the nearby falls.

When the song had ended, Moytoy asked Nagoochee what he would have, and before the people assembled there, the warrior asked that Jocassee accompany him home to his lodge and thus complete their marriage. Stunned by the request, the Oconees erupted into a loud uproar. The irate Cheochee rushed toward his sister and pulled her by the hair back within the protective circle of his clan. Then breathing fire and theatenings, notwithstanding the presence of Moytoy, he brandished his knife and hatchet and challenged Nagoochee to combat at that very moment.

"Let the dog-hearted hunter of the Green Birds come forward," cried the young chief, "and the Brown Viper will kill him." His tongue then trilled a fierce ululation, and his warriors gave the dreaded war whoop.

On hearing these words, Nagoochee, remained calm and gave no sign of fear, although his manner also indicated that he did not wish to engage Jocassee's brother in combat. However, at that moment Moytoy intervened, compelling the two sides to keep the peace of the hunt and bidding them to return to their camps. Cheochee was denied his vengeance for the time being. Yet war's fierce fever burned in the veins of both parties throughout the remainder of the restless night.

Of the hostile parties, only Nagoochee did not want conflict, and as a result of his peaceful disposition, the Green Birds began to whisper. They knew that he loved Jocassee, but they could not believe that his feelings for her would paralyze his behavior as a warrior. On hearing some of the bits and pieces of words that came his way, Nagoochee himself puzzled over his inaction at the insults of Cheochee, and the more he thought, the more he longed for another opportunity to restore his reputation among his people.

The next day, still under the direction of Moytoy, the hunting party left the White Water branch of the Keowee River and headed east toward the Sarratay, another tributary of the same stream. With their banners before them and still near to each other, the Green Birds and the Brown Vipers joined the line of march with the rest of the Cherokee. The women, children, and old men had charge of the skins from the hunt, the provisions of food, and cooking utensils.

The main body of warriors soon moved ahead of the column to forage closer to the Sarratay for additional game. As was the custom, the hunters moved in the same direction but scouted independently of one another. Their course generally wound without interruption through the Sarratay Valley until they came to a large crag in the middle of the valley that divided it into two narrow, overgrown passes. These forced the hunters closer together, their parties having been separated by individual forays along the previous track. The mountain now brought everyone back together with very little observable order according to clan distinctions.

When the Oconees and the Eastatoees neared the mountain dividing the valley, some funneled through the left defile and some through the right. On emerging from the trees and brush of one pass, a group of seven Oconees found that they had entered an open space of a small prairie along the valley floor. They also discovered that two warriors of the Eastatoees had emerged along with them. To make matters worse, one of these warriors carried the banner with the symbol of the green bird at its top.

Here at last was the perfect chance for the Brown Vipers to wreak their revenge. They cast down the standard and threw the green parrot onto the muddy ground where they stomped it beneath their feet. Not satisfied with this insolence, they next hung the degraded emblem around the neck of the warrior who had carried it aloft, bound his and his companion's arms, and through them inserted the long pole that had held the standard so as to fasten the two together. With taunts and buffets from fists and feet, the Oconees then left to join the rest of the expedition and abandoned their enemies to fend for themselves as best they could.

The great body of the hunt now began to assemble on the banks of the Sarratay, where Moytoy had sent a message ahead so that at least a hundred canoes were ready to ferry the Cherokee across the river. They now poured into the place of rendezvous. All around was the revelry of high spirits—of leaping, songs, shouts, and whoops—as the people celebrated the success of the hunt and gathered by their clans on the bank where canoes were assigned to them.

With his band, Moytoy himself was already on the water, while the canoes of the other clans filled and embarked for the opposite bank. Yet the camp followers of the Oconees remained, including Attakulla and Jocassee who waited for the arrival of Cheochee and the other Brown Vipers. The Eastatoees likewise waited for Nagoochee and his band. But neither group came. The delay began to trouble the thoughts of the old chief and his daughter, and for good reason, too. For strife had now started in earnest between the warriors of the two clans.

When Nagoochee had passed through one of the defiles beside the mountain that divided the valley, he had paused at its end to gather his thirteen men before they joined the main body with Moytoy. The young warrior had collected all his small force except for two, and for these he waited and waited until at last he observed them stumbling with painful approach across the valley toward him. As they came closer and he and the other eleven clearly saw the beating and degradation their comrades had suffered, there was no quelling the Eastatoees' anger. It rose to a ferocious height and cried out for dreadful vengeance on the Oconee perpetrators.

Nagoochee and his men took positions within the thick foliage at the foot of a hill where Cheochee and his band had to pass. Although half the number of the Brown Vipers, the Green Birds determined to have justice and honor, even if their action brought them death, rather than endure further injury and dishonor. Crouched in the underbrush along the tree line, they watched the Oconees come down the valley. Closer and closer they came until their line was opposite to their enemies. At the war cry of Nagoochee, the Eastatoees then burst from the woods as they chanted their scalp songs. Any thought of Jocassee had abandoned their leader's mind and heart.

The Oconees hardly had time to turn and prepare their weapons for the headlong assault at the side of their column, and at first the element of surprise favored the smaller force of their foes. Hatchet and war club brought down two Brown Vipers in the rear, and knives removed their scalps as they lay dead or dying.

Yet Nagoochee furiously led the fray in the first onslaught. Running, he cast his hunting spear and pierced the chest of one warrior as blood gurgled frothily from his mouth and he breathed his last. Then wielding his tomahawk in his right hand, he split the head of another who sank dying on the grassy meadow. An Oconee thrust his dart tipped with buffalo horn toward Nagoochee's side, but the agile warrior artfully dodged the tip and tackled his assailant while at the same moment inserting his knife into the man's rib cage with such force that the blade entered the victim's heart so that death came lightening swift. Like wolves, suddenly surprising a she-bear that savagely guards her cubs, the Oconees shrank before Nagoochee's rage. The parties began to be almost equal in the fight.

Undaunted, however, Cheochee saw the way the battle went, and his skill and valor in war were as strong, if not stronger, than his hate for his foes. He rallied his men after that first rush, and they cast aside their bows and arrows to rely solely on the knife, hatchet, and war club, weapons best suited to the hand-to-hand combat that now engulfed them. With a swift crack to the head, he stunned a young warrior of the Green Birds and took his scalp where, with his life flowing out of him, he stretched unconscious on the ground. Then holding the bloody trophy aloft, Cheochee gave an ear-piercing shriek of triumph and in that moment spied Nagoochee.

The leader of the Green Birds now fought with Okonetee, a tall and mighty warrior of the Brown Vipers. Like a fire set by hunters in the dry thickets of the woods to clear the undergrowth, Cheochee rampaged through the combatants toward his enemy. At that instant, the tomahawk of Nagoochee cut the flank of Okonetee who bowed and twisted in pain only to receive a blow which broke his jaw as it clove the side of his head. Sinking to the ground, the tall warrior clasped the legs of Nagoochee in a death grip of tremendous strength, leaving little room for Nagoochee to maneuver as Cheochee pressed upon him.

The end was swift. Though the young warrior fought with vigor and valor, the entangling death spasms of Okonetee prevented a fair defense. Before any of his Green Bird companions could come to their leader's aid, with his knife Cheochee gave one fatal stab to the heart. Nagoochee fell to his knees. His vision swam, but he could still perceive through his dimming eyes a blade circle his head as someone pulled it back by his long, black hair. And then, before darkness closed round him completely, he saw his scalp dangling from the hand of Jocassee's brother.

Beside the River Sarratay sat Jocassee, pondering the whereabouts of her brother and her beloved. Then toward evening, she heard the triumphant songs of the Brown Vipers as they descended from the hills. With joy, they sang how they had killed their foes and how Nagoochee had died. Toward the canoes, Cheochee came, proclaiming a victory that tore his sister's heart in two. With fixed eyes, like one already dead, she saw the scalp dangling from her brother's neck. She gave no cry and spoke no word but silently stole into one of the canoes that was ready to cross the river. When the boat reached the middle, where the water was swiftest and deepest, she seemed to return to herself. She glanced once more at the bloody battle trophy and at her proud brother on the bank. Then quietly she slipped over the side and, before anyone was aware, sank into stream and disappeared, never to rise to the surface.

From that day, the Sarratay became the Jocassee to the Cherokee and later to the whites. Yet some of the Eastatoee women of the time said that Jocassee did not drown but that she walked beneath the river until she saw on a remote bank a warrior of the Green Birds summoning her to join him. The women also told how the two journeyed to a remote valley in the high mountains where no one lived. They built a lodge that no one would ever be able to find and where they now live in peace. And there each day the young man hunts the deer, and the young woman dresses the venison.

SOME HEROIC ACTS IN WARS WITH WHITES

The Cherokee had long chaffed from constant encroachments on their lands in the 1740s and 1750s by the English colonists of Virginia and the Carolinas. Despite ceding over eleven thousand square miles to South Carolina in treaties of 1721 and 1755, the nation continued to be pressed upon its borders by whites. In 1748, a company of Virginia frontiersmen led by Dr. Thomas Davis discovered the Cumberland Gap in the Appalachian Mountains and traveled to the headwaters of the Cumberland River. Two years later, Davis undertook a second expedition and reached the Kentucky River but stayed only temporarily because of difficulties with Indians. As claimants to these hunting grounds, the Cherokee became alarmed by Davis's forays to the western side of the mountains.

Despite uneasy relations with the colonists, the Cherokee remained allies with the British and their southern colonies during the greater part of French and Indian War that began with hostilities in the Ohio River Valley between Virginian and French troops and the northern Indian allies of both sides. England made a declaration of war in 1756 against France and formal conflict between the two empires began in Europe, North American, and other parts of the world. Known as the Seven Years War in Europe, the struggle for colonial dominance during the first four years favored the French to whom the Cherokee were well-disposed, especially those in the Overhill towns, because of proximity to the French along the Mississippi and the possibility of better trade relations, although these did not materialize to any great extent. The Cherokee also found the French more conciliatory and less arrogant than the British colonial officers stationed among them.

To strengthen ties with the Cherokee, James Glen, the royal governor of South Carolina, had supervised the building in 1754 of Fort Prince George adjacent to Keowee, the principal town of their Lower settlements. Its purpose was to protect them from their enemies the Creeks to the south and to improve trade. To cement the relationship further, Glen promised the Cherokee arms and ammunition and another fort to be constructed among the Overhill towns across the mountains on the Little Tennessee River. By the fall of 1756, Fort Loudoun was built near the town of Tommatly and garrisoned by two hundred men. It would protect the Cherokee from the French and their Indian allies. In return the Cherokee were to provide troops to aid the English in their war efforts to the north and to receive presents or payment for their services.

The Cherokee did indeed fulfill their part of the arrangement and in 1757 sent men to fight against the Shawano allies of the French in Virginia. The Cherokee, however, were not paid as had been promised. On their way home in 1758, they stole some horses from Virginia settlers as due recompense for fighting. The settlers used force to retrieve their property, and the result was bloodshed on both sides. One estimate is that forty Cherokee were killed, scalped, and mutilated after their own fashion in warfare by German settlers. These then sold the scalps to the Virginia government at the highest sum allowed by law and claimed they were taken from the Indian supporters of the French. Seeking redress from the provincial governments of Virginia and North and South Carolina, the Cherokee found none, and though the nation was divided about how to react, some of the younger warriors eventually decided for themselves to take blood vengeance for their slain relatives. The Cherokee began to attack whites on the Carolina frontier. Some of these had settled on Indian land as, for example, moving across the established border of Long Canes Creek in South Carolina.

Various attempts at reconciliation failed to diffuse the tensions. Governor Lyttelton of South Carolina halted the sale of all ammunition to the Cherokee. This embargo curtailed their ability to hunt for white-tailed deer and trade for European goods. By 1759, full-scale war had broken out between the colony and its former Indian allies. The English made three invasions of Cherokee country. The last two under regular British army officers Montgomery and Grant proved devastating. Montgomery destroyed all the Lower towns in the summer of 1760, and the next year Grant did the same to fifteen Middle settlements. Referred to as the Anglo-Cherokee War, the conflict lasted from 1759 to 1761 and was part of the larger French and Indian War.

In 1759, several bands of Cherokee warriors led by Moytoy of Settico, nephew of their former emperor by that name, raided eastward toward settlements in North Carolina along the Yadkin and Catawba Rivers and killed around nineteen men, women, and children. The warriors took ten scalps in these attacks. Some settlers took refuge in Fort Dobbs, a blockhouse surrounded by a stockade and ditch and located in the Yadkin-Pee Dee river basin near what is now Statesville in Iredale County. Several members of Daniel Boone's extended family took refuge there, although Boone, his wife, and children were in Virginia at the time.

War intensified along the frontier in early 1760, and by the spring, the

Cherokee had pushed the border back from Long Canes Creek in South Carolina to Orangeburg, a distance of one hundred miles. In 1760, small gangs of Cherokee warriors again raided eastward along isolated farmsteads in the Yadkin, Catawba, and Broad river basins. Settlers sought refuge in the nearest towns or barricaded themselves in their homes. Many left the frontier entirely, and over the course of several weeks half the white population of Rowan County, North Carolina, had fled. Scalping parties appeared along the outskirts of Salisbury and the Moravian community of Bethabara.

At Salisbury, news spread that a band of six to eight warriors was near. Armed local citizens discovered their location and began to track them, hoping to engage the Cherokee or drive them away. In the meantime, the warriors had found a deserted cabin and decided to spend the night there. During the wee hours of the morning, the whites had surrounded the cabin. Some were behind a stack of fodder, and others had cover from the roofs of some small outbuildings so as to command shots at the door and chimney of the cabin. The men then tossed firebrands on top of the roof to set it ablaze and either drive the Indians out or burn them within.

Knowing the desperation of their circumstances, one of the Cherokee inside the house, said to his fellow braves, "It is better for one to die than for all of us to perish. Follow what I tell you, and you will be saved. As soon as I remove the fire from the roof, be ready to run outside and escape as fast as you can." The others agreed.

Then to their surprise, he went out of the doorway and began to run in a zigzag manner from one side to another. All of the whites emptied their guns in his direction, with several finding their mark. The warrior fell and died.

Everything happened in an instant. The rest of the Cherokee immediately ran from the cabin and rushed between the posted guards of whites before they could reload. All the braves escaped without harm. The name of the warrior who sacrificed his life is remembered no longer, but no one can forget his heroic deed that saved his companions.

Cherokee women also showed great valor in war. During the American Revolution, the Indian nation sided with the British as its best defense against the steady inroads made by backwoods whites into Indian lands. British superintendents for Indian affairs—in the northern colonies, Sir William Johnson, and in the southern, Captain John Stuart—had been steadfast friends to the Indians and had held their loyalty through presents of trade goods, the prospect of plunder from colonial settlements, and the possibility of regaining lands they had lost. In June of 1775, a year before the American provinces had formally declared themselves independent, British agents were busy supplying Indian tribes from the Great Lakes to the Gulf of Mexico with tomahawks, firearms, and ammunition as well as offering bounties for American scalps. Moreover, colonists loyal to the crown sometimes decided to join with the various tribes in their depredations along the frontier.

Angered by the actions of the Cherokee, the colonial governments of Virginia, North Carolina, South Carolina, and Georgia decided to move collaboratively against them with the purpose to destroy their ability to trouble the frontier any further. In August of 1776, North Carolina sent a large provincial force against the Cherokee under the command of Griffith Rutherford. During the Anglo-Cherokee War sixteen years earlier, he had seen action as a militia captain when one of their war parties had assaulted Fort Dobbs on February 27, 1760, but had failed to capture it. Now a militia general, Rutherford led his army of 2,400 across the Blue Ridge through Swannanoa Gap where Interstate 40 now leads from McDowell into Buncombe County. From there, he descended the western side of the mountains. He then divided his army into smaller contingents to attack the Middle towns from his base camp at Nequassee, where Franklin is today. These units fought a series of skirmishes with the Cherokee. At Sugartown east of Franklin, one detachment of Rutherford's army encountered strong resistance and only through the arrival of a relief force avoided being pinned down. Advancing north, another segment of the undisciplined frontier army managed to kill and scalp an Indian woman and to lose only one soldier in an exchange of gunfire. This event caused the North Carolina Council of Safety to warn Rutherford to restrain his troops from killing women and children.

After leaving Nequassee and the Middle towns, Rutherford next marched west to lay waste to the Valley towns. He took a twelve hundred man detachment of his best troops. Without a knowledgeable guide, they became lost as they headed west toward the main settlement of Hiawassi. Veering off course by ten miles, only by accident did they avoided an ambush set by the Cherokee at Wayah Gap in the Nantahala Mountains.

A few days later an army from South Carolina did make its way to Wayah Gap. Unfortunately, its competence in finding this more direct route to the Valley towns led it to fall into the Cherokee ambush. Commanded by Colonel Andrew Williamson, this force of almost two thousand strong had hoped to rendezvous with Rutherford's men. When Williamson got to Nequassee, he learned from some of Rutherford's officers stationed at the base camp that their commander had already departed for the Valley settlements. Williamson immediately left, hoping to overtake the North Carolina detachment. Upon arriving at Wayah Gap, Williamson's men met strong and organized resistance from five hundred Cherokee who had gathered there to stop the white advance. The fighting that ensued became the fiercest of the campaign. In fact, the noise of battle was so loud that the contingent of North Carolinians remaining at Nequassee heard the musketry and rushed to aid Williamson's troops. By the time the relief force arrived, however, the engagement had ended with the Cherokee warriors driven from the scene. Colonial casualties in killed and wounded were numbered anywhere from thirty-two to forty. Based on the body count, some fourteen Indians had died before the rest had melted away.

After the Cherokee dispersal, one lone Indian was spotted behind a tree and shot by some of Williamson's soldiers. When they went to examine the body, the men were surprised to see that the brave was a woman who had painted her face with red and black stripes. She was armed with a bow and arrows and stripped down for battle like the male warriors. Before being killed, she had already been wounded in the leg. Thus unable to retreat with the rest, she had remained behind to endure her fate.

At another engagement during the Revolutionary War, a woman named Gantunlati or Wild Hemp saw her husband fall in battle as he defended their settlement from attack. The other Cherokee warriors were in retreat. Wild Hemp took up her husband's tomahawk and killed his slayer. Shouting "Kill! Kill! Kill!" she then charged at the enemy so furiously that the men on her side regained their courage, renewed the fight, and drove off the attackers.

Because of her bravery, Wild Hemp received much honor from her people. She could participate in the war dance with the male warriors and attend their councils. She could sit with the war chief and peace chief near the sacred fire of the townhouse. She held the power of life and death over war captives, whether they would be burned at the stake or spared by her pardon. With her title of Ghighau or Beloved Woman, Wild Hemp had attained the highest distinction that the Cherokees could bestow upon females.

CATEECHEE OF KEOWEE: A BALLAD
OF THE CAROLINA BACKCOUNTRY

Introduction

The intricate relationships in the seventeenth and eighteenth centuries between the many eastern Indian nations of North America, the settlers and traders in the English and French colonies, and the policies of their colonial and home governments across the distant Atlantic form the background of the legend of Cateechee. For nearly three quarters of a century, the English and the French in a series of wars and diplomatic efforts vied for control of the continent. Sweden had previously lost its small colony to the Dutch who, in turn, lost theirs to the English. Spain's might had waned; its influence had become minimal; and its sphere of action was far to the south in Florida, the West Indies, and Mexico. France, in Canada and Louisiana, and England, along the Atlantic seaboard, were the only major powers in North America.

Between 1689 and 1763, the two nations fought four wars in Europe and North America. The first was the War of the Palatinate in Europe, called King William's War in America, which lasted from 1689 to 1697. The War of the Spanish Succession followed from 1702 to 1713 and was known in the colonies as Queen Anne's War. Next came the War of the Austrian Succession, named King George's War in America, lasting from 1744 to 1748.

This third conflict served as the larger setting to the negotiations that James Glen, the royal governor of South Carolina, engaged in with various Native American groups having connections through either trade or war or both with the English colony. With a combination of diplomatic initiatives and strong-armed tactics, Glen hoped to halt the constant wars among the far-flung native groups, especially the Creek and Cherokee, and to neutralize the French influence with them that came from both Louisiana and Canada. (For a fuller account of Governor Glenn's treaty negotiations with various Native American peoples connected to South Carolina, see Sirmans, 265–308.)

The governor's efforts were only partially successful. The frontier possessed few of the benefits of law and order, and there were too many constituents and factions to please, both Indian and white. Despite the 1748 peace treaty of Aix-la-Chapelle that ended King George's War, outbreaks of violence continued among the Cherokee, other native tribes, and the colonies of France and England, although the Cherokee were generally allies of the English.

By 1756, France and England were again at war. Known as the Seven Years War in Europe, the conflict was called the French and Indian War in America. The Cherokee attacks in February and March of 1760 on the backcountry settlement of Cambridge and the trading post at Fort Ninety Six and the subsequent Anglo-Cherokee War (1759–1761) with the colony of South Carolina are properly seen as part of this struggle between two great global powers of the time. It is this backdrop against which the story of Cateechee or Issaqueena was first imagined and set.

Part I: Capture

In seventeen and forty-eight,
A restless truce prevailed
Between the British and the French,
As peace seemed doomed to fail.

On Carolina's far frontiers
Both vied to find allies
Among the native nations there
Or strengthen former ties.

James Glen, the royal governor,
Went to the Cherokee
And told their headmen and their kings,
"The Creek, or Muskogee,

"You've long held as your enemies,
And often have made war,
But now the time has come for change.
Fight with the Creek no more.

"Both Creek and Cherokee are children
Of our great King George.
As brothers, you must live in peace
And thus your friendship forge.

"If you must raid and war with others,
Fight those who love the French.
Go west, and with the Choctaw blood
Your warriors' weapons drench."

These words the King of Keowee,
Kuruga, heard Glen speak
And raided to the south no more
His former foes, the Creek.

But still the men of Keowee
For war and honor itched.
Their victims' scalps on poles and belts
The warriors' fame enriched.

Kuruga has the war post struck
With his keen tomahawk
And summoned warriors to his side
The Choctaw towns to stalk.

They trekked through mist-filled mountains,
Through rivers, swamps, and wood,
And down the western slopes they stole
To where a village stood.

The sun had set and night had come
And midnight had come, too.
Kuruga held his warriors back
Till dark was nearly through.

Then just before the morning's break,
They left their hiding place
And moved upon the Choctaw town
With silent, stealthy pace.

And, as the sun came up at dawn,
Loud rang the dread war cry,
And fire devoured the village huts
Beneath the smoke-filled sky.

By tomahawk, the Choctaw fell,
Awakened while they dreamed.
They tried to flee the flames and death
That through their village streamed.

As King Kuruga led the fray,
He came upon a girl.
His tomahawk he raised aloft.
He meant to split her skull.

But to the Cherokee's surprise,
She cried, "I dare you spill
My maiden's brains upon the ground,
If girls, brave king, you kill?"

And as the maiden spoke these words,
She stared into his eyes.
Kuruga dropped his tomahawk,
Diverted from its prize.

Her fearlessness had stayed his hand
And spared her from the slaughter.
The king so liked her dauntlessness
He took her as his daughter.

Some Choctaw had escaped the fight
And fled away unharmed
To rouse their nearby settlements
And raise a swift alarm.

So King Kuruga bound the girl
And with his men did flee
Across the mountains and the glens
And back to Keowee.

He gave the captive to his wife.
"I took her in my wars,"
He said. "This Choctaw girl's my daughter,
And so she, too, is yours."

His wife then asked, "What is your name?"
"Doe's Head," replied the child.
"Or 'Issaqueena' in Choctaw."
"Not so," her mother smiled.

"Cateechee we will call you here—
'Doe's Head' in Cherokee.
You keep your name but not your tongue.
You are in Keowee."

In Keowee, Cateechee grew
And learned the women's skills.
She hoed the corn and dressed the deer
The men killed in the hills.

But deep within her hidden heart,
Cateechee felt alone
And longed for her return to those
Whom she could call her own.

Part II: Young Lovers

Some ninety miles along the trail,
Southeast of Keowee,
White settlers built a fort for trade
With Creek and Cherokee.

A trader of the settlement,
James Francis had two sons.
To trade in Indian towns, both thought
More profits might be won.

They loaded down two pack horse trains
And set off eagerly,
With Henry heading to the Creek
And Allan, the Cherokee.

When Allan came to Keowee,
He met Cateechee there
And found the lovely Choctaw girl
Far, far beyond compare.

They talked and grew to love each other
Beneath the Piedmont moon,
And Allan pledged to take his love
Back to her people soon.

"If you become my wedded wife,
For you all things I'll do,
But let me to my land return
To make a home for you."

So back he went to Ninety Six.
He found a hilltop site
Among the soaring poplar trees
To house his love's delight.

Where Allan Francis raised his cabin,
He named it Poplar Hill,
And he would bring Cateechee there,
And all his vows fulfill.

Yet neither of these lovers cared
The winds of war were brewing
Among the towns of Cherokee
For trespasses accruing.

Between the English and the natives,
Outrages rankled each
Of solemn oaths and treaties made
Each thought the other breached.

In seventeen and fifty-one,
White traders stole deer hides.
They took three hundred thirty-one.
The felons went untried.

The English said they would build forts
To guard the Cherokee—
Prince George near Keowee,
Loudoun in Tennessee.

Protection, true, but inroads, too,
Upon their hunting grounds,
Let settlers draw more closely to
The Lower Indian towns.

Both sides retaliate and slay
First one and two, then more.
The body counts of murders mount
Until there's open war.

White traders use false yards and scales
To measure deerskin hides
And sell their cloth and other goods
Beyond the legal price.

The trader Elliot admits,
In answer to Old Hop's complaint,
Of mixing red paint with red lead
And selling poison paint.

Two traders at Great Tellico
Must flee the hostile town.
A third, attacked and almost stabbed,
Escapes to Fort Loudoun.

John Kelly slain at Hiawasee,
His body quartered in four parts,
His head and hands on poles displayed,
His scalp declares war's start.

From Keowee, Kuruga sends
Fleet-footed scouts to spy
Upon the post at Ninety Six.
No one knew they were nigh.

The houses scattered through the hills,
The stockade gates unclosed,
The fort would make an easy mark
And should fall unopposed.

This news Kuruga's scouts told him
Within the council house:
"The time is ripe for our attack,
If you our warriors rouse."

And while the king and his chief men
Smoked from their pipes of war,
They planned the way that their foray
Left Ninety Six no more.

And when the glowing bowls died down,
Cateechee filled them back
And overheard the warriors' plans
Of their surprise attack.

She heard how in the dark of night,
When no moon shed its light,
Kuruga would his forces lead
And strike with all his might.

Her frightened heart then ceased to beat.
She feared her true loved one
In Ninety Six would die that night
And see no more the sun.

Part III: War

The headmen all, their clans have called
And to the warpath taken.
Young Seroweh of Estatoee
Has left Fort Prince George shaken.

The Overhill from Settico
To North Carolina raid.
For white attacks on Estatoee,
A score of scalps they take.

Surprise assault upon Long Canes
Leaves fifty-six whites slain.
If not forewarned at Fort Loudoun,
The fate might be the same.

Cateechee's heart seems torn apart
By duty and by love.
She chooses love above her clan
And thinks no more thereof.

One evening late in secret haste,
Cateechee steals away,
And to the horse corral she goes
As night diminished day.

The guards know her and let her pass.
She takes Kuruga's horse
And wends her way out of the town
To where the river coursed.

She crosses shallow Keowee,
And in her horse's side,
She digs her heels to press her mount
To start the long night ride.

From Keowee to Ninety Six
Is crisscrossed by defiles
Of numbered streams that score the trail
And tell the traveled miles.

By these swift rivulets that run
Across her horse's path,
Cateechee counts the distance placed
From King Kuruga's wrath.

At Six Mile Creek, she's gone six miles,
And Twelve Mile River makes six more.
At Eighteen Creek, she rests her horse,
Then onward as before.

The icy stars of February
Gleam coldly from above,
As Three and Twenty Creek brings her
Still closer to her love.

Cateechee now at Six and Twenty
Draws from her reservoir
Of heart and strength, as yet the length
Is scores of miles yet far.

Cateechee on her mission must
Now firmly set her mind.
She knows Kuruga or his men
Give chase not far behind.

So through the night and all next day,
She stays her steady course
And reaches Ninety Six's fort
Upon her footsore horse.

Her Allen greets her near the gate.
Cateechee hardly speaks,
Exhausted from the long road's ride
And crossing wintry creeks.

She warns of matters dark and dire
Among the Cherokee,
From Overhill and Middle towns
To Lower Keowee.

She tells about the massacre
Occurring at Long Canes.
She tells of Seroweh's attempt
To storm Prince George in vain.

The settlers hear and in their fear
Their preparations make.
They gather in their palisade
And close the wooden gate.

Saluda's able fighting men,
Attend their captain's call.
James Francis has at his command
Now forty-five in all.

Of these defenders of the fort,
The whites are thirty-three,
Yet rounding out the roll, a dozen slaves
Who know not liberty.

Armed men, along the firing step,
Patrol the parapet.
Inside the gate, the brass six pounder,
Is primed and ready set.

Kuruga's forces soon arrive.
Their number is two score.
They spy from preparations made
Cateechee's warned of war.

And so the bravest of the brave
The king now gathers round
To plot a plan, as best they can,
To seize the closed compound.

A sally Seroweh will lead,
Young Warrior of the fight,
To storm the post by quick assault
In dawn's dim early light.

Thus on the morrow's darkened morn,
Young Warrior screams his cry,
And from the tree line, his bold men
Like furies stream and fly.

But for this fight, throughout the night,
The garrison has waited,
And sleepless, Captain Francis' men
The charge anticipated.

Light casualties attend each cause.
Young Warrior's slain are two,
And two are wounded in the fort
Before the battle's through.

Repulsed, Young Warrior and his band
To other means resort,
And so they burn the barns and homes
Around the little fort.

They take what stores that they can carry
And lay waste to the rest
Before they make their swift retreat
Along the trail northwest.

They then return to Keowee,
Where more fierce warriors come.
To swell their ranks for new assaults,
Called by the warpath's drum.

His numbers now two hundred fifty,
Kuruga feels secure
The little post at Ninety Six
No longer will endure.

Young Seroweh still heads this force,
Once more attacks at dawn;
But after heavy fire, once more
Young Warrior has withdrawn.

The garrison to taunt their foe
An Indian scalp hoists high
Atop the flagpole of the fort
To draw the warriors nigh.

Another of the Indians slain
Becomes a gruesome sport.
James Francis feeds the carcass to
The dogs inside the fort.

Young Seroweh, too wary, though,
To let his men be marks,
Keeps them behind the line of trees
To let their flintlocks bark.

The fire continues day and night.
The wooden walls hold fast.
The morrow's rain brings two more men
Who through the gates have passed.

The Cherokee cannot prevail.
With thirty-six long hours done,
Cateechee and the trading post
Kuruga has not won.

With ambuscades and further raids,
His vengeance now he wreaks
Throughout the region of Saluda
For nearly three grim weeks.

The houses burned, the cattle killed,
And scalps and captives taken,
From Ninety Six to the Congarees,
The frontier seems forsaken.

At last the royal governor
For British troops requests
To aid the feeble colony
And end the fierce contest.

Montgomery leads his Highlanders,
With scouts and rangers, too,
And lays waste to the Lower towns
Then deems his mission through.

No peace unfolds from his retreat
Down country to Charles Town,
And some war chiefs think now they can
Defeat the British Crown.

Another Scots commander comes,
James Grant with greater force,
And to the Middle mountain towns
He sets his army's course.

Past summits like great sugar loafs
And through thick valley brush,
They're crushed between the Cowee Range
And where swift waters rush.

Then on the column's left-hand side
From Cowee River's bank,
The flintlocks of the Cherokee
Pepper the English flank.

And on the column's other side,
Shots ring from forest slopes
To mingle with the wild war whoops
Inciting native hopes.

This crossfire in the wooded narrows,
Checks for a while Grant's way,
And if not for low lead and powder
Had made a bloodier fray.

Grant's vanguard reaches open ground.
He forms his battle lines,
But to the rear at his supplies
His foes set their designs.

Along the pack train's hemmed-in spot,
The battle grows intense.
Swift-thinking Grant acts fast to send
More men for its defense.

Provincial troops rush to the back
Where panicked horses rear,
And just as fast as they appear,
The Indians disappear.

The Cherokee no more assault.
The King's men win the fray
To forward march to Etchoe
As twilight ends the day.

From June to July, one month's time,
Grant breathes fire all around,
Destroys the corn and other crops,
And burns the Middle towns.

The Cherokee must sue for peace.
They lose vast hunting grounds
Some twenty miles from Keowee,
Kuruga's Lower town.

Along the trail from Keowee
The Cherokee have sent
An eagle tail, their solemn sign,
Of peaceable intent.

Part IV: Interlude and Recapture

Between Montgomery's retreat
And Grant's decisive blows,
The Lower towns of Cherokee
No more great menace posed.

So to their home on Poplar Hill
Cateechee and Allan went,
Their cabin spared the hostile flames
Of savage war's ferment.

And yet Kuruga in his pride
Felt he had been defamed.
The daughter he had made his own
Had brought his honor shame.

Thus in the interlude of war,
He watched at Poplar Hill,
And with one warrior in the night,
He went when all was still.

And through the chinks by dim firelight,
They saw the couple sleeping.
Then King Kuruga tripped the latch
And to their bed came creeping.

Cateechee's ears pricked up in fear.
She'd heard soft footsteps tread.
She stirred as Allan then awoke.
Both saw paint black and red.

She recognized Kuruga's face
Behind the painted shape
And knew from his raised tomahawk
There would be no escape.

"Cry out and die," the king warned both.
Your silence lets you live.
Arise and quickly come with me,
And I your wrongs forgive."

And, as Kuruga spoke these words,
The other warrior looked
Throughout the low-lit hut and all
The weapons took.

He and Kuruga bound the pair.
Then through the low-set door,
They fled in secret silence as
The couple walked before.

And when they came to Keowee,
Before night fires ablaze,
Within the council house, the clans
Proclaimed Kuruga's praise.

Untied, the two were captives still,
Bound by the village eyes,
And to their captors' rules and ways
The captive pair complied.

In trade, young Allan had been fair
And long had been a friend.
In time, the steadfast watchfulness
Began to see an end.

On hunts he went with other men.
A winter hut he made
Of wattle daubed with clay, where he
And his Cateechee stayed.

And, since the pair did not escape,
The Wolf took Allan in,
And in this clan of Cherokee
He was now kith and kin.

The women picking fruit in spring,
A thunderstorm arose,
And flashes forked across the skies
While trees heaved in fierce throes.

Seized by great fear of rolling thunder
And black clouds overhead,
All helter-skelter back to their shelters,
The women lightning fled.

And yet Cateechee stayed behind,
Unnoticed in the storm
Of toppling trees and swirling leaves
That threatened or gave harm.

Within the village, Allan asked,
"Why is my wife not home?"
And in the forest downpour rushed
To find where she had gone.

About one mile, he found Cateechee
Huddled beneath a tree.
At once both knew their chance had come
To flee from Keowee.

Nearby, the pathway led southeast
And ran to Ninety Six,
The way Kuruga likely would
Upon his quarry fix.

The mountains, though, that westward stretched
More deeply stood inside
The wilder lands where fewer clans
Of Cherokee abide.

In cool spring rain, still drizzling down,
They left toward mountains vast.
There they might hide and bide their time
And any search outlast.

Part V: Escape and Reunion

Soon Allan and Cateechee came
Before an ancient height,
Rock-ribbed with freshets tumbling forth
Suffused with prismed light

The couple thought themselves secure,
Their freedom undefiled,
From King Kuruga's scouring bands,
On this steep stronghold wild.

Here, with green sapling spears,
Oak bark, and light pine boughs,
They fashioned round a hollow stump
A little rustic house.

Next Allan felled a tall, thick tree
Beside the Tugaloo,
And with a hatchet and hot coals
He fashioned a canoe.

They'd shoot the little Tugaloo,
Its swollen rapids ride,
To where it offered tribute to
The great Savannah's tide.

Cateechee fished and gathered greens
And other forest food,
And for four weeks upon their peace
No searcher did intrude.

That month, Kuruga hunted south
In lands no longer held,
Through peace and war, its masters once,
The Cherokee expelled.

No trace of these two fugitives,
He sent some warriors back
Who found on Stumphouse Mountain's heights
Faint signs of human tracks.

Dim print in sodden earth, snapped vine,
Crushed sprout, or broken stalk—
No better guide the hunters need
And let the mountain talk.

They came upon the bark-clad hut.
Cateechee was not there,
But from the glinting steel of knives,
She soon became aware.

She saw the warriors searching near
And softly stole away.
But not to Allan did she go.
She went some miles away.

Kuruga's men, though, found her track
And after her pursued,
And from their fast approach, she knew
Their chase she'd not elude.

From heights above where Allan was,
A creek plunged down the crest.
Behind these falls, a deep rock reft
Had held a wild duck's nest.

Cateechee once had spied the fowl
Fly through the misty spray,
And there she headed with all speed
As spring skies darkened gray.

She reached the lip of the steep cliff
And backward glanced to find,
Through foliage that disclosed and hid,
The men not far behind.

One moment on the brink, then gone!
They came where she had leapt
And, gazing down the rocky gorge,
Saw where white water swept.

Then clambering down the tumbled rocks
That framed the chasm's walls,
They searched the pools and broken trees
Spewed by the gushing falls.

No woman dead among the rocks,
Was it some fiendish crone,
Like old Spear-Finger changing form
Now back as flesh of stone?

Her shapes—the owl, the crow, the cat,
Or misty purple lights—
Or luring shifts to human guise
That haunt the mountain heights,

Hungry ever for her victims,
Ranging stream and darkened wood,
With forefinger, gnarled and flinty,
Human liver her prized food.

Stabbing each whom she draws near—
Stone Dress, with her sharp witch's claw—
Through the heart or through the neck,
Filling all with curdling awe.

Searching through the gorge's shadows,
Their thoughts on ancient tales,
The braves uneasy left the falls
And followed homeward trails.

Cateechee waited silently
Within the mountain cleft,
Then climbed back up the rocky cliff
Once all the warriors left.

She raced down to the Tugaloo—
A startled deer alarmed—
And Allan told how from the scouts
She had escaped unharmed.

No time to spare, they launched their craft
And paddled night and day
Down Tugaloo and broad Savannah
Beyond Kuruga's sway.

Down the Savannah at Fort Moore,
The way-worn pair arrived,
Where Henry, Allan's brother, gave
Glad thanks that both survived.

Their troubles almost past, one month
They stayed to gather strength.
Then southwest through the Creek domains,
They journeyed for some length.

By night, they hid among the reeds
Of tall and dense canebrakes
That gave them shelter but concealed
Thick canebrake rattlesnakes.

At last, they came unto a land
Of low and boggy earth,
A land that once upon a time
Had seen Cateechee's birth.

Now tongues and dress returned to mind,
Despite the years' long growth,
And by these signs, Cateechee knew
Her Allan kept his oath.

They dwelt among her Choctaw kin
In happiness and peace,
And through the years, the love they had
Did nothing but increase.

In time, Cateechee's fame grew great,
And later ages would
The summit Stumphouse Mountain name
Where her crude hut once stood.

And where she took her lover's leap,
The falls derives its fame,
From Issaqueena in Choctaw,
Cateechee's other name.

Sources Used
in the Retellings

I have divided into two parts the following notes on sources for each of the selections retold in this collection. The notes are intended for anyone who may want to deconstruct my adaptations or access references from which I derived background details to embed within the retellings.

The first part, labeled *Core Story,* indicates the basic source(s) that provides the overall plot of a particular selection. More often than not, the core story derives from Mooney's *Myths of the Cherokee* (1900). However, other core sources include Adair's *The History of the American Indians* (1775), Curtin's anthology of *Seneca Indian Myths* (collected in 1883 and published in 1922), Daniel's *Cateechee of Keeowee* (1898), and Simms' "Jocassee" from *The Wigwam and the Cabin* (1856). Occasionally, there are two sources for a core story when I have fused variants within Mooney or variants from other sources. These fusions are chiefly from Haywood's *The Natural and Aboriginal History of Tennessee* (1823) and Lanman's *Letters from the Allegheny Mountains* (1849). Blended with Daniel's *Cateechee of Keowee* are many details from Herd's summary of the legend in *The South Carolina Upcountry* (1981).

The second part, *In-Text Amplifications,* includes sources that, although not part of the original stories or a major variant, are intended to elaborate and clarify geographical, cultural, historical, political, or social references contain within the selections. I have embedded information from these sources into the plots to provide contemporary readers the kind of background knowledge that native listeners likely would have possessed when they heard one of the core stories told generations ago. These supplementary sources derive from Mooney's Notes and Parallels and his Glossary at the end of *Myths of the Cherokee* or from his prior work, *The Sacred Formulas of the Cherokee* (1891). Additional in-text amplifications come from earlier accounts composed during the eighteenth century about the Cherokee and other Southeastern Indians. These works provide some of the first ethnographic records of Native Americans by European eyewitnesses. Along with Adair's 1775 history, mentioned in the previous paragraph, significant sources include Bartram's 1791 *Travels,* containing his observations of indigenous people of the Southeast. Sizeable portions of this work describe the Cherokee. With other selected unpublished manuscripts by Bartram, these writings are now collected in one book, *William Bartram on the Southeastern Indians* (1995). Additional documentary works are Beverley's 1722 *The History of Virginia in Four Parts*; Lawson's 1709 *A New Voyage to Carolina*; the 1765 *Memoirs of Lt. Henry Timberlake*; and the 1970 *Colonial Records of South Carolina*, edited by McDowell. Besides these primary documents from the eighteenth century, I have also supplemented the story adaptations with information based on the research of contemporary anthropologists, archaeologists, and historians. Particularly invaluable have been the various works of Charles Hudson, the preeminent authority on the indigenous peoples of the Southeast, both before and after European contact.

For in-text amplifications, I have given the sources in alphabetical order by the author's last name in boldface. Topics from sources are then arranged in sequence by page number(s) from lowest to highest. Because some sources contain several topics within the particular pages listed, there is inevitable overlap among topics. To have categorized the sources by topic was an option that I considered, but such an approach would have entailed greater overlap and would have been more cumbersome than the current format. Topics may appear to readers inconsistently listed by different descriptors. The reason, however, for this seeming inconsistency is that I have listed the topics in a manner more nearly approaching the way they are delineated in each particular retelling. Full reference information on sources, whether for a core story or its in-text amplifications, may be found in the Bibliography.

The Three Worlds

Core Story: **Mooney** #1, 239–240.

In-Text Amplifications: **Buttrick**—original firmament above mountain tops and creation of seven heavens, 6. **Ethridge**—doors to the Below World, inhabitants of the three worlds, milky way as the "Path of the Souls" to other worlds, prevention of the island from rocking by four cords suspended from the sky vault, the sacred cedar tree connecting the three worlds; This World balanced between Upper and Lower Worlds, 20–22. **Hudson**, *Southeastern*—center of This World occupied by the Cherokee, earth as a circular island created from mud spreading in the four cardinal directions, Sun's day and night journey through sky vault, 122; turkey buzzard as symbol of healing as well as death, 129–130; cedar as a sacred wood, seven as highest level of purity, 134; seven Cherokee directions, 513 (N28). **Mooney**, *Myths*—cedar wands decorated with scalps, sacred nature of cedar as a medicine tree because of fragrance and slow decay, taboo against burning cedar except as incense to drive away evil ghosts, cedar's red color derived from blood of powerful magician, 421; solid rock arch of the sky vault, 440; *Kalanu* or The Raven, 524.

Fire

Core Story: **Mooney** #2, 240–242.

In-Text Amplifications: **Adair**—thanksgiving sacrifice to Fire of first fruits, 150; meat sacrifice by hunters to Fire, 159; sacrifice to Fire of war captives for success in battle, 188. **Bartram**—purification and renewal through Fire at the Feast of the First Fruits (Green Corn Ceremony) or busk, 125–126; use of the old Fire to light the new Fire in the council house rotunda, 149. **Corkran**, "Cherokee Sun and Fire Observances"— archetypal association of heat, life, light, fire, and the sun, 33; Fire and the protection of a newborn from snakes, meat sacrifice by hunters to Fire, sacrifice to Fire at the Festival of First Fruits, Smoke as Fire's messenger, white robe of the *Uku* [*Uka*] or Fire King, 36;

Fire formed by the same Creator God who created the Sun and Moon, Fire in the war chest of the war priest's waiter or helper, Fire symbolizing Cherokee continuity of past and present, 37; red priest, white priest, 38. **Corkran**, "The Sacred Fire of the Cherokees"—Fire of the town house or temple as Sacred Fire which never goes out, 21–22; Fire as a messenger to "great man above," 22–23; Sacred Fire of war, 24; Fire as a purifier, 25. **Hudson**, *Knights of Spain*—Sun as deity among Mississippian chiefdoms antecedent to the Cherokee and other Southeastern tribes, 26. **Hudson**, *Southeastern*—sky vault, 122; epithets for Fire as "Ancient Red" and "Ancient White," 126; This World and Upper World, 125–126; motif of cross within circle on water spider's back to represent Sacred Fire, 135; ancient time, 156; replacement of polluted old Fire by pure new Fire in the Green Corn Ceremony, 313; relighting of Fire to symbolize cleansing of the past year, 374–375. **Mooney**, *Myths*—*Galunlati* or the Above World, 231; home of the Thunder Boys or Little Men in the far west beyond the door of the sun, 248; lightning and rainbow as clothing of the Thunderers, 257, 442; extinguishing old Fire and lighting new Fire, 396; large hairy water spider, 431; *Kanati* the Great Thunder and His sons the Thunder Boys, 435, 441; *Kalanu* or The Raven, 524; *tusti* or small bowl, 540. **Payne**—lighting the new Fire of the new year, 178; poetic, mystical language of Indian ceremonies, 183; Fire as divine, 192. **Strickland, Rennard**—pardon of sin through the agents of Fire and Smoke, 11; association of Fire and Smoke with Spirit Beings, 22; Sacred Fire and the continuation of the Cherokee, 189.

Corn and Game

Core Story: **Mooney** #3, 242–248.

In-Text Amplifications: **Duncan** and **Riggs**—Pilot Knob, Pisgah National Forest, and Shining Rock Wilderness, 94. **Hudson**, *Knights*—*barbacoa* as a place Indians of the Southeast stored food, 156; *Southeastern*—association of water and disorder, taboo of mixing separate categories like blood with water, Wild Boy as unruly, 148; taboo of upsetting order and balance, 121, 159; the Thunder Boys as helpers, 155, mindreading as a sign of witchcraft, witchcraft as a captital crime, summary execution of witches, 363–364. **Lawson**—Indian cribs or food storehouses set on tall poles above the ground, 23. **Mooney**, *Myths*—movement of sky vault, Sun's eastern door, and Sunrise Place, 256; *Aniwaya* or Wolf People as the watchdogs of *Kanati*, 264–264; magical powers of trees struck by lightning, 422, 435; bears as originally humans, 323–324; seven as a Cherokee sacred number, 431; corn or *Selu* as "The Old Woman," location of *Kanati's* cave on Mount Mitchell, 432; ball play as a figure of speech for battle, 433, 464; Twilight Land or Darkening Land where it is always growing dark, 435; Little Men as helpful workers of great wonders, 438; association of honey locust tree with lightning and the Thunderers, 465.

Disease and Medicine

Core Story: **Mooney** #4, 250–252.

In-Text Amplifications: **Adair**—bear skins for beds and rugs, 77; beasts of prey as unclean food except bears, swiftness and wisdom as qualities in venison, 171; smoke and fire to drive bears from winter holes, 318; bear oil sweetened with sassafras and wild cinnamon, 405. **Bartram**—anointing stretched ear lobes with bear oil, 120; corn fritters fried in bear oil and eaten with jelly made of smilax root and honey, 165–166. **Duncan** and **Riggs**—Clingmans Dome, Great Smoky Mountains, Kituhwa townhouse, 73. **Hudson**, *Southeastern*—ancient versus recent time, animal retaliation on humans, Cherokee concept of balance, and plant cures, 156–157. **Lawson**—feasting on hot bread and bear oil, 62; bear oil to relieve aches and pains, 122; bear cub furs to make hats and muffs, 123; sweetness of bear grease, 216. **Mooney**, *Myths*—no separation of humans and animals, 261; larger, stronger, wiser animals of ancient time, 262; attributes of Little Deer or *Awi Usdi*, characteristics of master hunters, curse of rheumatism, hunter's prayer to deer for pardon, 263–264; bears' four townhouses and fall dances, residence of the old White Bear chief, 264; human destruction of insects and worms or *tsgaya* and their diseases, 308; description of Lake Atagahi and healing of wounded bears, 321–322; Cherokee deer songs, 435. **Perdue**, *Slavery*—why humans kill bears without fear of reprisal, 5–6.

The Bear and the Bear Songs

Core Story: **Mooney** #75, 325–327.

In-Text Amplifications: **Adair**—elders' belief in exclusive consumption of bear meat and dulling effect on human nature, 171. **Hudson**, *Southeastern*—bear as anomalous creature with human and animal characteristics, 139. **Mooney**, *Myths*—animal reincarnation and final resting place in the Darkening Land, 261–262; bear as human with speaking ability, 264; fall bear festival and bear dances, four peaks and council houses of the bear clan in the Great Smoky Mountains, *Gategwa-hi* or Thicket Place, *Kituhwa* or Mulberry Place, *Tisitu-yi* or Rabbit Place, *Uya-hye* or another high summit in the Great Smoky Mountains 472–473; *yanu* or bear(s), 547.

Tobacco

Core Stories: **Lanman**, 118–121; **Mooney** #6, Second Version, 255.

In-Text Amplifications: **Bartram**—red stone catlinite pipe bowls of the calumet, 247 (N69). **Duncan** and **Riggs**—dwelling places of Cherokee dwarves or Little People according to tribal elder Jerry Wolfe, 66. **Ethridge**, "Tobacco Among the Cherokees"—uses of tobacco in numerous aspects of Cherokee life, 76. **Mooney**, *Myths*—Istati or Chota as peace capital in the Overhill territory, 14; ceremonial and medicinal uses of tobacco, 424; old, wild tobacco versus new, cultivated tobacco introduced from the West Indies, 424, 439. **Timberlake**—seating accommodations in the townhouse at Chota, 17.

The Pleiades and the Pine Cone

Core Story: **Mooney** #10, 258–259.

In-Text Amplifications: **Adair**—scraped canes adorned with white feathers and green sprigs, 141; chants to *Yohewah* during sacred dancing, 142; dancing in circles with white feathers on scraped white canes, 152; religious singing during sacred dancing, 153; description of the game of chunkey, 394–395. **Corkran**, "The Sacred Fire of the Cherokees"—Sacred Fire of townhouse or temple associated with Upper World of "great man above," 22–23. **Hudson**, *Southeastern*—keeping score in chunkey, 423; lighting of cross-shaped four logs of new fire and sacrificing four perfect ears of corn; various purification rituals associated with feather dance such as ceremonial scratching, drinking black tea and vomiting, going to water; war whoop of turkey gobble, and whooping calls to honor birds during feather dance, 476–477. **Mooney,** *Sacred Formulas*—the *adawehi* or magicians and supernatural beings, 346. **Strickland, Rennard**—Fire as earthly manifestation of Sacred Fire of the Spirit Beings [of the Above World], 22. **Timberlake**—Cherokee chunkey poles of ten feet in length, 38.

The Great Yellow Jacket Ulagu

Core Story: **Mooney** #13, 260.

In-Text Amplifications: **Duncan** and **Riggs**—Franklin, Macon County, Wayah Gap, 158, 160–161. **Hudson,** *Southeastern*—monsters, This World, portals to the Under World, 130–131; *hilahiyu* or ancient time versus recent time, 156. **Mooney,** *Myths*—destruction of monster animals, 443–444; *hilahiyu* or ancient time, 522; Briartown Creek, *Kanugulayi* or Briar Place, Macon County, Nantahala River, 524; *Tsagunyi* or insect place, 537; *Ulagu* or yellow jacket queen, 541. *North Carolina State Road Atlas*—Cullasaja River, Franklin, Macon County, Little Tennessee River, 75.

The Leech Place

Core Story: **Mooney** #77, 329–330.

In-Text Amplifications: **Duncan** and **Riggs**—Leech Place or *Tlanusiyi*, Murphy, Valley Towns, 177–181. **Hudson,** *Southeastern*—danger, monsters, Under World, water, 166. **Mooney,** *Myths*—causeway, deep pool, Leech Place or *Tlanusiyi*, Murphy, subterranean connection between rivers, winged leech, 474–475. *North Carolina State Road Atlas*—Hiawassee River, Lake Hiawassee, town of Murphy, Valley River, 73–74. **Oliphant**—Valley Towns as heavily populated region with rich hunting grounds, 3–4.

The Uktena and the Shawano Conjuror

Core Story: **Mooney** #51, 298–300.

In-Text Amplifications: **Adair**—abodes and dangers of enormous mythical snakes in Cherokee country, 256–257. **Fogelson**—possibility of many *Uktena*, quartz-crystal stones of *Uktena*, 76. **Hudson,** "Uktena: A Cherokee Anomalous Monster"—power of crystals in predicting recovery of sick, death in battle, or length of life, 63. **Mooney,** *Myths*—Cherokee and Shawano as British allies in Revolutionary War, 55; anger of Sun at humans; disease sent to kill people, help from Kanati's sons or Little Men or Thunderers, Moon's death from rattlesnake, *Uktena's* jealousy, 252–253; the Above World of *Galunlati*, 231; danger, description, dimensions, power, and value of *Uktena*, 297–298; red streak of Agan-uni-tsi's transparent crystal or *ulunsuti*, 298; chronic warfare between Cherokee and Shawano, locations of Shawano and reputation for conjury, 370–371; Shawano use of sounds of flying squirrel and wild turkey as war stratagems, 372–373; *Gahuti* or Cohutta Mountains, Murphy as Leech Place at juncture of Valley and Hiawassee Rivers; roving life of Shawano and subsequent skill in magic, 461; Ohio River area as eventual home of Shawano, 494.

The Red Man and the Uktena

Core Story: **Mooney** #52, 300–301.

In-Text Amplifications: **Adair**—remote locations of great mythic snakes like *Uktena*, 256. **Hudson**, *Southeastern*—remote dwelling places of *Uktena*, 145, 514; *Uktena* as harmful yet full of great magic, 148. **Mooney**, *Myths*—lightning as brightest color of Red Man's clothes; Red Man equivalent to Great Thunderer, 257; vital spot of heart of *Uktena* in seventh circle from head, 297; magical powers of trees splintered by lighting, 422, 435; Great Thunderer equivalent to Kanati, 435; less powerful crystals from *Uktena* scales, powerful crystal or *Ulunsuti* from forehead of *Uktena*, 458–460; **Timberlake**—various hues of *Uktena* crystals, 24.

Ustu-tli, the Great Snake of the Cohutta Mountains

Core Story: **Mooney** #54, 302–303.

In-Text Amplifications: **Adair**—mythic snakes of huge and cumbersome size in remote mountains of Cherokee, 256. **Bartram**—bear, deer, turkey among chief animal foods of Southeast Indians, 164. **Hodler** and **Schretter**—elevation and location of Cohutta range in North Georgia, 16–19. **Lawson**—bear, deer, turkey as game animals, 17, 216–217. **Mooney**, *Myths*—great snakes as large as tree trunks, 297; *Gahuti* or Cohutta Mountain as haunt of both Uktena and Ustu-tli, 462; *Gahuti* or Cohutta Mountain meaning "poles of the shed roof," 518. **Mills**—peaks of the Blue Ridge Province, 11. **Rozema**—Cohutta Mountain same as Fort Mountain, 309. **Seabrook**—extent of Blue Ridge Mountains, 1. **Usery**—Appalachian and Blue Ridge Mountains in Georgia, 1. **Warren**, "Chattahoochee National Forest"—Cohutta Wilderness of Chattahoochee National Forest in North Georgia, 627.

The Great Hawks

Core Stories: **Mooney** #64, 315–316, and # 65, 316.

In-Text Amplifications: **Duncan** and **Riggs**—Citico (also Settico) and Little Tennessee River on Map 2, 212; Citico, Overhill Towns, Tellico Lake, 211, 214. **Fogelson**—Eastern Cherokee conjurors and predator animals killing dangerous ones, 74. **Hudson**, *Southeastern*—*Tlanuwa* as monstrous bird of prey, peregrine falcon, 129; caves, monsters, rivers, Under World, 130; balance of cosmic forces, opposition of Upper World and Under World, *Tlanuwa* and *Uktena* as deadly enemies, 136; *hilahiyu* or ancient time, 156. **Mooney**, *Myths*—ancient time after the creation, goshawk, holes in the rock, juncture of Citico Creek and Little Tennessee River, *Tlanuwas'* cave and cliff, 466; Blount County, cave, Citico Creek, Little Tennessee River, *Tlanuwa, Tlanuwayi*, 535. **Timberlake**—Kitchin's 1760 Map of the Cherokee Nation, Settico [Citico], xvi.

The Hunter in the Dakwa

Core Story: **Mooney** #68, 320–321.

In-Text Amplifications: **Duncan** and **Riggs**—Overhill Towns, Tellico Dam and Lake, Toqua, 211, 214; Little Tennessee River and Toqua on Map 9, 212. **Hudson**, *Juan Pardo*—*dakwa*, Little Tennessee River, monstrous mythic fish, Toqua, 95. **Mooney**,

Myths—men swallowed by fish, 469–470; *dakwa, dakwa-yi* as great mythic fish, 514. **Timberlake**—Timberlake's 1762 map of the Overhill Cherokee country, Toqua, 16.

Spear-Finger, the Nantahala Ogress

Core Story: Mooney #66, 316–317.

In-Text Amplifications: **Duncan** and **Riggs**—cascading waters, dense rhododendron thickets, difficult terrain, entangled undergrowth, steep sides of Nantahala Gorge, 130–131. **Hudson**, *Southeastern*—Spear-Finger as a shape shifter, 175–176. **Mooney**, *Myths*—Nantahala from *nundayeli* meaning "middle sun" or noonday sun, perpendicular cliffs allowing only midday sun to penetrate deep gorge, 528. *Nantahala Gorge*—flora, scenery, and seasons in Nantahala Gorge, 1–4.

The Stone Man of the Mountains

Core Story: **Mooney** #67, 319–320.

In-Text Amplifications: **Ethridge**—seven as sacred number of ritual purity, 20–21. **Fogelson**—otherworldly power drained by menstruating woman, 70. **Hudson**, *Southeastern*—number seven associated with highest ritual purity and sacredness, 134. **Mooney**, *Myths*—seven as sacred Cherokee number, 432; Spear Finger as Dressed-In-Stone's possible mate, 467; dangerous and uncanny nature of menstrual blood to indigenous peoples, 469. **Walker, Barbara**—male fear of mysterious menstrual or moon blood in early human societies, 635; power of menstrual blood to conquer death, 637; hysterical fear of menstrual blood in some cultures, 641.

The Raven Mockers

Core Story: **Mooney**, #120, 401–403.

In-Text Amplifications: **Faulkner**—*asi* or conical winter houses joined to the main house, warmth of winter houses, 87; interior earth ovens of winter houses, 88–89; use of winter house for sleeping, 91. **Fogelson**—"skillies" as inherently evil shape-shifting witches who stalk infirm victims at night, 63. **Hudson**, *Southeastern*—the old, sick, and feeble as easy victims for witches, 179; witch as intrinsically evil and unforgivable, 182; association of duck-root with witchcraft, purple as the color of witchcraft, shaman's use of duck-root decoction to discover and thwart witches, 182–183. **Mooney**, *Myths*—*asi* or hot house as sleeping quarters of Cherokee, especially the old, in winter, 462, 510.

The Immortals and the Water Cannibals

Core Story: **Mooney** #87, 349–350.

In-Text Amplifications: **Hudson**, *Southeastern*—water cannibals as a type of witch, 175. **Mooney**, *Myths*—appearance, behavior, and location of the *Nunnehi* or Immortals, "those who live forever"; differences between Immortals and Little People who are fairies the size of children; features of bald mountains; *Nunnehi* as friends of the Cherokee, 330–331; location of *Tikwalitsi* or Tuckalechee near Bryson City on the Tuckasegee River, 483.

The Man Who Traveled to the World Below

Core Story: **Mooney** #84, 345–347.

In-Text Amplifications: **Duncan** and **Riggs**—Tallulah Falls as dwelling place of Little People, twelve miles south of Clayton, Georgia, waterfall as portal to other worlds, 327–328. **Hudson**, *Southeastern*—turtle and frog as anomalies inhabiting edge of This World and World Below, 139; fearsome anomalies of the abominable *Uktena*, 144–145. **Hudson**, "Uktena: A Cherokee Anomalous Monster"—characteristics of the *Uktena*, 62–63, **Lanman**—avoidance of Tallulah Falls for fishing and hunting by the Cherokee, lost hunters destroyed by Little People, 41–42. **McCallister**—"Niagara of the South," waterfalls in Tallulah Gorge, 1–2. **Mooney**, *Myths*—characteristics of the *Uktena*, 297;differences between Immortals and fairies or Little People, resemblance of Immortals to other Indians, 331; characteristics and dwelling places of Little People, story of lost hunter found by Little People, 333; inferior or lesser thunder spirits of cliffs, mountains, and waterfalls like Tallulah, 441. **Morrison**—Rabun County waterfalls, damming the Tallulah River, pre-dam water flow in Tallulah Gorge, 1–2. **Schoolcraft**—etymology of *Tallulah*, 159–160. **"Tallulah Gorge," Brown's Guide**—formation, topography, and various waterfalls of Tallulah Gorge; orientation of Chattahoochee and Tallulah Rivers, N. pag. **"Tallulah Gorge," Official Guide to Georgia**—formation of Tallulah Gorge and topography, N. pag. **Warren**, "Tallulah Gorge"—formation of Tallulah Dome from sandstone and other rock, collision of continental plates, 677.

Judaculla, the Slant-Eyed Giant of Tanasee Bald

Core Story: **Mooney** # 81, 337–341

In-Text Amplifications: **Anderson**—Judaculla's farm of one hundred acres of cleared land, 638–639. **Faulkner**—*asi* as small conical house used for sleeping quarters, 77, 91. **Hudson**, *Southeastern*—inappropriate mixing of categories like blood and water, 148. **Mooney**, *Myths*—Tanasee Bald as Judaculla's residence, 477; *tsul-kalu* or "he has them slanting" as Cherokee name of Judaculla, 477, 538–539; Indian mounds and burial places on Pigeon River, 479; Judaculla Mountains as the habitation of Satan or an evil spirit, 479–480; footprints of Judaculla's children at Cold Mountain, 480; probable location of Kanuga near Waynesville, North Carolina; meaning of Kanuga as "a scratcher" used in purification rituals, 524. *North Carolina State Road Atlas*—Locations of Waynesville, West Fork of Pigeon River, Cold Mountain, Tanasee Bald, and Devil's Courthouse, 76. **Wilburn**, "Judaculla Place Names"—Judaculla as powerful master of game animals who could also control weather phenomena, prehistoric Cherokee town of Kanuga on West Fork of Pigeon River, 23; south and west slope of Richland Balsam Mountain as location of Judaculla's farm, Tanasee Bald and the Devil's Courthouse in relation to Richland Balsam, Tanasee Bald as dwelling place of Judaculla, 24. **Walker, Barbara**—ancient human belief in mystery of menstrual or moon blood in formation of babies, 635.

Legends of Pilot Knob

Core Story: **Mooney** # 82 and 83, 341–345.

In-Text Amplifications: **Hudson**, *Southeastern*—ancient tobacco used as medicine by Cherokee priests, 353–354. **Mooney**, *Myths*—mountain people or spirits as possibly the Immortals or *Nunnehi*, 335; location of Pilot Knob north of Brevard; resemblance of rock cliffs at Pilot Knob to windows, doors, and roof in sun's rays, 477; requirement to fast for seven days before joining spirit people, 480; sacredness of ancient tobacco, 481.

Yahula

Core Story: **Mooney** #86, 347–349.

In-Text Amplifications: **Adair**—trade goods of bullets, combs, flints, gunpowder, knives, liquor, looking glasses, red paint, scissors, shirts, 262; deerskins, liquor, pack-horses, 366–367. **Bartram**—cowhide whips, horses with ringing bells, packhorse caravan in single file, 97; average packhorse load of 150 pounds, 107; trade goods of deerskins, furs, hides, honey, oils, tallow, wax, 157. **Duncan** and **Riggs**—*Nunnehi* or Immortals associated with circular stone structures on hills, 317–318; Dahlonega as terminus of Southern Appalachian Mountains, 320. **Hudson**, *Southeastern*—*Nunnehi* as protectors, their dwelling places and townhouses in bald mountains, 169–170; trade goods of agri-cultural tools, ammunition, beads, brass bells and kettles, cloth, deerskins, Indian slaves, Jew's harps, knives, rum, tomahawks, 436–437. **Mooney**, *Myths*—Immortals as helpers and "people who live anywhere," mountain dwelling places, 330–331; value of red paint, 455; Immortals as "those who live forever," 475; Dahlonega meaning "yellow money" or gold, 514; *Nunnehi* as "dwellers anywhere" and invisible spirits, 528.

The Unseen Helpers

Core Story: **Curtin**, 394–395.

In-Text Amplifications: **Adair**—adoption or torture as fate of war captives of south-ern tribes, 188; size of war parties, 378, 380; ropes made of green bark, 398. **Ethridge**—control of fur trade by Iroquois, "Great League of Peace and Power," 93. **Faulkner**—*asi* or little hot house, 87. **Gallay**—connections between Iroquois and Tuscarora, 265–266; Tuscarora and formation of Six Nations in 1715, 285. **Josephy**—Iroquois tradition of Deganawidah, Hiawatha, and Thadodaho on Great Law of Peace and white pine as Tree of Peace, 47–50. **Lawson**—ropes made from green braided elm bark, 100; Seneca as the most warlike of Iroquois, 207. **Mooney**, *Myths*—Sir William Johnson and 1768 Cherokee-Iroquois peace treaty, 38, 352–353; Cherokee as "cave people," five day's dis-tance between Cherokee and Iroquois territories, founding of Iroquois Confederacy, legendary origins of Cherokee and Iroquois conflict, Seneca as most numerous and war-like of Iroquois Confederacy, Seneca as "people of the great hills," Tennessee River as Cherokee-Iroquois boundary, war parties as small as one person, 351–352; nineteenth century Cherokee descendants among Seneca, Oconostota as head of Cherokee peace delegation, 353, 507; Hodenosaunee or "the People of the Long House," expansionist aspirations of Iroquois Confederacy, 483–484; power of War Women or Beloved Women, 489–490. **Oliphant**—Oconostota titled Great Warrior and Warrior of Chota, 208. **Pearson**—Five Nations and Iroquois Confederacy, palisaded towns or castles of the Iroquois, torture or adoption as fate of war captives, 113; southward expansion of Iroquois toward Cherokee lands, 148; long-distance raids between Iroquois and Chero-kee, 167. **Schoolcraft**—small encounters between Cherokee and Iroquois for prestige, 252–253. **Timberlake**—power wielded by War Women, 37.

The Lost Cherokee

Core Story: **Mooney** #107, 391–392.

In-Text Amplifications: **Alderman**—Transylvania Company's meeting with Cherokee at Sycamore Shoals, number of Cherokee in attendance, kinds of trade goods offered for vast tract of Cherokee lands, 37; Dragging Canoe's speeches at Sycamore Shoals, 38–40; Dragging Canoe's refusal to sign the purchase agreement with Henderson, 40. **Buttrick**—Cherokee prophesy of loss of lands and conquest, 13. **Davis**—Cherokee migrations west prior to Trail of Tears of 1838, 144. **Hoig**—Colonial Governor Francis Nicolson's 1721 treaty with Cherokee from thirty-seven towns and land cession of 1721, Wrosetasatow named supreme chief, 18–19; Cherokee territorial cession to Richard Henderson or "Carolina Dick" of the Transylvania Company, 58. **Hudson**, *Knights*—Indian foodstuffs of various nuts and oils, 201; *Southeastern*—various Indian preserved foods, 300–308. **McDowell**—collusion between Cherokee headmen and white traders for large land cessions, xxxix–xli; French sympathies among Overhills at Great Tellico, 202–204. **Mooney**, *Myths*—Cherokee leanings toward the French, Fort Toulouse on the Coosa River, French attempts to control the Mississippi, Colonial Governor Nicholson's 1721 treaty with Cherokee representatives and land cession, Wrosetasatow named supreme chief, 34–35; British protection against white encroachment onto Indian territory, illegality of Henderson's purchase of Cherokee lands, Proclamation of 1763, 46–48; further encroachments on Cherokee lands, Indian Removal Act of 1830, Treaty of New Echota of 1835, 123. **Oliphant**—French sympathies among Overhill settlements, 4, 9, 32; war title of *Outacite* or Mankiller, 5; British policy of protection of Indians culminating in the Proclamation of 1763, 25, 28–29. **Thornton**—fifty-three Cherokee towns in the 1721 census, 25–27; eighteenth century treaties and Cherokee land cessions, Fort Toulouse and French influence among the Cherokee after 1714, 1721 land cession to colony of South Carolina, 1775 land cession to Richard Henderson and Transylvania Company, 40–43; Cherokee migrations west of the Mississippi prior to the Trail of Tears, 43–44, 47–50; nineteenth century treaties and Cherokee eastern land cessions, 1835 Treaty of New Echota and signatories, 54–58. **Timberlake**—war title of *Outacite* or Mankiller, 36–37, 122 (N121). **Walker, Felix**—Kentucky as "the Bloody Ground" because of wars over hunting rights, 150.

Ga'na and the Cherokee

Core Story: **Mooney** #98, 367–370.

In-Text Amplifications: **Adair**—button snakeroot tea or black drink, fasting, purging, purification, 146–147; downy feathers as part of warriors' martial array, sexual abstinence before war, war medicine ark or bundle, war priest, 193–197; parched corn for war supplies, war methods and rituals, war waiter, 376–378; battle trophies and dismemberment of enemies, death whoops, forms of ambush, weapons of war, war whistles as signals, 381–382; ball play and gambling, 392–393; eagle feathers (N42), red and white symbolism in war and peace, 484 (N43). **Bartram**—twelve tail feathers of an eagle, 67; ball game dance, dancers' dress, town houses, 84–87; **Beverley**—towns with palisades, 136–137; war paint mixed with down and animal hair, 149; consultation of priests and conjurors before major undertakings, 167. **Fogelson**—ball play, conjuror rivalry, going to water, scratching, 64. **Haywood**—Cherokee fortified towns, 235.

Hoig—Cherokee town with palisade, 17. **Hudson**, *Southeastern*—sixteenth century Spanish accounts of Cherokee palisaded towns, 117; seventh height of This World, 122–123; sun as female and the apportioner, 126; river as Long Man, 128; *dalala* or the red-bellied woodpecker associated with war and turkeys associated with scalps, 130; eagle as peace symbol, 163–164; sacred crystal, 168; war leaders, 243–244; colors, raids, scalping, war preparations, 247–253; cracked hominy or parched corn, 304–305; ball play and associated rituals, 408–421. **Lawson**—town houses, 42–43; dances, feasts, songs, 177; war paint, 201; Iroquois or "Sinnagars" (Seneca) as the "most warlike *Indians*," removal of top of skull in scalping; war as a way of life, war trophies of body parts and teeth, 207. **Mooney**, *Myths*—Iroquois League and Seneca, 208; ceremonies of going to water, scratching, and other purification, 230; procurement of sacred eagle feathers and seasons related to the eagle and the snake, 281–283; scratching, 476; fasting, 480; Hodenosaunee League, Iroquois and Cherokee border, Seneca as guardians of the western door of longhouse, 483–485; wampum, 488–489; adoption of relatives, ceremonial dance of approach or welcome, darts tipped with buffalo horn, foot races, Ga'na or Arrow, going to water, the great eagle *Shadagea*, Santee, towns with palisades, white path of peace, white wampum belt, 492–494; *Nunnahitsunega* or the white path of peace, 528. **Mooney**, *Sacred Formulas*—ball play, going to water, scratching, shaman, 334–336; rituals in preparation for war and shaman, 388–391; ball play, shaman, and seventh height, 397. **Oliphant**—Chota, townhouses, warfare and military titles, the *Uka* or Fire King, 4–8; eagle as peace symbol, 184 and 188. **Payne**—love of gambling among Indians, 186. **Timberlake**—ceremonial dance of approach or welcome, Chota townhouse, eagle tails, foods, 15–21; gambling, running, weapons of war, 27; war songs, 30–31; military titles, 36–37; ball play, purification drink, various dances including war dance, 38–41; description of battle, 46–47; black drink, 123–124 (N130). **Woodward**—account by Colonel Chicken of fortified towns of Chota and Great Tellico, 32.

The Mohawk Warriors

Core Story: **Adair**, 378–380.

In-Text Amplifications: **Adair**—hymns to invoke *Yohewah* or God, 101–103; great distances traveled with much difficulty to seek retaliation, law of corporate vengeance, red paint on trees to signal retaliation, scalps as esteemed war trophies, shed blood crying out for shed blood, taunting tortured captives, 182–187; stealthy means of travel by scouting war parties, various sizes of war parties, 377–378; burning and other tortures, curing scalps, death songs, dismemberment of war captives, manner of victorious war party's entrance to a settlement, painting scalps red, scalping technique, war poles, women's role in torture, 382–385; pacification of slain relatives' spirits, songs of triumph to *Yohewah*, victory dances imitating wild cats, 390; Cherokee displeasure at Carolinians who returned enemy prisoners, 392. **Alderman**—reprieve of captive Mrs. William Bean by *Ghighau* or Honored Woman Nancy Ward, 47–48. **Bartram**—blood to appease slain relatives, burning of captives, 114; curing scalps, sites for burning captives, war poles (slave posts) decorated with skull and scalps, 154–155. **Duncan** and **Riggs**—map of Keowee and Lower Towns, 17. **Gallay**—John Stewart's 1711 and 1712 letters from Carolina to Queen Anne describing Southeastern Indian vengeance, torture, warfare, 177–191. **Lawson**—war based on revenge, 208; Iroquois comment on inability to live without war, Tuscarora, 207–208. **Mooney**, *Myths*—Cherokee comment on inability to live without war, Cherokee involvement in Tuscarora War, 379. **Schoolcraft**—danger of starvation by war parties, distances traveled in intra–Indian wars, small size of war parties, 157, 252–253. **Timberlake**—Beloved Men and Women, Beloved Women's power to grant reprieve to war captives by waving a swan's wing, 37; reprieve of captive Lydia Bean by War Woman Nancy Ward, 122 (N122). **Woodward**—war as "beloved" occupation of Cherokee, 35.

The False Warriors

Core Story: **Mooney**, #102

In-Text Amplifications: **Adair**—hostilities between Overhills and northern Indians, 248; desire of Overhills to move settlements down the Little Tennessee River, French influence and trade with Overhills, sympathy among the Overhills toward the French, warlike nature of Overhills, 258–262; French influence and potential civil war among Cherokee regions, 265–266. **Bartram**—hostilities and Virginians indisposed to trade with the Overhills, 82–83. **Brown, M. L.**—repair of firearms by Native Americans, 43–44; decoration of gunstocks by Native Americans, gunsmiths highly esteemed among Native Americans, 157; stock as weakest part of rifle, 244. **Duncan and Riggs**—locations of Middle Cherokee towns, including Cowee, along the Little Tennessee and other rivers, 141–176; locations of Overhill Cherokee towns, including Chilhowee, along the Little Tennessee and other rivers, War Trail or Warriors' Path, 233–243. **Hoig**—French and northern Indian attempts to sway the Cherokee, 32. **Hudson**, *Southeastern*—scalp painting and poles, warriors' return following raids, 249–252; scalp dance and celebration, 257. **Lawson**—Indians as superior gunstockers, 175. **Mooney**, *Myths*—Great Indian War Path, 206–207; Cherokee and Shawano enmity, Shawano incursions by way of the Pigeon River Valley, 370–373; comment of captive Shawano warrior, Cowee or *Kawiyi* as "place of the Deer clan," Cowee's importance as a Middle town and proximity to Franklin, number of houses in Cowee; 377–378; ball play allusion to war, 433; scalp dance, 496; *Kuwahi* or "the Mulberry Place" at Clingmans Dome, 526. **Oliphant**—independence of Cherokee settlements within each region (e.g., Overhill) to declare war, Middle towns along the upper Little Tennessee and tributaries, Overhill towns along the lower Tennessee and tributaries, 2–4; French influences among the Overhills, 12; French and Shawnee agents among the Overhills, Overhill discontent with English in South Carolina and Virginia, Shawnee raids on the Cherokee, 22–23. **Whisker**—ability by Native Americans to repair and restock firearms, 2; Native American esteem for gunsmiths, 20.

Jocassee

Core Story: **Simms**, 209–233.

In-Text Amplifications: **Chambers**—Sir Alexander Cumming's 1730 coronation of Moytoy as Cherokee "emperor" and supreme commander, N. pag. Hudson, *Southeastern*—thin slabs of smoked venison, 300. **Hoffman**—Upper Whitewater Falls and River, 1184. **Hoig**—opossum wig as crown of Tannassy, 20. **Hudson**, *Southeastern*—scalping technique, 249–251. **McDowell**—names of Lower and Middle Cherokee towns, 151. **Milling**—former Lower Cherokee settlements located in present-day South Carolina, 271. **Mooney**, *Myths*—Lower Cherokee settlement of Seneca, 50; *wissactaw* or sweetened cornmeal mixed with water, 481; Cherokee woman's freedom to accept or reject marriage offer, presentation of gifts by intended husband to parents of Cherokee bride, 481–482; darts tipped with buffalo horn, 495. **"Oconee County"**—Duke Energy's power-generating complex at Keowee-Toxaway in South Carolina, 680. **Oliphant**—Lower Cherokee settlement of Coonasatchee or Sugar Town, 3; lack of internal unity among Cherokee towns, 21; Alexander Cumming's selection of Moytoy of Great Tellico as Cherokee "emperor," 67–68. **Owsley**—scalping of living victims, 126–127. **"Pickens County"**—location of Lakes Jocassee and Keowee in Oconee and Pickens Counties, 723. **Williamson**—scalping of living victims, 195.

Some Heroic Acts in Wars with Whites

Core Stories: **Haywood**, 239–240; **Mooney** #110, 394–395.

In-Text Amplifications: **Adair**—blood vengeance for slain relatives, failure of colonial governments to redress Cherokee grievances, horse stealing by warriors in Virginia, scalping of Cherokee by German settlers, 264. **Alderman**—honors and powers accorded to *Ghighau* or Beloved Women, 3. **Hairr**—Interstate 40 at Swannanoa Gap on border of McDowell and Buncombe Counties, 491. **Haywood**—powers of War Women or Pretty Women, 278. **Lee**—1754 construction of Fort Prince George, 63; global conflict between England and France in the French and Indian War, 64; Governor Glen's promise to build Fort Loudoun, its location and purpose, 66, 70; Cherokee resentment at failure to be paid as English allies, 70; arms embargo by Governor Lyttelton, 76; failures at reconciliation, full-scale war with South Carolina, 1760 Cherokee attack on settlers at Long Canes Creek, 77–78; Cherokee raids and scalping parties in Rowan County near Salisbury and Bethabara, 80; Montgomery's 1760 and Grant's 1761 invasion and devastation of Cherokee territory, 80–81, 86–87; **Lofaro**—Fort Dobbs as a refuge for settlers including Daniel Boone's family, 17. **MacDonald, James**—Rutherford's 1760 service as a provincial captain at Fort Dobbs, 30; Cherokee resistance to Rutherford's forces at Sugartown; Nequassee as Rutherford's base camp, Rutherford's failure to find Wayah Gap; warnings by North Carolina Council of Safety to Rutherford about army's atrocities against women and children, Williamson's engagement with Cherokee at Wayah Gap and losses on both sides, 81–84. **Mooney,** *Myths*—discovery of the Cumberland Gap by Dr. Thomas Davis, white encroachments onto Cherokee lands, Cherokee preference toward French trade, 38–39; Cherokee alliance with English during greater part of the French and Indian War, 40–44; British agents among Cherokee prior to the Revolutionary War; Cherokee alliance with Great Britain during the American Revolution, English colonial sympathizers fighting with the Cherokee, 47; Griffith Rutherford's 1776 invasion of Middle towns through the Swannanoa Gap, number of colonial dead and wounded at Wayah Gap, 49. **Oliphant**—Moytoy's raids and scalping along the North Carolina frontier, 72–73; Cherokee attacks from the border of Long Canes Creek to Orangeburg, 17–18, 110–111. **Timberlake**—Beloved Woman as highest honor for Cherokee women, privileges of War Women, 36–37; reasons for Cherokee preference for the French over the English, 37. **Thornton**—1721 and 1755 Cherokee land cessions to South Carolina, 41. **Wilburn**, "Nununyi, the Kituhwas, or Mountain Indians and the State of North Carolina"—coalition of Virginia, North Carolina, South Carolina, and Georgia against Cherokee during American Revolution, 54.

Cateechee of Keowee: A Ballad of the Carolina Backcountry

Core Story: **Daniel,** *Cateechee of Keeowee: A Descriptive Poem;* **Herd,** 84–90.

In-Text Amplifications: **Adair**—great distances traveled by warriors making raids, 185–186; Cherokee disgruntlement over poor treatment by English during French and Indian War, German settlers butchering and scalping about forty Cherokee warriors, 262–264; incompetence and weakness of South Carolina in the early stages of the Anglo-Cherokee War, 268. **Brown, John P.**—gross abuse in 1759 of Cherokee women at Keowee by officers from Fort Prince George, 11. **Brown, M. L.**—use of flintlocks in colonial wars by mid-eighteenth century, 173. **Cann**—settlement in mid–1700s around Ninety Six by James Francis and Robert Gowdy's trading post at Ninety Six, construction of 1759 stockade at Ninety Six, 1760 Cherokee February and March attacks at Ninety Six, 3–5. **Causey**—home of Allan and Cateechee at Poplar Hill, 24. **Chacon** and **Dye**—scalps as tokens of recognition and prestige by Cherokee warriors, 633–634. **Corkran,** *Carolina Indian Frontier*—January 19, 1760, attempt by Seroweh to enter For Prince George, 57. **Corkran,** *Cherokee Frontier*—Cherokee trade with Charleston merchants and trading path to Keowee, 6–7; Justice James Francis' refusal to punish 1751 theft by white traders of three hundred deerskin hides, Seneca and Cherokee retaliatory raids in 1751 around Ninety Six to punish white offenses, 25; Robert Gowdy as Cherokee trader, 30; murder and mutilation of John Kelly, 191; dispatches to Fort Loudoun about Cherokee anger and unrest, 191–192; Seroweh's use of scalps to proclaim war in Cherokee towns, 192; Cherokee backcountry raids after first attack at Ninety Six, 193–194. **Edgar**—Cherokee attack on wagon train and mutilations at Long Canes Creek, 206. **George**—traditional explanations for distance between Keowee and Ninety Six, 6–19; Hunter's 1730 map with streams bearing the names of numbers between Keowee and Ninety Six, 16–17. **Hatley**—Dividing Paths as South Carolina trade routes to Cherokee and Creek settlements, xiv; corn cultivation as part of Cherokee women's work, 8–9; Ninety Six as backcountry trading center established by Robert Goudy and James Francis, 85; young Cherokee squaw's warning of impending attack on Ninety Six, 89–90; Cherokee fears about Fort Prince George and Fort Loudoun, 96–97. **Hoig**—discussion of threats between Captain Demere, Oconostota, Old Hop, and Standing Turkey at Fort Loudoun, 35–36; Grant's 1761 destruction of Middle towns, 43. **Hudson,** *Southeastern*—Spear-Finger as liver-eater, shape-shifter, and undead being, 178–179; red and black war paint, 244. **Ivers**—Fort Moore near Augusta on the Savannah River, Savannah Trading Path to the Creek, 28. **Lee**—strong French sympathies at Great Tellico of the Overhills, 73; Settico's 1759 involvement in raids in North Carolina along the Catawba and Yadkin, Catawba, and Broad Rivers, 74–75; settler encroachment on Cherokee, strong French sympathies at Great Tellico of the Overhills, 73; lands as chief reason for hostility, 75; early 1760 raids by Cherokee scalping parties around Salisbury and Bethabara and throughout Yadkin, Catawba, and Broad Rivers, 80; account of Colonel Montgomery's 1760 and Lieutenant Colonel Grant's 1761 campaign against the Cherokee towns, 81–90. **McDowell**—Governor Glen's letters encouraging Cherokee-Creek alliance against French and their Choctaw allies, 10–12, 25–27; value of Fort Prince George in protecting Cherokee at Keowee, 17, 35; report of Ludovic Grant on dishonesty of white traders, 41–42; Governor Glen's desire to build forts in Cherokee country for protection against French and Indian enemies, 47–48; Cherokee complaints of white encroachment on lands, 95; value of Fort Loudoun in protecting Overhills from enemies, 99; Lower Cherokee fear of enslavement by whites and rumors of warriors' intent to kill whites, 117–118; list of Lower Cherokee towns and number of gunmen in each, 151; Captain Demere's conclusions on the low character of white traders, 282; evacuation of Great Tellico by two white traders and attempted stabbing of Cornelius Coakley, 306; selling of poison war paint by Elliot, 334; murder and mutilation of four-member Cherokee hunting party by lawless whites, 425–426; Lower towns' anger over murder of Indians and stealing of hides in 1758, 444; attack in February 1760 by Cherokee at Gowdy (Goudy) Fort at Ninety Six, burning of buildings around Ninety-Six, fear of Cherokee, flight of settlers from the Carolina backcountry, Cherokee raids throughout Saluda area, 495–496; Long Canes massacre with fifty-six killed, including women and children, and February 1760 attack by Young Warrior (Seroweh of Estatoee) at Ninety Six, 499; Captain Francis' letter to Governor Lyttelton on two Cherokee attacks at Fort Ninety Six, Indian carcasses fed to dogs by Ninety-Six defenders; Indian scalps displayed over Fort Ninety Six, white reinforcements during second Cherokee assault, thirty-six hour attack by over two hundred Cherokee warriors at Ninety Six in 1760 March incident, 504–505; Indian spying around colonial fort, 505–506. **Milling**—Cherokee and white atrocities prior to the Anglo-Cherokee War, 281; Cherokee killing of whites along Catawba and Yadkin Rivers in North Carolina, 294. **Mooney**, *Myths*—1740 opening of trading path from Augusta to Lower Cherokee towns, 36; Wolf as one of seven Cherokee clans, 212–213. **Oliphant**—Cherokee unease over settler expansion into territories, 15–18; abuses by white traders, 20; abandonment of the Carolina backcountry, attack on Fort Prince George by Seroweh or Young Warrior of Estatoee, fifty some white fugitives slain at Long Canes Creek, two attacks at Ninety Six, incompetence of South Carolina Governor Lyttelton in conducting the Anglo-Cherokee War, use of British regulars, 110–112; Colonel Montgomery's 1760 campaign against the Cherokee, 114–135; Lieutenant Colonel Grant's 1761 campaign against the Cherokee, 140–166; white eagle feather as a sign of peace, 167. **Perdue**, *Cherokee Women*—work by women in preparing skins, tending corn, and cooking, 17–18. **Timberlake**—agriculture and food preparation as Cherokee women's activities, 123 (N126).

Notes

PREFACE

1. James Mooney, *Myths of the Cherokee*, 1900, in *James Mooney's History, Myths, and Sacred Formulas of the Cherokees* (Fairview, NC: Historical Images, 1992), 411–412.

2. James Walter Daniel, *Cateechee of Keeowee: A Descriptive Poem* (Nashville, TN: Publishing House of the Methodist Episcopal Church, South, Barbee, and Smith, 1898), 17.

3. Daniel, 7, 10.

4. Terry L. Norton and Betty Lou Jackson Land, *50 Literacy Strategies for Beginning Teachers, 1–8*, 3d ed. (Boston: Pearson, 2012), 77.

5. Virginia Tufte, *Artful Sentences: Syntax as Style* (Cheshire, CT: Graphics, 2006), 217.

6. Hugo Friedrich, "On the Art of Translation," trans. Ranier Schulte and John Biguenet, in *Theories of Translation: An Anthology of Essays from Dryden to Derrida,* ed. Ranier Schulte and John Biguenet (Chicago: University of Chicago Press, 1992), 15–16.

7. Dennis Tedlock, "On the Translation of Style in Oral Narrative," in *Translation—Theory and Practice: A Historical Reader,* ed. Daniel Weissbort and Astradur Eysteinsson (New York: Oxford University Press, 2006), 454.

INTRODUCTION

8. Oliver La Farge, "Myths That Hide the American Indian," in *Historical Viewpoints, Volume One: To 1877, Notable Articles from American Heritage*, ed. John A. Garraty (New York: Harper and Row, 1970), 14.

9. Kenneth L. Donelson and Alleen Pace Nilsen, *Literature for Today's Young Adults,* 7th ed. (Boston: Pearson, 2005), 300.

10. George McMichael, et al., *Anthology of American Literature, Volume I, Colonial Through Romantic* (New York: Macmillan, 1974). 2.

11. Ron Querry, "Discovery of America: Stories Told by Indian Voices," in *American Diversity, American Identity: The Lives and Works of 145 Writers Who Define the American Experience,* ed. John K. Roth (New York: Holt, 1995), 1.

12. Margot Edmunds and Ella F. Clark, *Voices in the Wind: Native American Legends* (New York: Castle, 2003), xiii.

13. Evelyn Wolfson, *From Abenaki to Zuni: A Dictionary of Native American Tribes* (New York: Walker, 1988), 13.

14. Alvin M. Josephy, Jr., *500 Nations: An Illustrated History of North American Indians*, 1994 (New York: Gramercy, 2002), 8–9.

15. Charles F. Kovacik and John J. Winberry, *South Carolina: A Geography* (Columbia: University of South Carolina Press, 1989), 60.

16. Walter Edgar, *South Carolina: A History* (Columbia: University of South Carolina Press, 1998), 12–13.

17. John R. Swanton, "The Yuchi," in *Early History of the Creek Indians and Their Neighbors* (Washington, D.C.: Bureau of American Ethnology, No. 73, 1922), 286–312.

18. Douglas Summers Brown, *The Catawba Indians: The People of the River* (Columbia: University of South Carolina Press, 1966), 378.

19. Edgar, 14–15.

20. Lawrence Lee, *Indian Wars in North Carolina* (Raleigh, NC: Carolina Charter Tercentenary Commission, 1963), 45.

21. Lee, 44–45.

22. Lee, 33.

23. Lee, 26.

24. Alan Gallay, *The Indian Slave Trade: The Rise of the English Empire in the American*

South (New Haven, CT: Yale University Press, 2002), 288–291.

25. Michael Wood, *Conquistadors* (Berkeley: University of California Press, 2000), 49.

26. Wood, 50.

27. Charles C. Mann, *1491: New Revelations of the Americas Before Columbus,* 2d ed. (New York: Vintage, 2011), 102–104.

28. Thomas Parramore, et al., "Tuscarora Indians," in *Encyclopedia of North Carolina,* ed. William S. Powell (Chapel Hill: University of North Carolina Press, 2006), 1140–1141.

29. Stanley W. Hoig, *The Cherokee and Their Chiefs: In the Wake of Empire* (Fayetteville: University of Arkansas Press, 1998), 62–64.

30. John P. Brown, "Eastern Cherokee Chiefs," *Chronicles of Oklahoma* 16.1 (March 1938): 20–21; Hoig, 63–64.

31. Hoig, 15.

32. Charles Hudson, "Uktena: A Cherokee Anomalous Monster," *Journal of Cherokee Studies* 3.2 (Spring 1978): 65.

33. James Adair, *The History of the American Indians,* 1775, ed. Kathryn E. Holland Braund (Tuscaloosa: University of Alabama Press, 2005), 416.

34. Adair, 416.

35. Felix Walker, "Narrative of an Adventure in Kentucky in the Year 1775," *Debow's Review* 16.2 (February 1854): 150–151.

36. Walker, 150.

37. James C. Kelly, "Notable Persons in Cherokee History: Attakullakulla," *Journal of Cherokee Studies* 3.1 (Winter 1978): 9–12.

38. Hoig, 3.

39. William L. McDowell, ed., *Colonial Records of South Carolina, Series 2, Documents Relating to Indian Affairs, 1754–1765* (Columbia: University of South Carolina Press, 1970), xl–xli.

40. Dee Brown, *Bury My Heart at Wounded Knee: An Indian History of the American West* (New York: Holt, Rinehart, and Winston, 1970), 138–142.

41. Dee Brown, 300–305.

42. George Ellison, "Introduction: James Mooney and the Eastern Cherokees," in *James Mooney's History, Myths, and Sacred Formulas of the Cherokees* (Fairview, NC: Bright Mountain, 1992), 10.

43. Edgar, 15.

44. John Lawson, *A New Voyage to Carolina,* ed. Hugh Talmage Lefler (Chapel Hill:

University of North Carolina Press, 1967), 35.

45. Edgar, 15.

46. Mooney, *Myths of the Cherokee,* 234–235; John R. Swanton, "Comparison of Myths," in *Tales of the Southeastern Indians* (Washington, D.C.: Bureau of American Ethnology, No. 88, 1929), 267–275.

47. Zena Sutherland, *Children and Books* (New York: Longman, 1997), 191.

48. Donna E. Norton, *Multicultural Children's Literature: Through the Eyes of Many Children,* 3d ed. (Boston: Pearson, 2009), 91.

49. Richard Erdoes and Alfonso Ortiz, eds., *American Indian Myths and Legends* (New York: Pantheon, 1984), v–x.

50. Mooney, *Myths of the Cherokee,* 5–7.

51. Edmunds and Clark, xiv–xvi; Erdoes and Ortiz, xiv; Barbara Kiefer, Susan Hepler, and Janet Hickman, *Charlotte Huck's Children's Literature,* 9th ed. (Boston: McGraw Hill, 2004), 308–312; Norton, *Multicultural Children's Literature,* 86–92; Sutherland, 190.

52. Edmunds and Clark, xiv.

53. Edgar, 15.

54. Henri Frankfort and H. A. Groenenwegen Frankfort, "Myth and Reality" in *The Intellectual Adventure of Ancient Man: An Essay on Speculative Thought in the Ancient Near East* (Chicago: University of Chicago Press, 1946), 4–6, 15.

55. *Ovid's Metamorphoses,* 1955, trans. Rolfe Humphries (Bloomington: Indiana University Press, 1983), 61.

56. Padraic Colum, *The Golden Fleece and the Heroes Who Lived Before Achilles,* 1921 (New York: Aladdin, 2004), 11.

57. Mooney, *Myths of the Cherokee,* 345–347.

58. Thomas B. Leekley, *The World of Manabozho: Tales of the Chippewa Indians* (New York: Vanguard, 1965), 7–9.

59. Erdoes and Ortiz, xii–xiii.

60. Mooney, *Myths of the Cherokee,* 273–274.

61. Mooney, *Myths of the Cherokee,* 277.

62. Mooney, *Myths of the Cherokee,* 327.

63. Mooney, *Myths of the Cherokee,* 329.

64. Mooney, *Myths of the Cherokee,* 431.

65. Mooney, *Myths of the Cherokee,* 327–329.

66. Mooney, *Myths of the Cherokee,* 316.

67. Mooney, *Myths of the Cherokee,* 320.

68. Mooney, *Myths of the Cherokee,* 324.

69. Thomas Bulfinch, *The Age of Fable or*

Beauties of Mythology, 1855 (Philadelphia: Henry Altemus, 1903), 27, 178–179, 192–193.

70. Kiefer, Hickman, and Hepler, 308.

71. Mooney, *Myths of the Cherokee,* 349.

72. Alan C. Purves, *The Scribal Society: An Essay on Literacy and Schooling in the Information Age* (White Plains, NY: Longman, 1990), 52, 56.

73. Mooney, *Myths of the Cherokee,* 330–335.

74. Mooney, *Myths of the Cherokee,* 506–548.

75. Mooney, *Myths of the Cherokee,* 428–505.

76. Qtd. in Edmonds and Clark, xvi.

77. Anne Pellowski, *The World of Storytelling* (New York: Bowker, 1977), 110.

78. Pellowski, *World of Storytelling,* 109–111.

79. La Farge, 13.

80. La Farge, 13.

81. Michael O. Tunnell and James S. Jacobs, *Children's Literature Briefly Considered,* 4th ed. (Upper Saddle River, NJ: Pearson, 2008), 188, 192–193.

82. Donna E. Norton, *Multicultural Children's Literature,* 79–84.

83. Hudson, *Southeastern Indians,* 1976 (Knoxville: University of Tennessee Press, 2007), 314–315.

84. Gallay, 307.

85. Robert Beverley, *The History of Virginia in Four Parts,* 2d rev. ed., 1722 (Richmond, VA: J. W. Randolph, 1855), 142.

86. Adair, 185–186.

87. Mooney, *Myths of the Cherokee,* 234–235.

88. Mooney, *Myths of the Cherokee* 187, 235.

89. Mooney, *Myths of the Cherokee,* 234–235.

90. Charles Hudson, *Knights of Spain, Warriors of the Sun: Hernando de Soto and the South's Ancient Chiefdoms* (Athens: University of Georgia Press, 1997), 13–26.

91. Robbie Ethridge, *From Chicaza to Chickasaw: The European Invasion and the Transformation of the Mississippian World, 1540–1715* (Chapel Hill: University of North Carolina Press, 2010), 89, 116.

92. Ethridge, *From Chicaza to Chickasaw,* 116.

93. Ethridge, *From Chicaza to Chickasaw,* 96–115.

94. Mooney, *Myths of the Cherokee,* 196.

95. Mooney, *Myths of the Cherokee,* 27–29.

96. Charles Hudson, *The Juan Pardo Expeditions: Exploration of the Carolinas and Tennessee, 1566–1568* (Washington, D.C.: Smithsonian Institution, 1990), 3, 95.

97. Hudson, *Juan Pardo Expeditions,* 25–26.

98. Sarah Ellis, "Spanish Fort Discovered at Dig Site in N. C. Foothills," *The Rock Hill Herald,* 24 July 2013: B4.

99. Hudson, *Juan Pardo Expeditions,* 146–147, 175.

100. Mooney, *Myths of the Cherokee,* 29.

101. Hudson, *Juan Pardo Expeditions,* 182.

102. Hudson, *Southeastern Indians,* 112.

103. Qtd. in Hudson, *Juan Pardo Expeditions,* 182.

104. Hudson, *Juan Pardo Expeditions,* 181–182.

105. Grace Steele Woodward, *The Cherokees* (Norman: University of Oklahoma Press, 1963), 35.

106. Woodward, 30.

107. Duane King, Ken Blankenship, and Barbara Duncan, *Emissaries of Peace: The 1762 Cherokee and British Delegations—An Exhibit of the Museum of the Cherokee Indian* (Cherokee, NC: Museum of the Cherokee Indian, 2006), vii.

108. Robert Conley, *The Cherokee Nation: A History* (Albuquerque: University of New Mexico Press 2005), 40–41.

109. George Chicken, *Journal of the March of the Carolinians into the Cherokee Mountains in the Yemassee Indian War, 1715–1716, from the Original MS,* ed. Langdon Cheves, in *Charleston, S.C., Yearbook – 1894* (Charleston, SC: Walker, Evans, and Cogswell, 1895), 342.

110. Chicken, *Journal of the March,* 342.

111. Chicken, *Journal of the March,* 344.

112. George Chicken, *Journal of Colonel George Chicken's Mission from Charleston, S.C., to the Cherokees, 1726* [1725] ed. Newton D. Mereness, in *Travels in the American Colonies* (New York: Macmillan, 1916), 107–108.

113. Chicken, *Journal of Colonel George Chicken's Mission,* 112–113.

114. Tobias Fitch, *Journal of Captain Tobias Fitch's Mission from Charleston, S.C., to the Creeks, 1726* [1725] ed. Newton D. Mereness, in *Travels in the American Colonies* (New York: Macmillan, 1916), 178–181.

115. Ethridge, *From Chicaza to Chickasaw,* 93, 113.

116. Fitch, 188–189.

117. Gallay, 346.

118. Edgar, 136.

119. Hudson, *Southeastern Indians*, 436–437.

120. Hudson, *Southeastern Indians*, 316.

121. McDowell, 10–11.

122. McDowell, 15.

123. Russell Thornton, *The Cherokees: A Population History* (Lincoln: University of Nebraska Press, 1990), 45–46.

124. David H. Corkran, "Cherokee Sun and Fire Observances," *Southern Indian Studies* 5 (October 1955): 35–36.

125. Theda Perdue, *Slavery and the Evolution of Cherokee Society, 1540–1866* (Knoxville: University of Tennessee Press, 1979), 23, 26.

126. Perdue, *Slavery and the Evolution of Cherokee Society,* 33–34.

127. Russell J. Snapp, *John Stuart and the Struggle for Empire on the Southern Frontier* (Baton Rouge: Louisiana State University Press, 1996), 123, 196–198, 201–205.

128. R. Halliburton, Jr., *Red over Black: Black Slavery among the Cherokee Indians* (Westport, CT: Greenwood, 1977), 10–11.

129. Hoig, 2.

130. Ethridge, *From Chicaza to* Chickasaw, 83–84.

131. Conley, 103–106.

132. Thornton, 52–53.

133. Thornton, 55–56.

134. Conley, 83.

135. Woodward, 140.

136. Querry, 2.

137. Querry, 2.

138. Querry, 2.

139. Alice Marriott and Carol K. Rachlin, *American Indian Mythology* (New York: Crowell, 1968), 12.

140. Marriott and Rachlin, 12–13.

141. Marriott and Rachlin, 14.

142. Marriott and Rachlin, 14.

143. Tedlock, 454.

144. Mooney, *Myths of the* Cherokee, 229.

145. Mooney, *Myths of the Cherokee*, 236.

146. Mooney, *Myths of the Cherokee*, 236.

147. Mooney, *Myths of the Cherokee*, 237.

148. Mooney, *Myths of the Cherokee*, 237.

149. Mooney, *Myths of the Cherokee*, 236–238.

150. Donna E. Norton, *Multicultural Children's Literature*, 82.

151. Ruth Sawyer, *The Way of the Storyteller*, 1942 (New York: Viking, 1962), 59.

152. Sawyer, 59.

153. Augusta Baker and Ellin Greene, *Storytelling: Art and Technique* (New York: Bowker, 1977), 45.

154. Margaret Read MacDonald, *The Storyteller's Start-Up Book: Finding, Learning, Performing, and Using Folktales, Including Twelve Tellable Tales* (Little Rock, AR: August House, 1993), 11.

155. Sawyer, 142.

156. Baker and Greene, 40.

157. Sawyer, 142.

158. Jamake Highwater, *Anpao: An American Indian Odyssey* (New York: HarperCollins, 1977), 241.

159. Highwater, 239.

160. Jack F. Kilpatrick and Anna G. Kilpatrick, *Friends of Thunder: Folktales of the Oklahoma Cherokees*, 1964 (Norman: University of Oklahoma Press, 1994), xvi.

161. Kilpatrick and Kilpatrick, xvi.

162. Kilpatrick and Kilpatrick, 22–23.

163. Barbara R. Duncan, ed., *Living Stories of the Cherokee* (Chapel Hill: University of North Carolina Press, 1998), 1.

164. Barbara R. Duncan, 2.

165. Barbara R. Duncan, 22–23.

166. Barbara R. Duncan, 23–24.

167. Ranier Schulte and John Biguenet, Introduction, in *Theories of Translation: An Anthology of Essays from Dryden to Derrida* (Chicago: University of Chicago Press, 1992), 6.

168. Octavio Paz, from *Translation: Literature and Letters,* trans. Irene del Corral, in *Theories of Translation: An Anthology of Essays from Dryden to Derrida*, ed. Ranier Schulte and John Biguenet (Chicago: University of Chicago Press, 1992), 152.

169. Paz, 154.

170. Terry Eagleton, *Literary Theory: An Introduction*, 2d ed. (Minneapolis: University of Minnesota Press, 1996), 64.

171. Eagleton, 64–65.

172. Eagleton, 64.

173. Louise M. Rosenblatt, *The Reader, the Text, and the Poem: The Transactional Theory of the Literary Work* (Carbondale: Southern Illinois University Press, 1978), 10–12.

174. Rosenblatt, 16–18.

175. Louise M. Rosenblatt, "Literature: The Reader's Role," *English Journal* 49.5 (May 1960): 305.

176. Albert J. Harris, and Edward R. Sipay, *How to Increase Reading Ability: A Guide to Developmental and Remedial Methods*, 9th ed. (New York: Longman, 1990), 559.

177. Harris and Sipay, 559.

178. Gale E. Thompkins, *Language Arts: Patterns of Practice,* 6th ed. (Upper Saddle River, NJ: Pearson, 2005), 8–9.

179. Dorothy G. Singer and Tracy A. Revenson, *A Piaget Primer: How a Child Thinks* (Madison, CT: International Universities Press, 1997), 11–15.

180. Harris and Sipay, 558–559; Barbara Taylor, et al., *Reading Difficulties: Instruction and Assessment,* 2nd ed. (New York: McGraw Hill, 1995), 17–18.

181. E. D. Hirsch, Jr., *Cultural Literacy: What Every American Needs to Know* (Boston: Houghton Mifflin, 1987), 39–41.

182. Marjorie Y. Lipson and Karen K. Wixson, *Assessment and Instruction of Reading and Writing Difficulties: An Interactive Approach,* 4th ed. (Boston: Pearson, 2009), 42–44.

183. Harry Daniels, "Introduction: Psychology in a Social World," in *An Introduction to Vygotsky,* ed. Harry Daniels (New York: Routledge, 1996), 4.

184. Harry Daniels, "Pedagogy," in *The Cambridge Companion to Vygotsky,* ed. Harry Daniels, Michael Cole, and James V. Wertsch (New York: Cambridge University Press, 2007), 310.

185. Dorothy Strickland, Lee Galda, and Bernice Cullinan, *Language Arts: Learning and Teaching* Belmont, CA: Thompson Wadsworth, 2004), 250.

186. Richard T. Vacca, Jo Anne L. Vacca, and Maryann Mraz, *Content Area Reading: Literacy and Learning Across the Curriculum,* 10th ed. (Boston: Pearson, 2011), 120.

187. Harris and Sipay, 604; Vacca, Vacca, and Mraz, 120.

188. Harris and Sipay, 556, 559, 604.

189. Daniels, "Pedagogy," 311.

190. Charles Lanman, *Letters from the Allegheny Mountains* (New York: Putnam, 1849), 119.

191. Mooney, *Myths of the Cherokee,* 300–301.

192. Mooney, *Myths of the Cherokee,* 256–257.

193. Mooney, *Myths of the Cherokee,* 441.

194. Mooney, *Myths of the Cherokee,* 242–248.

195. Betty Rose Nagle, "Introduction," in *Ovid's Fasti: Roman Holidays,* trans. Betty Rose Nagle (Bloomington: Indiana University Press, 1995), 31–32.

196. Mooney, *Myths of the Cherokee,* 369.

197. Hudson, *Southeastern Indians,* 408–421.

198. Mooney, *Myths of the Cherokee,* 315–316.

199. Mooney, *Myths of the Cherokee,* 335–336, 341–345.

200. Mooney, *Myths of the Cherokee,* 229.

201. Mooney, *Myths of the Cherokee,* 232.

202. Mooney, *Myths of the Cherokee,* 230–231.

203. Mooney, *Myths of the Cherokee,* 237.

204. Mooney, *Myths of the Cherokee,* 236.

205. Edward P. J. Corbett, *Classical Rhetoric for the Modern Student,* 2d ed. (New York: Oxford University Press, 1971), 460–461.

206. Sheridan Baker, *The Complete Stylist* (New York: Crowell, 1966), 320.

207. Tufte, 217–218.

208. Corbett, 463.

209. Sheridan Baker, 328.

210. Corbett, 473.

211. Corbett, 464.

212. Corbett, 464.

213. Corbett, 466–467.

214. Tufte, 176.

215. Tufte, 177.

216. Corbett, 470–471.

217. Corbett, 470.

218. Sheridan Baker, 321.

219. Mooney, *Myths of the Cherokee,* 431.

220. Ethridge, *From Chicaza to Chickasaw,* 20.

221. James Mooney, *The Sacred Formulas of the Cherokees,* 1891, in *James Mooney's History, Myths, and Sacred Formulas of the Cherokees* (Fairview, NC: Historical Images, 1992), 339.

222. Sheridan Baker, 328; Corbett, 472.

223. Sheridan Baker, 328; Corbett, 473.

224. Corbett, 472–474.

225. Mooney, *Myths of the* Cherokee, 230, 454.

226. Adair, 378–380.

227. Sheridan Baker, 331; Corbett, 466.

228. Tufte, 23–24.

229. Corbett, 459–460.

230. Simms, 209.

231. Simms, 209.

232. John Caldwell Guilds, "William Gilmore Simms and the Portrayal of the American Indian: A Literary View," in *An Early and Strong Sympathy: The Indian Writings of William Gilmore Simms,* ed. John Caldwell Guilds and Charles Hudson (Columbia: Uni-

versity of South Carolina Press, 2003), xxvii, xxix.

233. Sean R. Busick, *A Sober Desire for History: William Gilmore Simms as Historian* (Columbia: University of South Carolina Press, 2005), 63–64.

234. Busick, 65.

235. Busick, 67.

236. Charles Hudson, "William Gilmore Simms and the Portrayal of the American Indian: An Ethnohistorical View," in *An Early and Strong Sympathy: The Indian Writings of William Gilmore Simms*, ed. John Caldwell Guilds and Charles Hudson (Columbia: University of South Carolina Press, 2003), xlii.

237. Hudson, xliii.

238. Simms, 218.

239. Simms, 224.

240. Mooney, *Myths of the Cherokee*, 264–265.

241. Hudson, "William Gilmore Simms," xlix–l.

242. E. Don Herd, Jr., "Cateechee, Issaqueena, and Ninety Six," in *The South Carolina Upcountry, 1540–1980: Historical and Biographical Sketches,* Vol. I (Greenwood, SC: Attic, 1981), 98.

243. Daniel, 70.

244. Daniel, 71.

245. Herd, 91; Buzz Williams, "Trailing Issaqueena a.k.a. Cateechee," *Chattooga Quarterly* (Spring 2007): 8.

246. Herd, 91.

247. McDowell, 495.

248. John Oliphant, *Peace and War on the Anglo-Cherokee Frontier, 1756–63* (Baton Rouge: Louisiana State University Press, 2001), 111.

249. Qtd. in Herd, 104–105.

250. Elizabeth F. Ellet, *The Women of the American Revolution,* Vol. III (New York: Baker and Scribner, 1850), 88–89.

251. Tom Hatley, *The Dividing Paths: Cherokees and South Carolinians Through the Era of the Revolution* (New York: Oxford University Press, 1993), 33, 89.

252. Daniel, 19.

253. Daniel, 12.

254. Ethridge, *From Chicaza to Chickasaw,* 94; Hudson, *Southeastern Indians,* 254–255.

255. Daniel, 35.

256. Daniel, 31–32, 34–35.

257. Daniel, 32.

258. Daniel, 33–34.

259. Daniel, 34, 37.

260. Daniel, 74.

261. Mooney, *Myths of the Cherokee,* 524.

262. Henry Timberlake, *The Memoirs of Lt. Henry Timberlake: The Story of a Soldier, Adventurer, and Emissary to the Cherokees, 1756–1765,* ed. Duane H. King (Cherokee, NC: Museum of the Cherokee Indian Press, 2007), 36–37.

263. Oliphant, 5.

264. Duane H. King in Timberlake, 122.

265. F. Muench, *Palmetto Lyrics* (Charleston, SC: Lucas and Richardson, 1896), 45–47.

266. F. Muench, 24–25.

267. Herd, 109.

268. Bruce E. Baker and Shelby Stephenson, "Country Music," in *Encyclopedia of North Carolina,* ed. William S. Powell (Chapel Hill: University of North Carolina Press, 2006), 302.

269. Michael C. Scoggins, *The Scotch-Irish Influence on Country Music in the Carolinas: Border Ballads, Fiddle Tunes and Sacred Songs* (Charleston, SC: History, 2013), 17–22.

270. Scoggins, 22–25.

271. Scoggins, 31.

272. John Henry Logan, *A History of the Upper Country of South Carolina from the Earliest Periods to the Close of the War of Independence* (Charleston, SC: S. G. Courtenay; Columbia, SC: P. B. Glass, 1859), 168.

273. Logan, 174.

274. Snapp, 31.

275. McDowell, 149, 160.

276. Baker and Stephenson, 302.

277. Scoggins, 44.

278. Samuel Kercheval, *History of the Valley of Virginia,* 2d ed. (Woodstock, VA: John Gatewood Printer, 1850), 244.

279. Kercheval, 244.

280. Kercheval, 244.

281. C. Hugh Holman, *Handbook to Literature* (Indianapolis: Bobbs-Merrill, 1972), 52.

282. Oscar Wilde, *The Critic as Artist,* in *The Complete Works of Oscar Wilde: Stories, Plays, Poems, and Essays* (New York: Harper and Row, 1989), 1028.

Bibliography

Aarne, Antti, and Stith Thompson. *The Types of Folktale: A Classification and Bibliography.* 2d rev. ed. Helsinski: Academia Scientiarum Fennica, 1961.

Adair, James. *The History of the American Indians.* 1775. Ed. Kathryn E. Holland Braund. Tuscaloosa: University of Alabama Press, 2005.

Anderson, William L. "Judaculla Rock." In *Encyclopedia of North Carolina,* edited by William S. Powell, 638–639. Chapel Hill: University of North Carolina Press, 2006.

Baker, Augusta, and Ellin Greene. *Storytelling: Art and Technique.* New York: Bowker, 1977.

Baker, Bruce E., and Shelby Stephenson. "Country Music." In *Encyclopedia of North Carolina,* edited by William S. Powell, 302–303. Chapel Hill: University of North Carolina Press, 2006.

Baker, Sheridan. *The Complete Stylist.* New York: Crowell, 1966.

Bartram, William. *William Bartram on the Southeastern Indians.* Ed. Gregory A. Waselkov and Kathryn E. Holland Braund. Lincoln: University of Nebraska Press, 1995.

Beverley, Robert. *The History of Virginia in Four Parts.* 2d rev. ed., 1722. Richmond, VA: J. W. Randolph, 1855.

Brown, Douglas Summers. *The Catawba Indians: The People of the River.* Columbia: University of South Carolina Press, 1966.

Brown, Dee. *Bury My Heart at Wounded Knee: An Indian History of the American West.* New York: Holt, Rinehart, and Winston, 1970.

Brown, John P. "Eastern Cherokee Chiefs." *Chronicles of Oklahoma* 16.1 (March 1938): 3–35. Web. 15 June 2013. http://digital.library.okstate.edu/chronicles/vO16/.

Brown, M. L. *Firearms in Colonial America: The Impact on History and Technology, 1492–1792.* Washington, D.C.: Smithsonian Institution, 1980.

Bulfinch, Thomas. *The Age of Fable or Beauties of Mythology.* 1855. Philadelphia: Henry Altemus, 1903.

Busick, Sean R. *A Sober Desire for History: William Gilmore Simms as Historian.* Columbia: University of South Carolina Press, 2005.

Buttrick, Daniel Sabin. *Antiquities of the Cherokee Indians. Compiled from the Collection of Rev. Daniel Sabin Buttrick, Their Missionary from 1817 to 1847.* Vinita, OK: Indian Chieftain, 1884. Ed. Jeffrey Fuller-Freeman, 2003. Web. 8 August 2013. http://etext.lib.virginia.edu.

Cann, Marvin. *Old Ninety Six in the South Carolina Backcountry: A Historical Guide.* 2000. Fort Washington, PA: Eastern National, 2010.

Causey, Beth G. "The Legend of Cateechee of Keowee." In *South Carolina Legends,* 15–33. Mount Pleasant, SC: Hope, 1969.

Chacon, Richard J., and David H. Dye. "Conclusions." In *The Taking and Displaying of Human Body Parts as Trophies by Amerindians,* edited by Richard J. Chacon and David H. Dye, 630–653. New York: Springer, 2007.

Chambers, Ian. "Alexander Cumming—King or Pawn? An Englishman on the Colonial Chessboard of the Eighteenth-Century American Southeast." All-UC Economic History and All-UC World History Groups Conference on Middle Men and Networks: Economic, Social, and Cultural Foundations of the Global Economy. University of California, Riverside: November 3–5, 2006: N.p. Web. 7 Jan. 2014. www.

iga.ucdavis.edu/Research/All-UC/conference/2006-fall.

Chicken, George. *Journal of the March of the Carolinians into the Cherokee Mountains in the Yemassee Indian War, 1715–1716, From the Original MS.* Ed. Langdon Cheves. In *Charleston, S.C., Yearbook—1894,* 313–354. Charleston, SC: Walker, Evans, and Cogswell, 1895.

_____. *Journal of Colonel George Chicken's Mission from Charleston, S.C., to the Cherokees, 1726* [1725]. In *Travels in the American Colonies,* edited by Newton D. Mereness, 93–172. New York: Macmillan, 1916.

Colum, Padraic. *The Golden Fleece and the Heroes Who Lived Before Achilles.* 1921. New York: Aladdin, 2004.

Conley, Robert. *The Cherokee Nation: A History.* Albuquerque: University of New Mexico Press, 2005.

Corbett, Edward P. J. *Classical Rhetoric for the Modern Student.* 2d ed. New York: Oxford University Press, 1971.

Corkran, David. H. *The Carolina Indian Frontier.* Columbia: University of South Carolina Press, 1970.

_____. *The Cherokee Frontier: Conflict and Survival, 1740–62.* Norman: University of Oklahoma Press, 1962.

_____. "Cherokee Sun and Fire Observances." *Southern Indian Studies* 5 (October 1955): 33–38.

_____. "The Sacred Fire of the Cherokees." *Southern Indian Studies* 5 (October 1953): 21–26.

Curtin, Jeremiah. "A Warrior Cared for by Wolves." In *Seneca Indian Myths,* 394–398. New York: Dutton, 1922. Web. 22 June 2013. http://www.sacred-texts.com.

Daniel, James Walter. *Cateechee of Keeowee: A Descriptive Poem.* Nashville, TN: Publishing House of the Methodist Episcopal Church, South, Barbee and Smith, 1898.

Daniels, Harry. "Introduction: Psychology in a Social World." In *An Introduction to Vygotsky,* edited by Harry Daniels, 1–27. New York: Routledge, 1996.

_____. "Pedagogy." In *The Cambridge Companion to Vygotsky,* edited byHarry Daniels, Michael Cole, and James V. Wertsch, 307–331. New York: Cambridge University Press, 2007.

Davis, Kenneth Penn. "Chaos in the Indian Country: The Cherokee Nation, 1828–35." In *The Cherokee Nation: A Troubled History,* edited by Duane King, 129–147. Knoxville: University of Tennessee Press, 1979.

Donelson, Kenneth L., and Alleen Pace Nilsen. *Literature for Today's Young Adults.* 7th ed. Boston: Pearson, 2005.

Duncan, Barbara R., ed. *Living Stories of the Cherokee.* Chapel Hill: University of North Carolina Press, 1998.

Duncan, Barbara R., and Brett H. Riggs. *Cherokee Heritage Trails Guidebook.* Chapel Hill: University of North Carolina Press, 2003.

Eagleton, Terry. *Literary Theory: An Introduction.* 2d ed. Minneapolis: University of Minnesota Press, 1996.

Edgar, Walter. *South Carolina: A History.* Columbia: University of South Carolina Press, 1998.

Edmonds, Margot, and Ella E. Clark. *Voices in the Wind: Native American Legends.* New York: Castle, 2003.

Ellet, Elizabeth F. *The Women of the American Revolution.* Vol. 3. 4th ed. New York: Baker and Scribner, 1850.

Ellis, Sarah. "Spanish Fort Discovered at Dig Site in N.C. Foothills." *The Rock Hill Herald,* 24 July 2013: B4.

Ellison, George. "Introduction: James Mooney and the Eastern Cherokees." In *James Mooney's History, Myths, and Sacred Formulas of the Cherokees,* 1–32. Fairview, NC: Bright Mountain, 1992.

Erdoes, Richard, and Alfonso Ortiz. *American Indian Myths and Legends.* New York: Pantheon, 1984.

Ethridge, Robbie. *From Chicaza to Chickasaw: The European Invasion and the Transformation of the Mississippian World, 1540–1715.* Chapel Hill: University of North Carolina Press, 2010.

_____. "Tobacco Among the Cherokees." *Journal of Cherokee Studies* 3.2 (Spring 1978): 76–86.

Faulkner, Charles H. "Origin and Evolution of the Cherokee Winter House." *Journal of Cherokee Studies* 3.2 (Spring 1978): 87–93.

Fitch, Tobias. *Journal of Captain Tobias Fitch's Mission from Charleston to the Creeks, 1726* [1725]. In *Travels in the American Colonies,* edited by Newton D. Mereness, 173–212. New York: Macmillan, 1916.

Fogelson, Raymond D. "The Conjuror in Eastern Cherokee Society." *Journal of Cherokee Studies* 5.2 (Fall 1980): 60–87.

Frankfort, Henri, and H. A. Groenenwegen

Frankfort. "Myth and Reality." In *The Intellectual Adventure of Ancient Man: An Essay on Speculative Thought in the Ancient Near East.* Chicago: University of Chicago Press, 1946: 3–27.

Friedrich, Hugo. "On the Art of Translation." Trans. Rainer Schulte and John Biguenet. In *Theories of Translation: An Anthology of Essays from Dryden to Derrida,* edited by Rainer Schulte and John Biguenet, 11–16. Chicago: University of Chicago Press, 1992.

Gallay, Alan. *The Indian Slave Trade: The Rise of the English Empire in the American South.* New Haven, CT: Yale University Press, 2002.

George, David P., Jr. *96 Decoded: A Mystery Solved.* N.p., 2007.

Guilds, John Caldwell. "William Gilmore Simms and the Portrayal of the American Indian: A Literary View." In *An Early and Strong Sympathy: The Indian Writings of William Gilmore Simms,* edited by John Caldwell Guilds and Charles Hudson, xiii–xxxiii. Columbia: University of South Carolina Press, 2003.

Hairr, John. "Gaps." In *Encyclopedia of North Carolina,* edited by William S. Powell, 490–491. Chapel Hill: University of North Carolina Press, 2006.

Haywood, John. *The Natural and Aboriginal History of Tennessee, Up to the First Settlements by the White People, in the Year 1768.* Nashville, TN: George Wilson, 1823.

Halliburton, R., Jr. *Red over Black: Black Slavery Among the Cherokee Indians.* Westport, CT: Greenwood, 1977.

Harris, Albert J., and Edward R. Sipay. *How to Increase Reading Ability: A Guide to Developmental and Remedial Reading Methods.* 9th ed. New York: Longman, 1990.

Herd, E. Don, Jr. "Cateechee, Issaquena, and Ninety Six." In *The South Carolina Upcountry, 1540–1980: Historical and Biographical Sketches.* Vol. 1, 84–112. Greenwood, SC: Attic, 1981.

Highwater, Jamake. *Anpao: An American Indian Odyssey.* New York: HarperCollins, 1977.

Hirsh, E. D., Jr. *Cultural Literacy: What Every American Needs to Know.* Boston: Houghton Mifflin, 1987.

Hodler, Thomas W., and Howard A. Schretter. *The Atlas of Georgia.* Athens: Institute of Community and Area Development, 1986.

Hoffman, Joseph Paul. "Waterfalls." In *Encyclopedia of North Carolina,* edited by William S. Powell, 1183–1184. Chapel Hill: University of North Carolina Press, 2006.

Hoig, Stanley W. *The Cherokees and Their Chiefs: In the Wake of Empire.* Fayetteville: University of Arkansas Press, 1998.

Holman, C. Hugh. *A Handbook to Literature.* 3d ed. Indianapolis: Bobbs-Merrill, 1972.

Hudson, Charles. *The Juan Pardo Expeditions: Exploration of the Carolinas and Tennessee, 1566–1568.* Washington: Smithsonian Institution, 1990.

_____. *Knights of Spain, Warriors of the Sun: Hernando de Soto and the South's Ancients Chiefdoms.* Athens: University of Georgia Press, 1997.

_____. *The Southeastern Indians.* 1976. Knoxville: University of Tennessee Press, 2007.

_____. "Uktena: A Cherokee Anomalous Monster." *Journal of Cherokee Studies* 3.2 (Spring 1978): 62–75.

_____. "William Gilmore Simms and the Portrayal of the American Indian: An Ethnohistorical View." In *An Early and Strong Sympathy: The Indian Writings of William Gilmore Simms,* edited by John Caldwell Guilds and Charles Hudson, xxxiv–li. Columbia: University of South Carolina Press, 2003.

Ivers, Larry E. *Colonial Forts of South Carolina, 1670–1175.* Columbia: University of South Carolina Press, 1970.

Josephy, Alvin M., Jr. *500 Nations: An Illustrated History of North American Indians.* 1994. New York: Gramercy Books, 2002.

Kelly, James C. "Notable Persons in Cherokee History: Attakullakulla." *Journal of Cherokee Studies* 3.1 (Winter 1978): 2–34.

Kercheval, Samuel. *A History of the Valley of Virginia.* 2d ed. Woodstock, VA: John Gatewood Printer, 1850.

Kiefer, Barbara, Susan Hepler, and Janet Hickman. *Charlotte Huck's Children's Literature.* 9th ed. Boston: McGraw Hill, 2004.

Kilpatrick, Jack F., and Anna G. Kilpatrick. *Friends of Thunder: Folktales of the Oklahoma Cherokees.* 1964. Norman: University of Oklahoma Press, 1994.

King, Duane, Ken Blankenship, and Barbara Duncan. *Emissaries of Peace: The 1762 Cherokee and British Delegations—An Exhibit of the Museum of the Cherokee Indian.* Cherokee, NC: Museum of the Cherokee Indian, 2006.

Kovacik, Charles F., and John J. Winberry. *South Carolina: A Geography*. Columbia: University of South Carolina Press, 1989.

La Farge, Oliver. "Myths That Hide the American Indian." In *Historical Viewpoints, Volume One: To 1877, Notable Articles from American Heritage*, edited by John A. Garraty, 12–25. New York: Harper and Row, 1970.

Lanman, Charles. *Letters from the Allegheny Mountains*. New York: Putnam, 1849.

Lawson, John. *A New Voyage to Carolina*. Ed. Hugh Talmage Lefler. Chapel Hill: University of North Carolina Press, 1967.

Lee, Lawrence. *Indian Wars in North Carolina*. Raleigh, NC: Carolina Charter Tercentenary Commission, 1963.

Leekley, Thomas B. *The World of Manabozho: Tales of the Chippewa Indians*. New York: Vanguard, 1965.

Lipson, Marjorie Y., and Karen K. Wixson. *Assessment and Instruction of Reading and Writing Difficulties: An Interactive Approach*. 4th ed. Boston: Pearson, 2009.

Lofaro, Michael. *Daniel Boone: An American Life*. Lexington: University of Kentucky Press, 2010.

Logan, John Henry. *A History of the Upper Country of South Carolina from the Earliest Periods to the Close of the War of Independence*. Charleston, SC: S. G. Courtenay; Columbia, SC: P. B. Glass, 1859.

MacDonald, James M. *Politics of the Personal in the Old North State: Griffith Rutherford in Revolutionary North Carolina*. Diss. LSU, 2006. Baton Rouge: Louisiana State University, 2006. Web. 7 Dec. 2013.

MacDonald, Margaret Read. *The Storyteller's Start-Up Book: Finding, Learning, Performing, and Using Folktales, Including Twelve Tellable Tales*. Little Rock, AR: August House, 1993.

Mann, Charles C. *1491: New Revelations of the Americas Before Columbus*. 2d ed. New York: Vintage, 2011.

Marriott, Alice, and Carol K. Rachlin. *American Indian Mythology*. New York: Thomas Y. Crowell, 1968.

McCallister, Andrew B. "Tallulah Falls and Gorge." *New Georgia Encyclopedia*. 13 Dec. 2013. Web. 16 Dec. 2013: 1–2. http://www-georgiaencyclopedia.org/articles/geography.

McDowell, William L., ed. *Colonial Records of South Carolina. Series 2. Documents Relating to Indian Affairs 1754–1765*. Columbia: University of South Carolina Press, 1970.

McMichael, George, et al. *Anthology of American Literature. Volume I, Colonial Through Romantic*. New York: Macmillan, 1974.

Milling, Chapman J. *Red Carolinians*. Chapel Hill: University of North Carolina Press, 1940.

Mills, Hugh H. "Blue Ridge Province." In *Encyclopedia of Appalachia*. Ed. Rudy Abramson and Jean Haskell. Knoxville: University of Tennessee Press, 2006: 11–12.

Mooney, James. *Myths of the* Cherokee. 1900. In *James Mooney's History, Myths, and Sacred Formulas of the Cherokees*, 4–576. Fairview, NC: Bright Mountain, 1992.

_____. *The Sacred Formulas of the Cherokee*. 1891. In *James Mooney's History, Myths, and Sacred Formulas of the Cherokees*, 301–397. Fairview, NC: Historical Images, 1992.

Morrison, Mark. "Waterfalls." *New Georgia Encyclopedia*. 13 Dec. 2013. Web. 16 Dec. 2013: 1–3. http://www.georgiaencyclopedia.org/articles/geography.

Muench, F. *Palmetto Lyrics*. Charleston, SC: Lucas and Richardson, 1896.

Nagle, Betty Rose, trans. *Ovid's Fasti: Roman Holidays*. Bloomington: Indiana University Press, 1995.

"Nantahala Gorge." *The Blue Ridge Highlander*. Web. 24 June 2012. http://theblueridgehighlander.com.

North Carolina State Road Atlas. Alexandria, VA: American Map, 2009.

Norton, Donna E. *Through the Eyes of a Child: An Introduction to Children's Literature*. 8th ed. Boston: Pearson, 2011.

_____. *Multicultural Children's Literature: Through the Eyes of Many Children*. 3d ed. Boston: Pearson, 2009.

Norton, Terry L., and Betty Lou Jackson Land. *50 Literacy Strategies for Beginning Teachers, 1–8*. 3d ed. Boston: Pearson, 2012.

"Oconee County." In *The Encyclopedia of South Carolina*, edited by Walter Edgar, 679–680. Columbia: University of South Carolina Press, 2006.

Oliphant, John. *Peace and War on the Anglo-Cherokee Frontier, 1756–63*. Baton Rouge: Louisiana State University Press, 2001.

Owsley, Douglas W., et al. "Human Finger and Hand Bone Necklaces from the Plains and Great Basin." In *The Taking and Dis-*

playing of Human Body Parts as Trophies by Amerindians, edited by Richard J. Chacon and David H. Dye, 124–166. New York: Springer, 2007.

Ovid: Metamorphoses. Trans. Rolfe Humphries. 1955. Bloomington: Indiana University Press, 1983.

Parramore, Thomas, et al. "Tuscarora Indians." In *Encyclopedia of North Carolina*, edited by William S. Powell, 124–166. Chapel Hill: University of North Carolina Press, 2006.

Payne, John Howard. Letter to a Relative in New York, 1835: The Green-Corn Dance. In John R. Swanton, "The Green-Corn Dance." *Chronicles of Oklahoma*. 10.2 (June 1932): 171–195. Web. 10 Oct. 2013. http://digital.library.okstate.edu/chronicles/vO10/vO10.

Paz, Octavio. From *Translation: Literature and Letters*. Trans. Irene del Corral. In *Theories of Translation: An Anthology of Essays from Dryden to Derrida*, edited by Rainer Schulte and John Biguenet, 152–162. Chicago: University of Chicago Press, 1992.

Pellowski, Anne. *The World of Storytelling*. New York: Bowker, 1977.

Perdue, Theda. *Cherokee Women: Gender and Culture Change, 1700–1835*. Lincoln: University of Nebraska Press, 1998.

_____. *Slavery and the Evolution of Cherokee Society, 1540–1866*. Knoxville: University of Tennessee Press, 1979.

"Pickens County." In *The South Carolina Encyclodedia*, edited by Walter Edgar, 723–724. Columbia: University of South Carolina Press, 2006.

Purves, Alan C. *The Scribal Society: An Essay on Schooling in the Information Age*. White Plains, NY: Longman, 1990.

Querry, Ron. "Discovery of America: Stories Told by Indian Voices." In *American Diversity, American Identity: The Lives and Works of 145 Writers Who Define the American Experience*, edited by John K. Roth, 1–3. New York: Holt, 1995.

Rosenblatt, Louise M. "Literature: The Reader's Role." *English Journal* 49.5 (May 1960): 304–310, 315.

_____. *The Reader, the Text, the Poem: The Transactional Theory of the Literary Work*. Carbondale: Southern Illinois University Press, 1978.

Rozema, Vicki. *Footsteps of the Cherokees: A Guide to Eastern Homelands of the Cherokee Nation*. 2d ed. Winston-Salem, NC: John F. Blair, 2007.

Sawyer, Ruth. *The Way of the Storyteller*. 1942. New York: Viking, 1962.

Schoolcraft, Henry R. *Notes on the Iroquois; or Contributions to American History, Antiquities, and General Ethnology*. Albany, NY: Erastus H. Pease, 1847.

Schulte, Rainer, and John Biguenet. Introduction. *Theories of Translation: An Anthology of Essays from Dryden to Derrida*, 1–10. Chicago: University of Chicago Press, 1992.

Scoggins, Michael C. *The Scotch-Irish Influence on Country Music in the Carolinas: Border Ballads, Fiddle Tunes, and Sacred Songs*. Charleston, SC: History, 2013.

Seabrook, Charles. "Blue Ridge Mountains." *New Georgia Encyclopedia*. 23 August 2013. Web. 2 Jan. 2014: 1–3. http://www.georgiaencyclopedia.org/articles/geography.

Simms, William Gilmore. *The Wigwam and the Cabin*. Rev. ed. New York: W. J. Widdleton, 1856.

Singer, Dorothy G., and Tracey A. Revenson. *A Piaget Primer: How a Child Thinks*. Madison, CT: International Universities, 1997.

Sirmans, M. Eugene. *Colonial South Carolina: A Political History, 1663–1763*. Chapel Hill: University of North Carolina Press, 1966.

Snapp, J. Russell. *John Stuart and the Struggle for Empire on the Southern Frontier*. Baton Rouge: Louisiania State University Press, 1996.

Strickland, Dorothy, Lee Galda, and Bernice Cullinan. *Language Arts: Learning and Teaching*. Belmont, CA: Thompson Wadsworth, 2004.

Strickland, Rennard. *Fire and the Spirits: Cherokee Law from Clan to Court*. Norman: University of Oklahoma Press, 1975.

Sutherland, Zena. *Children and Books*. 9th ed. New York: Longman, 1997.

Swanton, John R. "Comparison of Myths." In *Tales of the Southeastern Indians*. Washington, D.C.: Bureau of American Ethnology, No. 88, 1929: 267–275. Web. Feb. 5, 2014. http://www.sacred-texts.com.

_____. "The Yuchi." In *Early History of the Creek Indians and Their Neighbors*. Washington, D.C.: Smithsonian Institute, Bureau of American Ethnology, Bulletin 73, 1922: 286–312. Web. Mar. 13, 2013. http://www.openlibrary.org.

"Tallulah Gorge." *Brown's Guide to Georgia.* Web. 1 July 2012. http://www.brownsguides.com.

"Tallulah Gorge." *Official Guide to North Georgia and North Georgia Mountains.* Web. 13 Dec. 2013. http://www.northgeorgia.com//attractions/tallulah-gorge.

Taylor, Barbara, et al. *Reading Difficulties: Instruction and Assessment.* 2d ed. New York: McGraw-Hill, 1995.

Tedlock, Dennis. "On the Translation of Style in Oral Narrative." In *Translation—Theory and Practice: A Historical Reader,* edited by Daniel Weissbort and Astradur Eysteinsson, 454–456. New York: Oxford University Press, 2006.

Thomkins, Gale E. *Language Arts: Patterns of Practice.* 6th ed. Upper Saddle River, NJ: Pearson, 2005.

Thornton, Russell. *The Cherokees: A Population History.* Lincoln: University of Nebraska Press, 1990.

Timberlake, Henry. *The Memoirs of Lt. Henry Timberlake: The Story of a Soldier, Adventurer, and Emissary to the Cherokees, 1756–1765.* Ed. Duane H. King. Cherokee, NC: Museum of the Cherokee Indian Press, 2007.

Tufte, Virginia. *Artful Sentences: Syntax as Style.* Cheshire, CT: Graphics, 2006.

Tunnell, Michael O., and James S. Jacobs. *Children's Literature, Briefly Considered.* 4th ed. Upper Saddle River, NJ: Pearson, 2008.

Usery, Lynn E. "Geographic Regions of Georgia: Overview." *New Georgia Encyclopedia.* 1 Oct. 2013. Web. 2 Jan. 2014: 1–2. http://www.georgiaencyclopedia.org/articles/geography.

Vacca, Richard T., Jo Anne L. Vacca, and Maryann Mraz. *Content Area Reading: Literacy and Learning Across the Curriculum.* 10th ed. Boston: Pearson, 2011.

Walker, Barbara G. "Menstrual Blood." In *The Woman's Encyclopedia of Myths and Secrets,* 635–645. San Francisco: Harper, 1983.

Walker, Felix. "Narrative of an Adventure in Kentucky in the Year 1775." *DeBow's Review* 16.2 (February 1854): 150–155.

Warren, Wallace H. "Chattahoochee National Forest." In *Encyclopedia of Appalachia.* Ed. Rudy Abramson and Jean Haskell, 627. Knoxville: University of Tennessee Press, 2006.

_____. "Tallulah Gorge." In *Encyclopedia of Appalachia,* edited by Rudy Abramson and Jean Haskell. Knoxville: University of Tennessee Press, 2006: 677.

Whisker, James B. *Arms Makers in Colonial America.* Selinsgrave, PA: Susquehanna University Press, 1992.

Wilburn, Hiram C. "Judaculla Place-Names and the Judaculla Tales." *Southern Indian Studies* 4 (October 1952): 23–26.

_____. "Nununyi, the Kituhwas, or Mountain Indians and the State of North Carolina." *Southern Indian Studies* 2 (October 1950): 54–64.

Wilde, Oscar. "The Critic as Artist." In *The Complete Works of Oscar Wilde: Stories, Plays, Poems, and Essays,* 1009–1059. New York: Harper and Row, 1989.

Williams, Buzz. "Trailing Issaqueena a.k.a. Cateechee." *Chattooga Quarterly* (Spring 2007): 6–8. Web. July 1, 2013. http://www.chattoogariver.org.

Williamson, Ron. "*Otinontsiskiaj ondaon (The House of Cut-Off Heads)*: The History and Archaeology of Northern Iroquoian Trophy Taking." In *The Taking and Displaying of Human Body Parts as Trophies by Amerindians,* edited by Richard J. Chacon and David H. Dye, 190–221. New York: Springer, 2007.

Wolfson, Evelyn. *From Abenaki to Zuni: A Dictionary of Native American Tribes.* New York: Walker, 1988.

Wood, Michael. *Conquistadors.* Berkeley: University of California Press, 2000.

Woodward, Grace Steele. *The Cherokees.* Norman: University of Oklahoma Press, 1963.

Index

Aarne, Antii 17
Above World *see* The Three Worlds
Adair, James 2–3, 5–6, 14, 24, 46
Agan-uni-tsi 86–88, 90
The Age of Fable or Beauties of Mythology 20
Algic Researches 2
All Bones *see* Flying Squirrel
Allan, Frank 52
ancient time 60, 62, 70; long ago 74, 76, 81, 84
Andersen, Hans Christian 35
Anglo-Cherokee War 4, 166, 168, 170
Ani-Tsaguhi *see* Bear tribe
Apportioner 140
Artful Sentences: Syntax as Style 6, 44
Arthur and Needham expedition 26
asi *see* winter house
Ataghi, the magic lake 70
Atahuallpa 13
Attakullakulla 14–15, 131
Awi Usdi *see* Little Deer
Ax, John 33, 43–44
Ayunini *see* Swimmer
Aztecs 13

background of experience 5–6, 21–22, 36–42;
    see also decontextualized stories; schema
    theory; topical knowledge
Baker, Augusta 35
Baker, Sheridan 47
balance: Cherokee concept of 36, 64, 73;
    improper comingling of elements 62, 114;
    Native American concept of 17
bald mountains 114–121
ball play 43, 46, 136–141; euphemism for war
    66, 155
ballads 54
Balsam Mountains 114–115, 117; Cold Moun-
    tain 117
barbacoa 65
Bartram, William 189
Bear songs 75–76
Bear tribe 70–71, 74–76
Beloved Men 140–142, 149, 159
Beloved Women 126, 150, 169

Below World *see* The Three Worlds
Beverley, Robert 24, 189
Biguenet, John 37
black as symbol of death 139–140, 142–143
black drink or tea 79–80, 122, 133, 143
Blankenship, Ken 27
blood vengeance 147–148, 151, 155
Blount, Chief Tom 13
Blue Ridge Mountains 25–25, 76, 90, 92
Boas, Frank 6, 33
Boone, Daniel 166
borderers *see* Scots Irish
Broad River 167
Brothers Grimm 18, 33
Brown, Dee 15
Brown, Douglas Summers 12
Brown, John P. 14
Bulfinch, Thomas 20
Bury My Heart at Wounded Knee 15
Busick, Sean R. 47–48

Cambridge *see* Ninety Six
cannibals 21, 97–98, 101, 103–104; Roasters
    68–69; water cannibals 106–107
captives 29, 49, 124, 135–136, 147–151, 157,
    172–173, 180
Carolina parrot 156, 158–159
Catawba River 166–167
Catawba tribe 10, 12, 24
Cateechee Chapter, Daughters of the Ameri-
    can Revolution 4
Cateechee of Keeowee: A Descriptive Poem 4,
    49–53, 169–189; *see also* Daniel, the Rev.
    James; Herd, E. Don, Jr.; Issaqueena;
    Issaqueena Falls; Muench, Francis; Sloan,
    Charles Reid
"Cateechee, the Indian Maiden" 52
cedar as sacred 59
Chattahoochee National Forest 90
Chattahoochee River 109
Chattooga River 108
Cheraw coalescence with Catawba 12; war
    with colony of South Carolina 12–13
Cherokee chiefs and headmen 14, 130

The Cherokee Nation 27
Cherokee population 31
Chickamaugans 14
Chickasaw 10, 13, 29
Chicken, Col. George 27–28
Chilhowee 152–156
Chimney Rock 42, 76
Choctaw 3, 10, 13, 49, 51, 171–173, 188
Choctaw prophet 51
Chota 26–27, 77, 134, 136–138, 140, 142, 145, 147
Chunkey game and stone 67, 79–80
Civil Rights movement 23
Clark, Ella F. 17, 22
classical mythology 18
Classical Rhetoric for the Modern Student 47
Clingmans Dome 70, 155
Cohutta Mountains 85, 87, 90–91
Colum, Padraic 18
Compact of 1802 32
The Complete Stylist 47
conjurors 58–59, 72, 75, 78, 84, 94, 101–102, 120, 138–141, 147–148, 157, 159; *see also* Agan-uni-tsi; Choctaw prophet; Gunska-liski; Thadodaho
Conley, Robert J. 27
considerate text 40
Coosa River 130
Corn *see* Selu
Cowee 152–156, 181
Creek 10, 13, 16, 24, 27–30, 171–172, 188
Cultural Literacy 39
Cumberland Gap 152, 165
Cumberland River 86, 152, 165
Cumming, Sir Alexander 159

Dahlonega 121–122
Dakwa 20, 95–96
D'Alembert, Jean-Baptiste Rond 6
dancing 70, 105, 109, 120–121, 134, 136–137, 160; feather 79–80; scalp 153–155
Daniel, the Rev. James 2–6, 41, 47, 49, 51–53, 189
Darkening Land 67, 69, 75, 85, 140
Daugherty (early trader) 53
Davis, Dr. Thomas 165
de Ayllon, Lucas 2, 26
DeBrahm, William 52
decontextualized stories 5, 21–23, 33, 35; *see also* background of experience; schema theory; topical knowledge
deer songs 69–70, 72
Deer tribe 71–72
deerskins 25, 28–29, 51, 166, 174–175
de Leon, Ponce 26
Demere, Captain Raymond 53–54
de Narvaez, Panfilo 26
de Soto, Hernando 24–26
Diderot, Denis 6

disease 7, 13, 26, 70–74, 77, 84, 86; rheuma-tism 71; smallpox 25–26, 29
Donelson, Ken L. 9
Dragging Canoe 14, 132
Dressed-in-Stone 100–102
Duke Energy 4, 156
Duncan, Barbara 27, 35–36

eagle as bird of peace 133; feathers 79, 133–135, 138, 182; Shadagea or Cloud Dweller 133–134
Edgar, Walter 12, 16–17, 28
Edmunds, Margot 17
Ellet, Elizabeth 50–51
Elliot, John 175
English influence on southeastern Indians 12–13, 15, 24–31, 33, 152, 169–170, 174
Erdoes, Richard 16–18
ethnopoetics 36; *see also* Tedlock, Dennis
Ethridge, Robbie 25, 31

Fasti 42
fasting 19–20, 58, 116–117, 120–121, 143, 147
Fire King *see* Uka
firearms 25–29, 153, 165–167
Fitch, Captain Tobias 28
La Florida 25
Flying Squirrel 41
foods 62, 65, 67, 70–72, 75, 79, 92, 98, 107, 113, 116, 118, 120, 122, 128–129, 135–136, 141, 143, 145, 159; *see also* wissactaw
Fort Dobbs 166, 168
Fort Loudoun 166, 174–176
Fort Moore 188
Fort Patrick Henry 14
Fort Prince George 54, 165, 174, 176, 178
Fort San Juan 25
Fort Toulouse 130
four *see* sacred numbers
four cardinal directions 57, 79
1491: New Revelations of the Americas Before Columbus 13
Francis, Allan 5, 49–52, 173–174, 178, 182–188
Francis, Henry 173
Francis, Capt. James 49, 173, 178; feeding slain Cherokee to dogs 180
Frankfort, H.A. Groenwegen 18
Frankfort, Henri 18
Franklin 82, 168
French and Indian War 165–166, 170
French Broad River 118, 152
French influence on southeastern Indians 13, 24, 27, 29–30, 33, 130, 152, 165, 169–171
Friedrich, Hugo 6
Friends of Thunder: Folktales of the Oklahoma Cherokee 35
From Abenaki to Zuni: A Dictionary of Native American Tribes 11

Gallay, Alan 13, 24
Galunlati *see* The Three Worlds
gambling 140–141
Georgia Gold Rush 121
Ghighau *see* Beloved Women
giant leech 83–84, 87
Glen, James (royal governor of South Carolina) 29, 165, 170–171
going to water 58, 79, 133, 136, 138, 143, 147
The Golden Fleece 18
Gowdy, Robert 50, 52, 54
Grant, Ludovic 29
Grant's campaign 166, 181–182
Great Buzzard, creation, and healing 57
Great Hawks 43, 92–95
Great Indian War Path 152
Great Law of Peace 123
Great River *see* Mississippi River
Great Smoky Mountains 70, 85, 87, 90, 152
Great Snake 90–92
Great Spirit 17, 79, 151
Great Tellico 175
Great Thunderer *see* Kanati
Great Warrior of Chota *see* Oconostota
Great Yellow Jacket 81–82
Greene, Ellin 35
Guilds, John Caldwell 47
Gunskaliski 103
Gunstocker 153–155; high esteem 153

Halliburton, R., Jr. 30
Hancock, Chief 14
Haywood, John 1–3, 189
Head Warrior of Tanassee 27–28
Henderson, Col. Richard "Carolina Dick" 131–132
Hepler, Susan 21
Herd, E. Don, Jr. 2, 50, 189
Hiawassee River 82–83, 87
Hickman, Janet 21
Hickory Nut Gorge 41–42, 76
Highwater, Jamake 35
Himes, Dell 36
Hirsch, E. D. 39
Historical Sketch of the Cherokee 2, 25–26
The History of the American Indians 14, 24, 46, 189
The History of Virginia in Four Parts 24
Hodenosaunee 124, 133; *see also* Iroquois
Hoig, Stanley 14–15
Holston River 14
Huascar 13
Hudson, Charles 8, 14, 16, 22, 25–26, 48–49
Hudson River 123

Immortals 21–22, 105–107, 118, 122–123
Incas 13
Indian removal 2, 32, 43, 118, 123, 132
The Indian Slave Trade 13

Iroquois 14, 24, 28, 123–124, 129, 133, 152
Issaqueena 49–52, 170, 173, 188; *see also Cateechee of Keeowee: A Descriptive Poem*
Issaqueena Falls 188
Issaquena, Legend of Upper South Carolina 52
Itagunahi *see* Ax, John

Jack the Giant Killer 54
Jackson, Andrew 31–32
Jefferson, Thomas 32
"Jocassee, a Cherokee Legend" 3–5, 47–49, 156–165, 189; *see also* Simms, William Gilmore
Jocassee River 157, 162, 164
Johnson, Sir William 125, 167
Jonah story *see* Dakwa
Josephy, Alvin M., Jr. 11
Judaculla 112–117; Judaculla Rock 117

Kanati 42, 60, 62–70, 85; Red Man 88–89
kanuga *see* scratching
Kelly, John 175
Kentucky River 165
Keowee River 16, 149, 156–157, 177
Keowee settlement 4, 47, 49–51, 148–150, 156, 162, 165, 171–173, 179, 182–184
Kercheval, Samuel 54
Kiefer, Barbara 21
Kilpatrick, Anna 35–36
Kilpatrick, Jack 35
King, Duane 27
King Crow 27
King George's War 170
King James I of England (James IV of Scotland) 53
King Kuruga 4, 49, 51, 52, 54, 171–173, 175–177, 179–180, 182–186, 188
King William's War 170
Kituwha *see* Clingmans Dome
Kovacik, Charles F. 12

La Farge, Oliver 9, 23
Lake Hiawassee 84
Lake Jocassee 4, 156
Lake Keowee 156
Lake Lure 76
Lake Zwerner 121
Lakota 15
land cessions by Cherokee 14–15, 130–132, 165; *see also* Henderson, Col. Richard "Carolina Dick"; Treaty of Long Island; Treaty of 1721
Lanman, Charles 1–3, 6, 41–42, 189
Laughing Boy 9
law of retaliation *see* blood vengeance
Lawson, John 16, 189
Lee, Lawrence 12
Leekey, Thomas B. 18
Lesser Thunderers *see* Thunder Boys

Letters from the Allegheny Mountains 41–42, 189
Literature as Exploration 38
Little Men *see* Thunder Boys
Little People 41, 77–78, 108–109
Little Tennessee River 14, 26, 82, 93, 95, 152, 166
Living Stories of the Cherokee 35
Logan, John 53
Long Canes Creek 166–167; massacre at 178
Long Man (The River) 139–140
Longfellow, Henry Wadsworth 2, 4
"Lover's Leap" 52
Lower Cherokee region 4, 11, 16, 27, 30, 49–52, 137, 148, 150, 156, 159, 166, 175, 182
Lower World *see* The Three Worlds
Loyalists and southeastern Indians 30, 168
Lucky Hunter *see* Kanati
Lyttelton, William Henry (royal governor of South Carolina) 50, 54, 166

MacDonald, Margaret Read 35
magic quartz crystals *see* Ulunsuti
Mann, Charles C. 13
Marriott, Alice 32
McKenny, Barbara 50–51
medicine bundle 143
medicine men *see* conjurors
menstruation 73, 101
Metamorphoses 18
Middle Cherokee region 11, 16, 30, 137, 152–156, 166, 168, 181
Mississippi River 10, 13, 24, 27, 130–132, 165
Mississippian culture 24–26, 31–32
Mississippian "shatter zone" 25
Mohawk 46–47, 123, 147–151; *see also* Iroquois
Moitoy *see* Moytoy of Great Tellico
Montgomery's campaign 166, 180–182
Moon as Sun's daughter 84–85
Mooney, James 1–3, 5–6, 16–20, 22, 24–26, 33, 37, 42–44, 46, 48–49, 189
Moyano, Sergeant 25
Moytoy of Great Tellico 3–4, 159–163
Moytoy of Settico 166
Muench, Francis 52–53
Multicultural Children's Literature 23
mythopoeic perspective 17–19, 21
Myths of the Cherokee 2–3, 17, 189
Myths of the Seneca 6, 189

Nagle, Betty Rose 42
Nantahala Gorge and River 20, 81, 85, 97, 99–100
Nantahala Mountains 168
"Narrative of an Adventure in Kentucky" 15
Natchez 16, 24; coalescence with Cherokee and Creek 29, 31
The Natural and Aboriginal History of Tennessee 189

Nequassee 168; *see also* Franklin
Neuse River 12–14
A New Voyage to Carolina 189
Nicholson, Francis (royal governor of South Carolina) 130
Nilsen, Alleen Pace 9
Ninety Six (Fort and Trading Post) 4, 15, 49–52, 54, 170, 173–180, 184
Norton, Donna E. 16, 23, 34
Notes on the Iroquois 3
Nunnehi *see* Immortals

Oconostota 14–15, 125, 131–132
Ohio River 10, 24, 27, 152, 165
Old Hop 29, 175
Oliphant, John 52
Overhill Cherokee region 11, 14, 16, 26–27, 30, 52, 134–135, 152–156, 165, 176
Ovid 18, 42

pack-horse trains 122–123, 181
Palmetto Lyrics 52
Pardo, Juan 25–26
Park, Andrew 53
Path of Souls 58
pathetic fallacy 4
Paz, Octavio 37
Pellowski, Anne 22–23
Perdu, Theda 30
Perrault, Charles 18
Piaget, Jean 5–6, 38–39
Pigeon River 112, 115, 117, 153
Pisgah National Forest 117
Pizarro, Francisco 13
pourquoi stories 7, 19
Pretty Women *see* Beloved Women
Price, Aaron, 50
priests *see* conjurors
prior knowledge *see* background of experience
Proclamation of 1763 132
purification rituals 43, 133, 136, 138, 143, 147; *see also* black drink; fasting; going to water; scratching
Purves, Alan 21

Qualla Boundary 2
Queen Anne's War 170
Querry, Ron 11, 32

Rachlin, Carol K. 32
Raven Mockers 102–105
reader-response theory 38–39; *see also* Rosenblatt, Louise
The Reader, the Text, and the Poem 38
reader's background *see* background of experience
reception aesthetics 38
red as war symbol 61, 142–143, 145, 150–151, 153

Red Cloud 15
Red Man 42, 88–89; *see also* Kanati
religious changes among southeastern Indians 31
Report of the General Survey of the Southern District of North America 52
retelling Native American folklore 1–2; accuracy and authenticity 1–7, 21–24, 32–33, 35, 40–43, 47–52; ownership or sovereignty 7, 34–36; plot structure 18–21; stereotyping 4–5, 9, 23, 51–52; style 4, 6, 44–47; types 16–17, 20–21
Revolutionary War 30, 83, 86, 122, 152, 167–169
rhetorical devices 44–47
Robin Hood 54
Rocky Broad River 76
Rosenblatt, Louise 5–6, 38–39
rum, effects of 30, 54
Rutherford's campaign 168

sacred fire 29, 45–46, 60–62, 79–80, 169; lighting 68, 89, 138
The Sacred Formulas of the Cherokee 46, 189
sacred numbers of four and seven 19–21, 36, 45–46, 57–59, 64–70, 73, 75, 78–79, 88, 89, 101, 105, 107, 109, 116–117, 120, 138–139, 141
Santa Elena 26
Santee tribe 136–142, 145–147
Sarratay River *see* Jocassee River
Savannah River 10, 86, 108–109, 148, 185, 188
Sawyer, Ruth 34–35
scalping 13, 59, 126, 144, 146, 148, 151, 163–164, 166–167, 171, 175–176, 180
Scheiermacher, Friedrich 6
schema theory 39–40
schemes see rhetorical devices
Schoolcraft, Henry 2–3
Schulte, Ranier 37
Scots Irish ("Scotch-Irish") 53–54
scratching 46, 80, 138–139
The Scribal Society 21
Selu 42, 62–70
Seneca 6, 10, 28, 123, 125–127, 133–135, 138–142, 146–147; *see also* Iroquois
Sequoyah 31
Seroweh 176–180
seven *see* sacred numbers
Seven Years' War *see* French and Indian War
Sevier, John 31–32
shaman *see* conjurors
Sharp, John 28
Shawano (Shawnee) 10, 84, 86, 90, 152–153, 156, 166
Shining Rock Wilderness 62
Simms, William Gilmore 2–6, 41, 47–49
Sitting Bull 15
sky vault 57–58, 69, 84

slavery and southeastern Indians 3, 7, 13, 25, 27–31, 51
Sloan, Charles Reid 52–53
Smith, John 10
Song of Hiawatha 2
South Carolina: A Geography 12
South Carolina: A History 12
The Southeastern Indians 24, 43
Spanish influence on southeastern Indians 3, 24–26, 30, 33
Spear-Finger 20, 97–102, 187
Spotted Tail 15
stereotyping 4, 9, 14, 23, 32, 48, 51–52
Stone-Dress *see* Spear-Finger
storytelling 7, 22–23, 33–36, 40–44
Stuart, Capt. John 30, 167
Stumphouse Mountain 50, 185–188
Sun worship 29, 31, 45; *see also* Apportioner
Sunland 67, 69
Sutherland, Zena 16
Swannanoa Gap 168
Swanton, John R. 16
Swimmer 33, 44

Tallulah Gorge and River 18, 108–112
Tellico Lake 94, 95
Tennessee River 14, 16, 152
Thadodaho 123–124
Thompson, Stith 17
This World *see* The Three Worlds
The Three Worlds 31, 42, 57–61, 62, 69, 73, 77, 79, 85, 92, 94, 101, 111–112
Thunder Boys 60, 62–70, 85
Thunder People or Spirits 18, 112
Timberlake, Lt. Henry 52, 189
Tlanuwa (peregrine falcon) *see* Great Hawks
tobacco 41, 76–78, 120
topical knowledge 40–42
Tories *see* Loyalists and southeastern Indians
torture 46–47, 86, 126, 144, 147–148, 157
Toxaway Creek 3
trade, influence on southeastern Indians 7, 13, 24–30, 51, 53, 122; *see also* deerskins; disease; firearms; pack-horse trains; rum; slavery
traders 149–150; character of 53–54, 175
Trail of Tears 132
transactional theory *see* reader-response theory
translation theory 6, 33, 37–38
Treaty of Aix-la-Chapelle 170
Treaty of Long Island 14
Treaty of New Echota 2, 132
Treaty of 1721 130, 132, 165
Tuckaseegee River 106, 115
Tufte, Virginia 6, 44
Tugaloo River 108, 185–188
turkey as bird of war 79, 138
Tuscarora 10, 13–14, 124, 148; *see also* Iroquois
Twilight Land *see* Darkening Land

The Types of Folktales: A Classification and Bibliography 17

Uka 61, 134–135, 142, 147–147
Uktena 42, 58, 84–88, 89–90, 94, 111; power of scales 89
Ulagu *see* Great Yellow Jacket
Ulster Plantation 53–54
Ulunsuti 58, 85–88
Underworld *see* The Three Worlds
Unicoi Mountains 152
Upper Cherokee *see* Overhill Cherokee
Upper World *see* The Three Worlds
Ustu-tli *see* Great Snake

Valley River 82–83, 87
Valley towns 30, 83, 137, 156
Vygotsky, Lev 5–6, 39–40

Walker, Felix 15
War of the Austrian Succession *see* King George's War
War of the Palatinate *see* King William's War
War of the Spanish Succession *see* Queen Anne's War
War Women *see* Beloved Women
warfare 4, 7, 12–15, 24–32, 49–52, 124–125, 146–156, 168–170, 174–182; ceremonies 77, 142–146, 149–151, 153–155, 171; war titles 52, 130, 142–143, 145; war trophies 146–148, 151, 175; war waiter 145; *see also* captives; medicine bundle; scalping; torture; wissactaw
The Way of the Storyteller 34
Wayah Gap 82, 168
Wayna Capac 13

white as peace symbol 61, 79, 134, 135; *see also* eagle as bird of peace; white wampum belt
White Bear 70–71
white wampum belt 135
White Water Falls 159
White Water River 159, 161–162
The Wigwam and the Cabin 3
Wild Boy *see* Thunder Boys
Wilde, Oscar 54
Wilde Hemp 169
Williamson, Colonel Andrew 168–169
Winberry, John J. 12
winter house 104–105, 113–114, 125, 142, 151
wissactaw 143, 160
witches 65–66, 98, 100, 187; *see also* Raven Mockers
wizards *see* conjurors
Wolf people 66–67
Wolfson, Evelyn 11
wolves as animal helpers 127–129
Women of the Revolution 50
Wood, Michael 13
Woodward, Grace Steele 26
The World of Manabozho: Tales of the Chippewa Indians 18
The World of Storytelling 22
Wrosetasatow 130

Yadkin River 16, 167
Yanu *see* Bear tribe
Yemassee War 28
Yohewah *see* Great Spirit
Young Warrior *see* Seroweh

zone of proximal development 39